the

Nine Fantasies

that will ruin your life

and the

Eight Realities

that will save you

the

Nine Fantasies

that will ruin your life

and the

Eight Realities

that will save you

By Dr. Joy Browne

THREE RIVERS PRESS
NEW YORK

Published by Three Rivers Press, a division of Crown Publishers, Inc., 201 East 50th Street, New York, New York 10022. Member of the Crown Publishing Group.

Random House, Inc. New York, Toronto, London, Sydney, Auckland
www.randomhouse.com

THREE RIVERS PRESS is a registered trademark of Random House, Inc.

Originally published in hardcover by Crown Publishers, Inc., in 1998.

Printed in the United States of America

Design by Lauren Dong

Library of Congress Cataloging-in-Publication Data
    The nine fantasies that will ruin your life (and the eight
    realities that will save you) / by Joy Browne. — 1st ed.
        1. Conduct of life.   2. Happiness.   I. Title.
    BF637.C5B78   1998
    158—dc21   98-36245

ISBN 0-609-80473-1

10 9 8 7 6 5 4 3 2 1

First Paperback Edition

To the child in all of us who wants desperately to believe and the adult that fashions a wonderful life from reality.

acknowledgments

The world was eagerly awaiting this book, and it appears exactly as it sprung from my head . . . well, that's the fantasy. The reality is that there are a number of very hard-working, good-hearted souls who helped me sculpt and polish this work into what it has become.

The book could not have occurred without Joni Evans: She held my hand through thick ideas and thin concepts and kept asking those irritating questions that made me think, work, and create. Joni did this over the holidays without so much as a peep. Her assistant, Tiffany Ericksen, supplied access, cold water, and endless enthusiasm. You go girls.

It's tough to be an editor. You've got to convince your author that she's got to cut, rework, trim, and rethink without throwing things, pouting, or calling her mom. Sue Carswell is smart, tough, and stubborn, and the perfect editor for someone like me. Her assistant, Rachel Kahan, can always be counted on for the perfect factoid, pithy comment, or historical note.

A fine-tooth comb never had more competition than from Donna Ryan, who caught the errors and sharpened my focus. The legendary Amy Boorstein had the final say and said, "Let there be a book."

Thanks also to Mary Schuck, who indulged my whims to help design a terrific cover, photographer Debra Feingold who made me look good, and Mario D'Aiuto, who supplied goodies over the holidays so I could keep writing with a minimum of self-pity.

Thanks to all the folks at Crown who have demonstrated unflagging enthusiasm from that first fateful five o'clock meeting. Chip Gibson and Steve Ross—as both pep squad and lunch hosts—you're the best. Thanks to Barbara Marks and her gang for doing such a good job getting the word out. I hope I have justified your enthusiasm and hard work.

I sincerely thank you all for turning my pride into prose and my fantasy into reality.

Dr. Joy Browne
New York City

c o n t e n t s

fantasies

L*ook, I know* you think fantasies are fun, sexy, and cool, whether you dream of being Cinderella or Prince Charming, or that your love will be passionate, available, rich, gorgeous, and lovable. Even if you think of yourself as too old or too sophisticated to believe in fairy tales, I'll bet you occasionally indulge in the giddy notion of someday playing for the L.A. Lakers or winning the gold in wrestling by overpowering that third-grade bully who still haunts your nightmares. Maybe in this alternate reality, you're accepting an Oscar or being crowned Miss America or doing something you won't admit to in public. Everybody indulges in fantasies from time to time, but as a lifestyle choice, we're talking *di-sas-ter!* Even if these seemingly harmless little devils don't ruin your life, they can cause a lot of avoidable misery. The alternative to fantasies is a happy and fulfilling life, so please listen up.

"Ruinous fantasy?" I can hear you saying. "She needs to get a grip." How can a fantasy be anything but pleasurable? How can such a whimsical idea cause anyone harm? Think about it: if you fantasize that you can fly and decide to test the idea from the observation deck of the Empire State Building . . . well, you get my point.

The purists among you will point out that it's not the belief that's so dangerous, but the action based on the belief, and you'd be right on the money. If I can persuade you to examine your beliefs, then your actions will follow a safer, saner, and more productive path. Okay? Okay.

THE SKINNY ON FANTASIES

Repeat after me: "Fantasies aren't real." If something isn't real, it's dangerous to believe it. Other people may tell us lies or try to convince us of their points of view. Their reasons may be lofty or lower than a snake's belly, but a fantasy is a lie we tell ourselves, and because it isn't true, it's toxic, no matter how harmless and whimsical it seems. Fantasies are a distraction from the business of running our lives successfully and realistically. I plan to wrestle these pesky critters to the ground so we can all get on with the pleasure of focused thoughts and energy.

Okay, I admit that fantasies may not actually kill you, but they can make you wish you were dead. They can effectively ruin your life by seducing you into painful and unnecessarily destructive situations. ("Fantasy," in fact, is an interesting word: it was originally spelled with a *ph* rather than an *f,* which suggests that it's related to "phantasm"—a ghost, an odd, capricious illusion rather than a reality.) Most of us think of fantasies as dreams that make us happy, but the fantasies discussed here will offer pleasure only temporarily and at great cost. They are familiar and comfortable, but they can be dangerous and counterproductive in the long run.

Fantasies are delusions that no amount of medication can cure; the sufferer requires a dollop of common sense. And you, fair reader, are in luck because "sensible" is my middle name. Whoops, no fantasies here: I have no middle name, but I am imminently practical and sane. These poisonous fantasies are a lot subtler than the delusion that you're Joan of Arc, but they're also a lot more common. Not to worry. I am going to tell you not only what these fatal notions are and how to avoid them but also how to substitute healthy, life-giving realities that will save you from self-induced misery and enhance your life.

All of us grow up believing certain things to be true. Parents, teachers, grandparents, older siblings, books, Sunday school teachers, baby-sitters, and best friends weave fairy tales about handsome heroes and beautiful maidens. These commonly held beliefs can be

- ✦ **Harmless:** The world is round. It's not. It's an oblate spheroid, which is fancy talk for a flattened ball. But who cares?
- ✦ **Silly:** If you make an unpleasant face, Jack Frost will come along and freeze it permanently.
- ✦ **Tantalizing:** If you kiss your elbow, you'll turn into the opposite sex.
- ✦ **Dangerous:** If you step on a crack, you'll break your mother's back.
- ✦ **Romantic:** If you sleep on a slice of wedding cake, you'll dream of your true love.
- ✦ **Hopeful:** A loose eyelash gives you a free wish.
- ✦ **Somewhat practical:** Walking under a ladder is bad luck. Sure, it's a mechanically unstable device, and stuff can fall down and clunk you upside the head.

If you're noting that some of these fantasies are superstitions, you're right. Superstition is just fantasy with attitude; it's a way of erroneously trying to control events. You don't have that control; none of us do, but you can adopt a clearer belief system that doesn't depend on superstition to get you in touch with who you are and what you want. This new system will allow you to fine-tune your behavior by dealing with what *is*, not with what you want. In a word: *reality*.

As wrongheaded as fantasies are, scores of them guide our lives and shape not only our perceptions but also our behavior. The examples mentioned above are purposely dramatic and fairly irrelevant.

Unfortunately not all dearly held beliefs are so harmless or silly. Certain more relevant assumptions constitute the value system by which we live and run our lives, form our associations, set our goals, raise our children, interact with strangers, and find comfort. These assumptions shape our existence.

THE REAL STORY ABOUT REALITY

We've become so used to the idea that the real world is dangerous that reality has gotten a really bad reputation. I'm going to show you that reality is a lot less scary than you've been led to believe and that it is actually potentially helpful, healthy, life-affirming, and *the* most useful game in town.

The question is how do you separate reality from fantasy? The first test of an idea in action is functional: is it working? Most of us aren't even aware of our belief system until something breaks down.

Every day on my nationally syndicated call-in psychology program, I bump up against callers from all over the Northern Hemisphere who are looking for sympathy when their favorite way of behaving—their applied value system—runs into trouble with somebody else's way of doing something. Approximately 95 percent of those who call want me to agree that they are right and that the person who is making them unhappy is wrong and should die a quick and possibly excruciating death. Instead of offering sympathy, which just makes people feel good about feeling bad, I gently but firmly guide them to a less painful way of dealing with spouses, bosses, kids, parents, employees, and even themselves.

As we believe, so we behave. In helping people find different ways of acting, I help them look at the source of their ineffective interactions to see that what they believe is causing their behavior to bomb. It's not easy. Our belief system is basic, dearly beloved, and largely unexamined by most of us. So before we even begin together, I want to warn you that there are several characteristic ways of responding when we are challenged. And I intend to challenge you.

The first response to a challenge is either to run or to fight. Running is moving away from the offending and offensive object (in this case, me), and fighting can take the form of either defending yourself or attacking me. It would be really cool if you could resist both of these impulses, at least temporarily. Just open your mind and your heart, and let's see if we can do this together.

I want you to get real! I want you to be willing to look at these nine fantasies that can ruin your life until you are willing to examine, adjust, and discard them. These fantasies are causing you to spend time and energy living in an imaginary world that will not allow you to be effective. These assumptions are pervasive, ubiquitous, and dangerous.

THE BIG UGLY NINE FANTASIES CONCERN . . .
+ **Home:** Functional families exist.
+ **Perfection:** Describes everybody . . . except me.
+ **Money:** Winning the lottery would free me.
+ **Truth:** It will set you free.
+ **Sex:** Men and women are from different planets.
+ **Innocence:** Ignorance is bliss.
+ **Righteousness:** Stick to your guns.
+ **Fairness:** Good always triumphs.
+ **Love:** Somewhere I have a soul mate.

These treacherous fantasies need to be dissected and expunged. I'm warning you up front that this process isn't easy, because these myths are deeply ingrained. They're also cleverly disguised as cute rather than malevolent creatures; one of the Seven Dwarfs rather than the Wicked Queen. Even a shiny red apple can turn out to be poisonous. Instead of becoming paranoid about apples, understand that the search for reality is a combination of detective work, excavation, and surgery.

Throughout this book, you'll get to move ahead at your own pace. I'll offer you lots of steps, vitamins, and promises of recovery. I'll show you where these deceptive, tempting fantasies originate, why you buy into them, how they can ruin your life, and how you can find 'em, examine 'em, dump 'em, or change 'em before they wound you.

For a moment let me take you to another time and place to help you better understand my point: Think of a Spanish conquistador in the New World, complete with shiny armor, curved helmet, and velvet breeches, sitting outside his tent at a carved mahogany table in an elaborately carved chair resembling a throne with a velvet cushion. There's a table set with a gleaming silver candelabrum, polished silver goblets and plates, heavy silver cutlery, and damask napkins. The meal has just begun when it starts to rain. The horses are suddenly spooked, attuned to approaching danger. Our conquistador hurriedly begins to gather up his belongings, stuffing the silver and cooking utensils into a tablecloth, taking the heavy table apart. Time is short. Our hero must quickly decide what's important, whether it's worth his time and effort to pack everything or whether he's endangering himself by wasting time on the things he *thinks* he needs. If he takes the time to pack everything, he very likely will not survive long enough to enjoy them. Finally, with what he considers the basics firmly strapped to his back, the candelabrum protruding awkwardly, he begins a laborious trek up the mountain to possible salvation. But the path is slippery, and he becomes bogged down by the weight of his possessions, the things he feels are crucial to his life. He must now decide either to hang on to the stuff he has always considered crucial and perhaps perish or to cut these items loose.

This stuff is what we psychologists call baggage—the things we carry around with us at great expense that seem necessary but that in reality are burdensome and often irrelevant to our journey. (Okay, if this scene seems familiar, you might want to rent a copy of *The Mission* with Robert De Niro and Jeremy Irons. I admit it, I'm a child of the movies, and my unconscious mind has definitely been tainted.) I want to teach you how to sort through your baggage. Do you really need the candelabrum, the silver goblets, and the mahogany table?

I want you to be lean and, if not mean, then prepared, aware, unburdened, and ready to do what you need to do to make yourself happy and sane. I want you to replace fantasy and mistaken dependence on reality and self-reliance. I don't want you naked, just stripped down to basics. Let old-fashioned, clunky armored extras be the stuff of costume dramas. I want you to star in your own story with a minimal amount of extraneous stuff bogging you down.

I can hear you grumbling: "Cut me some slack here, I *like* fantasy." Okay, so go to Disneyland or see a movie. I don't want you acting on the basis of nonsense, because it will make you more vulnerable than safe. It will also make you look like a doofus unnecessarily. Before I tell you that the cavalry is on the way with the eight realities that will save you, I want to clue you in. If you're willing to look at your fantasies and understand the need behind them, you can know more about yourself, the difference between what you have and what you want. This information can help you increase the possibility of actually *getting* what you want.

Are you beginning to see the path between fantasy and reality in terms of understanding who you are so you can get what you want? If so, this gets us to the good stuff, the toolbox of life: reality.

THE EIGHT REALITIES THAT WILL SAVE YOU CONCERN . . .
+ **Knowledge:** Never tell someone something they already know.
+ **Expectation:** Expectation is the death of serenity.
+ **Selfishness:** Selfish is cool. Mean is not.
+ **Responsibility:** Don't sweat your feelings. Focus on action.
+ **Romance:** It's the true poison of the twentieth century.
+ **Pain:** Go for short-term pain and long-term gain.
+ **Reason:** People do things for reasons.
+ **Attitude:** Hey, dude, it's everything.

In this book, I'm going to use questions and situations from my practice, from my life, and from callers to my radio program. All are compilations with "fantasy" names and places attached—so relax callers . . . no "real" lawsuits pending here! I hope you'll be reminded of *your* life. Together we will get our lives to work that much better. I promise.

Oh, and speaking of reality, here's how I came up with nine fantasies: I started by compiling a humongous list of all the destructive fantasies that I thought were lies, which totaled into the hundreds. I then sorted, combined, and eliminated them until I had what I considered the basic, crucial, and not inherently obvious elements necessary to living a productive, straightforward, regret-free life. Voilà! The nine!

My list of realities is a little shorter, but I am a clinical psychologist, and if I hadn't boiled things down to some pretty straightforward realities that actually work, I would have been out of business a long time ago. My original idea was to have the same number of fantasies and realities, but I ran smack dab into—yeah, you guessed it—reality. That's the problem with reality; it is what it is. Maybe reality is tougher, but it's shorter than fantasy. So there you are: *The Nine Fantasies That Will Ruin Your Life and the Eight Realities That Will Save You.*

1

there's no place like home

We all assume that everybody else's family is terrific and ours is dysfunctional. Don't believe it for a minute.

For most of human history, people have lived in extended families, the larger the better. Bigger families meant more hands to do the work, raise the kids, gather the crops, and fight the enemy. A larger population pool also meant that assaults from hostile neighbors, rampaging plagues, and infant mortality would be less devastating. Until the recent advent of the nuclear family, never had so few adults been entrusted with the responsibility of caring for and socializing offspring.

Fifty years ago the nuclear family comprised Mom, Dad, and kids (with or without a station wagon and a dog). Today nearly two-thirds of all children are raised in single-parent households. The nucleus is getting smaller and smaller. Now the Mom-and-Pop version of the nuclear family seems positively nostalgic, a shrine of togetherness.

As the family unit shrank, the importance of Mother as caregiver grew to nearly mythic proportions (in the larger extended family, child care was shared by older children and aunts) while the father figure (if and when he was present) assumed total economic responsibility. As traditional functions bash into modern structures, however, roles become distorted. On the one hand, the messy work of raising children remains, but the number of hands sharing the work keeps diminishing, creating a sentimental longing for the good old days, which never really existed. When the work of turning infants into responsible, potentially happy, self-sufficient adults is done by two or often one parent, the task is daunting enough. Add to all this shrinking nuclear unit stepparents and stepchildren, separated parents, same-sex partnerships, and unwed mothers, and you can see how irrelevant and burdensome the traditional view of family can be.

Let's look at the fantasy of the sentimentalized functional family that serves as the standard against which any real family, like yours or mine, can never measure up. If we can get beyond the fantasy, we'll see the reality: that family may be kindred spirits rather than kin, genuine feelings rather than genealogy. For the 17 percent of the population who live in a Father works–Mom at home with kids household, hurrah. For everybody else, let's worry more about function and less about form.

FAMILIES FUNCTION

✳

I come from a dysfunctional family, and . . . —MARTIN, 36, TUSCUMBIA, ALABAMA

Martin, stop. *Everyone* in America comes from a dysfunctional family. The term has no meaning anymore except as an excuse for bad behavior. Regardless of what you want to discuss with me, I want you to forget about using your family as an excuse for your problems. That's why adulthood was invented—to allow us to sort through what we were taught as children and pick and choose appropriate behavior. It's like a Chinese menu for life. Picking one item from column A and one from column B allows you to customize your existence without hollering at the cook. I also don't want you to beat up on yourself for falling into this trap, since you're certainly not alone. I just want you to climb out of it.

The American notion of family is perhaps the most romanticized, deep-rooted, and misery producing fantasy of the last hundred years. When soldiers returned from World War II, women were no longer needed in the workforce. As people moved from farms to urban and suburban centers, the basic need to maintain the larger extended family— with grandparents, aunts, uncles, cousins—as part of the social order really hit the wall.

Our society responded by idealizing the nuclear unit, with emphasis on the mom who stayed at home and kept the home fires burning. This comforting and idyllic, if inaccurate, model of family life has been perpetuated by television and the movies. Norman Rockwell, whose paintings of an America that never was adorned covers of the *Saturday Evening Post* for generations, gave us a sugar-coated version of an extended family so seductive that all of us now believe that everyone else's family functions better than ours. In case you've never seen one of Rockwell's paintings, the Thanksgiving dinner table is peopled by well-dressed, well-behaved brethren giving thanks for a golden turkey and all the trimmings, including the salad, which is always forgotten at my house.

In the Rockwell family there is no version of our own tipsy uncle Jack, there's no howling cousin Sammy who was just pinched by whiny sister Susie, and the turkey is not burned. Brother Bob has not brought the television into the dining room to watch the final quarter of the football game, and the baby is not wet and sobbing. In our house Thanksgiving dinner is a Maalox moment, especially when compared to Norman Rockwell's view.

Add to this the notion of dysfunction and you've got a domestic Molotov cocktail capable of inflaming ordinary daily frictions into catastrophe. The fantasy has become even more inflated in the last several years, since politicians coined the term "family values" as shorthand for "I'm a good guy, and my opponent is in favor of the downfall of Western civilization as we know it." Those who most adamantly espouse "family values" have forgotten that the traditional family usually included the beating of women and children and the early death of the father, undoubtedly caused by the lethal combination of mom's home cooking and the overwhelming responsibility of shouldering the economic burden for the entire family structure.

So, Martin, the best place to start with problem-solving is the here and now, understanding that who you are is partially determined by how you were raised. Now that you're all grown up, however, you get to raise yourself. You can understand why you do what you do and what you can do to change it. If you don't like the way you were raised, you can raise your children differently or keep the things that worked and discard those that didn't, keeping in mind that your children aren't you and that times do change.

As parents, we unthinkingly do exactly what our parents did, or else we do the opposite. As the oldest of six children, I had ample opportunity to view the parenting process. I had lots of responsibility toward the younger kids, but no real authority. I spent all my years at home sharing a room with a sister who was fifteen months younger than I was and with whom I had very little rapport. We had very different temperaments, and she was frequently angry with our parents or younger sibs, but could most easily take it out on me because I was neither a parent nor a younger child. (In a big family, if you hit a younger sib, you're sent to your room until you're forty, and being visibly angry toward a parent can get you grounded until you're one hundred and forty.)

Occasionally my sister and I would somehow bridge the chasm between our distinct and fairly incompatible personality styles and chat after lights-out. I can still hear my father hollering, "If I hear one more word out of there, I'm coming up and you'll both be sorry." Even as a young girl, I realized how precious those whispers were. I vowed that when I had children, I would never forbid them to talk in the dark. Unfortunately, I only had to wait till I was about twelve years old and baby-sitting to hear the same wretched words come out of my mouth: "One more word and I'm coming up there." *Sigh.* Memory is such that we are very likely to replicate the negative.

Even if you're one of those souls who long for the good old days, the current reality of single parenting, a 50 percent divorce rate, and the economic need for moms to work mean that June Cleaver is no more. One of the reasons *Leave It to Beaver* survives as a cultural icon forty years after it was made is that it plays into the fantasy that life was simpler, easier, and better back then. I personally think the cotton-candy notion is both nonsensical and dangerous, but whether it was ever true or not, it certainly isn't now.

FATHER KNOWS BEST

✳

My twelve-year-old son wants to shave his head. Do you think this is the first step toward civil disobedience? Do we let him? His mother cries all the time about it. —QUENTIN, 41, GRAY, TENNESSEE

Quentin, trust me, your wife isn't crying about hair loss. She may be crying about your son's looming independence, the loss of his baby curls, or her own aging process, but hair is just dead tissue with a great deal of social meaning. If your parents were living with you, they'd probably remind you of your shoulder-length hair in the 1970s or your dad's fight with his dad about his "ducktail" do. Your young son is going to belligerently tell you, "It's my hair to do with as I want, and you might think about the same *do*, because you're losing yours." All of this seemingly innocent, though sometimes snotty behavior—the purple hair, goatee, tattoos, body-piercings, T-shirts, short skirts, and nail polish—is just a warm-up for teenage rebellion. *All this from a haircut?* Sure, the first shot fired across the bow signals the beginning of a long-term conflict about rules and sovereignty and independence. The parent and child will never view each other exactly the same way again. Don't get between your son and his mom, and remember that hair—in an adolescent, at least—will grow back. Let it go.

✳

My thirty-eight-year-old brother still lives at home. He's never really had a job, and he's sponging off my parents. My mom is always complaining to me how lazy he is. When I tell her to toss him out, she tells me to mind my own business. She says I've never really liked him. Maybe she's right, but it seems like he's really taking advantage. —MIRANDA, 44, ALBANY, NEW YORK

Miranda, carrying on sibling rivalry when we have zits is one thing, but once we get wrinkles, don't you think it's time to let it go? This really isn't your business, even though it's your family. You can ask your mom not to complain to you, but asking her to love you best won't work any better at forty-four than it did at four. Twenty years ago, parents were worried about the empty-nest syndrome: how will we cope when the kids leave? Now they're concerned about the crowded-nest syndrome: how can we get them out of here?

As parents, we give our kids roots and wings, and the hard part is never the roots. Today's family roots have to be portable as well as sustaining. The old-fashioned family was less touchy-feely than our modern one and much more fundamentally economic: "Look, I pay the bills around here, so it's my way or the highway." Not only does the modern family emphasize emotions and self-esteem, but the financial aspects of the nuclear family have also altered significantly.

One of the reasons for the family as a social unit was economic. A large group of adults (aunts, uncles, grandparents, cousins, in-laws) could add financial stability during tough times as well as be a social unit that allowed for interaction and involvement. Today's nuclear family is a much more isolated and fragile economic unit, as you, your brother, and your parents are discovering.

That's not to say that the extended family was a walk in the park; young wives were often terrorized and tyrannized by their mothers-in-law (where do you think all those jokes originated?), younger sons didn't inherit property, and younger sisters couldn't marry until older sibs found matches. Talk about sibling rivalry with a vengeance.

Miranda, ask your mom not to complain to you about your brother, and be thankful you're so self-reliant. While you're at it, it's okay to ask your mom for a hug as long as you don't give her a lecture first.

✳

My boyfriend and I just got engaged. My parents have never liked him, and now that we're planning the wedding, they have said they will contribute only if we put down a deposit of 50 percent of all costs, because they don't think we'll go through with it. My fiancé is really insulted, and I'm caught in the middle.
—SANDRA, 28, BOISE, IDAHO

Sandra, the fun has just begun. You've bumped into the "Home, Sweet Home" fantasy at a hundred miles an hour. You want Mommy and Daddy to make a party for you and love your fiancé while also treating you like a big girl. When we throw in the expense of a wedding, the mix gets really lively—especially since all participants are stubborn, sensitive, and convinced they're right. You're looking for all of them to support your independence. Your parents don't want to lose you. Your boyfriend is saying, "Choose." And you're getting a headache.

Relax a bit if you can. Remember that the family is an economic unit. All the basic conflicts are being acted out here, which is what makes the mixture so potent. If the two of you plan to assume some of the costs, then write your folks a check. If the deal is that your parents always planned to pay, ask them if they'll refund your money as a wedding gift or put it in escrow. The two of you might decide to finesse the whole situation and elope. If you can, try not to take everything quite so personally. In reality, this is what family is all about—the tension between dependence and freedom and whether or not the wedding cake is chocolate.

A MAN'S HOME IS HIS CASTLE

✳

My wife and I are separating, and I told my folks that I wanted to bunk at home until I decide what I want to do. Mom said she and Dad are moving to Florida and they're going to rent the house for a year and then sell it. She says I'll have to make other arrangements. I told her they're my parents and they have to take me in. She just laughed, and I heard Dad saying to get off the phone, they were going to be late for their tone-and-stretch class. —LOREN, 34, CAMDEN, NEW JERSEY

Because the nuclear family is a relatively new development and most prominent in American life, the fantasies surrounding it are compounded by nostalgia, fear, dependency, competitiveness, and love. The idea that there will always be a home where you can go and be welcomed is charming and appealing but completely false. I think you've been seduced by the *Father Knows Best* syndrome. In that popular TV show, Robert Young dispensed white-collar suburban wisdom to cute, passive children who gratefully acknowledged their intellectual, emotional, and financial debt once a week within a thirty-minute window. American men ever since have been trying to figure out how that paragon wielded such total control over home and hearth, not to mention how he elicited his family's gratitude, respect, and affection. Listen up: that was television, not reality.

Loren, this notion of the ideal family—which may even be partially responsible for the breakup of your marriage—was totally fanciful. The TV dads in those earlier times lived in an antiseptic environment in which the major concerns were baby-sitting, bikes, and whose turn it was to do the dishes. They were absent during the day and appeared only long enough to dispense wisdom. Today this sort of male behavior would be seen as the cause of a wife's drinking and adultery with the tennis instructor. The perky older daughter would blame Dad for her father fixation and for her unrealistic demands on her suitors, whom he disdains. Sonny would see his inability to find and hold a job as a result of feeling castrated by his father's power, and the baby of the family would undoubtedly attribute her sexual identity confusion to having been called Kitten since birth.

Today's father had better be a lot more hands-on if he is to be taken seriously by his brood. Being an absentee provider who can defend himself by bringing home his paycheck is considered old-fashioned, paternalistic, and inadequate. But this new freedom always incorporates the ability to just say no—to being forever responsible for grown children's economic welfare, to eternal baby-sitting, and to adult children returning home to crash until they get their lives or finances in order. Dads have had to learn to be more giving, and they've been allowed to be a bit more selfish and to focus on their feelings as well as their finances.

As dads have changed, so have moms. Loren, your mother has learned that love doesn't mean being a doormat. It sounds as if her days of always considering your needs before her own have come and gone. The good news is that you won't have to deal with Saint Mom the Martyr. The bad news is you're going to have to find your own digs.

✳

My son puts up with an enormous amount of guff from his wife and kids. If I'd talked to my dad that way, I wouldn't have been able to sit down for a week. Hell, if my son had talked to me the way his kids talk to him, I would have given him the same sore butt my dad would have whopped on me. That's the problem with kids today—they have no respect for authority. Things were a lot better in this country when a man's home was his castle. —PATRICK, 63, CHICAGO

Patrick, you're certainly not alone in feeling a fond nostalgia for the days when a man's home was his castle. Unfortunately most of the people with whom you share this fantasy are men. This is a terrific philosophy if you happen to be the man, but it's not so great if you're unlucky enough to be a woman or a child.

Before you decide you'd look great in a crown, remember that being King Pat has some serious limitations. Not only does a king have to take care of his subjects (to avoid being overthrown), but you might remember the lessons of history, where unhappy younger brothers, jealous cousins, and ambitious offspring could get frisky and plot to stab King Dad in the back and usurp his throne. If this sounds like your normal family get-together . . . well, unless you inherited the royal treasury and a loyal army to maintain your position, you might want to give up the fantasy.

It sounds to me as if you're feeling unloved, Patrick. Is the boss pushing you around at work, so that you want to compensate by being powerful at home? Are you having a Rodney Dangerfield moment and feel like you're getting no respect?

Don't let your longing for the lord-and-master thing blind you to the present. The past always seems most appealing when the present is rapidly changing. Obviously the happier we are, the better the status quo seems to be. Conversely, when we're unhappy, we adopt the grass-is-greener perspective. It sounds to me as if you're not very happy at this moment. You may want to dig a bit deeper and see if there's not something lurking behind your kingdom fantasy.

NORMAN ROCKWELL LIED

✳

My mother's in a nursing home. None of my brothers or sisters ever come to visit her. Everyone else at Shady Acres is swamped with company. My family stinks. They always have and they always will. —ISADORE, 69, RICHMOND, VIRGINIA

Whoa, easy there, Isadore. I know it frightens you to see your mom deteriorate. Its tough to think about becoming an orphan at any age, but this displaced rage isn't going to help you, your mom, or your siblings. The assumption that everybody else's family works better than yours is self-defeating. You know your family from the inside and everyone else's from the outside. It may be time to organize your brethren to visit mom. If you seem patronizing or whiny, you'll make the task more difficult than it has to be. If they feel you're trying to foist Mom off on them or make them feel guilty, they're going to be less compliant than if you suggest that maybe you can all have lunch once a week and work out a schedule.

If it comforts you to believe that your family is lousier than everyone else's, ask yourself why. You can believe that functional families exist, but only if you intend to create one of your own. There also seems to be a lot of pressure on you, your brothers, and your sisters to be paragons of virtue, now that your childhood is but a memory. Simply speaking, you can't remake your family, but you can begin to relate to them as the adults they have become and begin to like them or not. You can also show your children how you would like to be treated when you're old by how you treat your mom. Isadore, it's obvious that you've got a lot on your plate right now. If you can let go of some of that anger, you'll be happier and more effective.

If you can give up the notion that there is only one way to be, you might more readily accept that there are lots of ways to be a parent and multiple ways to be a child. Home may not be sweet or stable, but it's not as toxic or hostile as it seems when measured against an unrealistic and futile fantasy. Instead of relying on faulty reporting and emotional balderdash, we need to focus on what is important today in terms of relating to *our* children, what we wish we had been told as children by our parents and how we wish we had been treated when we were kids. You may want to take the "pendulum theory" into account while you're at it: if your parents were strict, it's likely you'll loosen up and your kids will be tough to their kids who will loosen up . . . and so it goes.

If we can put aside our anger about how we were or weren't raised, we can then begin to understand that everybody feels the discrepancy between the perfect parent they longed for and the reality of parents doing the best they could with what they had. Each of us can then begin to do for ourselves what we wish had been done for us. We can raise our children as we wish we'd been raised—confident in the certainty that they too will probably feel gypped.

SHRINK-WRAPS

FALSE FAMILY FANTASIES

I want a girl like the one who married Dad: If you're noticing that you've run across this idea before when it comes to your love life . . . ta-da. You've been paying attention and a high five for you. This is the basis of that whole destructive notion. Let's all agree that Oedipus didn't have all that comfy a life. Let's further admit that the cult of Mom Worship in this society is based on trying to convince a lot of women that they shouldn't ask for anything more than gratitude for staying in an empty house all day and basing their total self-worth on someone else.

Home is where they've got to take you in: Sorry, Thomas Wolfe, I don't mean to be paraphrasing, but it's not true that you can't go home again. It's just that home is not what it once was. The point is, the vine-covered cottage that would always be there was probably never there, and it sure isn't these days. Mom and Dad are now in the midst of a trial separation. They have put the house on the market, and they're tired of taking care of kids. So get a job, get a life, and raise your own kids, who will treat you much the same way you've treated your folks.

The apple never falls far from the tree: Today's functioning family is tomorrow's therapy project, because the rules for parenting change every decade or so, which means everybody gets caught. There's a pendulum effect to parenting. When discipline is emphasized, the next generation rebels in favor of freedom, which then results in a longing for structure. If the point of the family is to socialize the child to function in society, the stress becomes obvious. When I was in college, a professor admitted he was trying to train us for jobs twenty years down the road he couldn't even imagine. Today he'd have to amend that statement to five years down the road.

How, then, does a family cope? Certainly not by looking backward. The past looks most seductive when the future is unsure, but clinging tenaciously to a completely unrealistic and inaccurate fantasy of the past in order to apply brakes to our headlong rush into the unknown won't work. The sad laments of family life gone wrong are all statements about the difficulty of change. Human beings are homeostatic by nature: the unknown feels frightening. Whether we look at concerns about our children's dress code or where to go for Christmas when parents are divorced, we're acknowledging the pain of change as well as its inevitability. Take deep cleansing breaths, everyone.

Spare the rod and spoil the child: Yeah, smacking someone around who is smaller and loves you is really loving and good role modeling. *Not!* The whole issue of spanking and corporal punishment is an important one which is slightly off the point here. The reason I include it at all is to offset the knee-jerk response that spanking is a good way to think about love, family, or discipline. Children certainly need rules and structure, but as a society, hopefully we are learning better techniques to teach respect. Fear just begets misery and anxiety. It's also self-perpetuating, mindless, and short-term.

TV SHOWS THAT PERPETUATE THE FAMILY FANTASY

+ *Leave It to Beaver*—Sibling rivalry: is gentle and fun . . . right!
+ *The Dick Van Dyke Show*—Happy homemaker: (Are we talking about dosage adjustment here?) *"Rob* . . . puhleeze, can I get out of these pedal-pushers?"

- *The Partridge Family*—Single mom: is always calm, cool, collected—only ruffled shirtwise—and never, ever out of tune!
- *I Love Lucy*—Cross-cultural marriage: never creates problems with in-laws or bigoted landlords.
- *The Brady Bunch*—Blended family: all disputes can be settled cutely and "permanently" in a half hour—including commercials.

MISLEADING "REALISTIC" FAMILIES
- *All in the Family*
- *Roseanne*
- *The Jeffersons*
- *Murphy Brown*
- *One Day at a Time*
- **Any soap opera**

2.
everybody's perfect ...
except me

Nobody's perfect, so relax and enjoy the imperfections.

T*he need to* be perfect is a terrible burden. It means there is no rest, no serenity, only striving and failing, since perfection can't change and to be alive means to change. So even if it were possible to be momentarily perfect, that would be the end of the line—as a verb, "to perfect" means "to finish." The gnawing sense of imperfection can taint the simplest pleasure and the greatest triumph. A dedication to perfectionism means that we are doomed always to be just a heartbeat away—from exposure. Perfection is unchanging; lives are ongoing.

In this fantasy, relationships must be perfect lest they reflect badly on us. So being critical of others is an integral part of maintaining the fantasy that you are perfect and others must strive to keep up with you. This whole process of the best defense being a good offensive is tiresome and joyless, but obsessive, because to fail means to be unworthy of love.

Zowie, how did such an optimistic country saddle itself with such a profoundly gloomy fantasy?

Before there was Madison Avenue's advertising influence or television, there was Hollywood and the dream machine that offered a gloriously perfect universe of beautiful people and clear lines between the good guys and the bad guys. Advertising and television took up the challenge of entertaining by distracting us from our comparatively mundane everyday lives. This made the unobtainable "perfect life" seem personal by bringing the message into our living rooms. The fantasy of perfect bodies, lives, and loves blemishes the reality of lives in progress.

✳

My younger sister and I fight all the time. She'll go off in a huff, so I have to be the peacemaker and call her back. When I do, everything goes just fine until I explain to her how rude she was to me. —MELINA, 37, SARASOTA, FLORIDA

Melina darlin', you're driving your sister crazy because you're acting as if you are perfect and deign to deal with her only because you are so incredibly wonderful. Every day my callers convince me, as you did today, to tell them they're being vicitimized by someone who should suffer a lifetime of ingrown toenails or worse. This doesn't make them bad. It is the result of the erroneous notion that there are only two groups—the blameworthy and blameless. All of us would rather be the blamer than the blamed. It becomes really important to be right because if we're not right, we're *wrong*. And who wants to be wrong? In order to feel safer, we attempt to divert attention elsewhere before our flaws can be scrutinized. In this way, we can pretend to be blameless while hiding our terrible secret: that we are not perfect.

The "best defense is a good offense" strategy is tempting. I criticize; therefore I'm above being criticized. So I'm safe. The problem, Melina, is that this technique doesn't work, as you've undoubtedly noticed. When you criticize your sister, she attacks you or retreats to fight another day. The two of you gain nothing. You just escalate your private war.

How did we come to use this belief in perfection as the key to social success?

All of us live in a capitalist society, Melina, which means we buy things that are not crucial for survival. If I can convince you that there is something wrong with you that will make you unlovable or unsuccessful, and then tell you that I have a magic potion that will cure the problem, you'll very likely be interested. On a very large scale, that defines the emotional underpinnings of our economic system. The "problem" may be the wrong car, the wrong look, or the wrong smell. The solution is a new car, suit, fragrance, or—in your case, Melina—the expensive grovel "I'm-so-sorry-I-hurt-your-feelings" bouquet as a peace offering. Growing up in America means growing up insecure because we believe there is an ideal way to be. In this cult of perfection, we pretend that perfection is obtainable, and we are afraid to admit that we're not perfect. This is the real subtext of the conflict between you and your sister. The drumbeat here is the unholy trinity:

1. What you have isn't enough to make you happy.
2. You can never be happy by yourself.
3. Attracting someone is dependent on looking or smelling or tasting different than you do.

The approach works only if you *believe* in the ideal. When there is a conflict, the only choice is to be perfect or to be a loser. So we pretend to be perfect, and we belittle our opponent as a way of deflecting attention from our own imperfection. Think about it. If you're feeling calm and confident, taking a good look at who you are feels warm and pleasant. Conversely, when you're convinced that you have zits, halitosis, and thinning hair, that same scrutiny feels excruciating, embarrassing, and threatening. You're quickly going to become convinced that everyone is going to hurt you, humiliate you, or leave you for someone who has perfect hair, teeth, breath, and whatever else you feel is lacking in you. The tragedy is that *everybody* feels that way. Whatever we are isn't enough, but everybody else is perfect.

Melina, perfectionism isn't only about advertising, which is why you and your sister are constantly playing "who's perfect and who's the unlovable nerd?" Every group—whether it's the marines, the Girl Scouts, or the church—has an ideal to which its members are encouraged to aspire. Years ago a sermon on Sunday reminded us that we weren't living up to the ideal, but now advertising can remind us seven days a week in the comfort of our living rooms that we don't have the perfect Evian body or Jell-O child.

Encouraging individuals to live up to a very high standard is normal. When your folks urged you to do your best, they weren't being nasty, just unrealistic. When your mom asked you why you couldn't be more like your sister, she sowed the seeds of today's dissension with your sister. Parents may mean well, but their admonitions combined with those impossibly perfect images are so overwhelming that we've lost our ability to distinguish between the possible and the impossible. The price of failure has never seemed higher.

In a contest held in Canada last year for aspiring models, 80 percent of the 20,000 applicants would be considered anorexic by their height-weight ratio. The five finalists all weighed less than 100 pounds and were at least five feet seven. It is chilling to realize that the notion of perfection has gotten so out of hand as to distort the perception of teenage girls so that they will never feel happy in their own bodies. There is something tragic about a pubescent girl searching for diet aids and fake breasts in a futile pursuit of an unobtainable look.

When you combine an excruciatingly small chance of success and a fear of failing, you get people who are afraid to look at themselves honestly for fear of what they will discover. The flip side of this ugly coin is a willingness to aggressively find fault with others as a way to feel superior and safe: "I may not be perfect, but I'm a lot better than you are, so I'm more nearly perfect by comparison."

Melina, if you accept your sister exactly as she is and love her, not in spite of her quirks but because of them, you'll have more time to study your own quirks and more fun when you're together. She might even give you a hug now and then.

COMMUNICATE DISAPPOINTMENT

✳

My twelve-year-old son is a really great kid, but his grades have fallen, so I told him he can't play sports, and now he's threatening to run away from home. I never let him watch TV until he's finished his homework, and I've hollered about how important school is till I'm blue in the face. —KEITH, 41, FORT WORTH, TEXAS

Keith, before we even get started here, there is no reason for any kid in America to watch the tube on a school night; that's why VCRs were invented. (Hey, before y'all start yelling at me, even my editor wanted me to take this out. I not only believe it but I practiced it when my daughter was in school.) No kid is going to perish from lack of a remote control, and the weekends can be for boob-tubing. If you tell your son he can't watch TV until his homework is done, he'll either fib or rush through it. The Browne family rule says "No TV." I also think you should spend time in the same room with a child while he's tackling his homework. You can balance your checkbook, do the crossword, or read T. S. Eliot. Just be there with him.

Now on to the harder stuff: you can see that perfectionism isn't limited to adults or young girls. You yourself might have fallen into the "perfect daddy reflected by the perfect kid" trap. *The Cosby Show* convinced an entire nation that it was possible to have cute, smart, respectful kids who were popular, athletic, and polite, with a wonderful sense of humor and great affection for their parents. Bill Cosby was and is just one in a long line of flickering images of parental and familial perfection that includes fathers with straight teeth who knew best.

These homey, familiar familial images were and are part of our life. TV life is not real life. Keith, your angel isn't going to develop independence and a clear sense of self in twenty-two minutes plus commercials, courtesy of a wry smile and the obvious affection of lovable old pretend dad. He's going to do it the old-fashioned way, by rebelling, talking back, and experimenting with music, clothes, and friends that drive you absolutely crazy.

His methods may vary, but he's behaving just like you did and your dad did and his dad did. What if you and your son took a walk together around the mall and tried to solve the school problem? Don't be put off by his sullenness—he's a kid. Ask him what you can do to help him. Tell him you were thinking about grounding him, but you'd like his opinion on what the problem is and what the solution might be. If nothing else, you'll learn a great deal about your son. Just for a moment, think about what your reaction would have been if your father had tried this technique.

Adolescence isn't easy, and it's not much fun, which is why all of us would rather succumb to the warm seduction of TV fantasy families. But that seductive video fantasy of family life can't alter human nature.

All kids, even teens, would rather be praised than punished, but they would rather be punished than ignored. At some point, every kid decides his parents are nincompoops. (Viewing your own dad as an example of perfect dolthood allowed the teenage you to develop personal values rather than swallowing your father's ideas whole.) If your primary method of parenting is to act like a warden and correct all mistakes before they get out of hand, you will have an incredibly angry, confused adolescent on your hands.

If we could shift from the perfection model of child rearing, where any minor deviation has to be instantly eradicated, to a kinder, gentler, more realistic style, we could catch kids doing good rather than bad. Instead of constantly communicating our disappointment, we could find behavior to praise. Remember how much a compliment meant to you as a kid? In any relationship it is depressing and unmotivating to feel that no matter what you do, it's not enough. What's even more depressing is how often we apply this same perfection mumbo jumbo to our own behavior as well. If we come up with a list of seven New Year's resolutions and accomplish six of them, guess which is the only one that you will note, remember, and highlight? Yep, you got it; the failure, not the successes. Not only do we poison our parenting and self-appraisal, but we carry this counterproductive perspective into our adult relationships as well.

When you communicate disappointment you are sending out a message of shame. Shame makes people feel small. For humans to change, they must summon energy from somewhere. If they feel small and belittled, they are unlikely to have the energy or the courage to find that energy.

Keith, this isn't to say that you should abandon all attempts at understanding your son's school problems and changing perspective. I'm not suggesting that you allow him to do as he wishes, but there are more effective ways of teaching about school responsibilities than depriving him of something he enjoys. When you ask people—adults or children— how they feel about a situation, instead of telling them how disappointed you are, you give them room to evaluate their own behavior and offer a solution that feels appropriate and possible to them rather than just dispensed by you. Guilt works as a motivating force only as long as the scold is standing around. If you allow people to make their own choices, then their conscience goes with them so you don't have to constantly be there to remind them of what's right. Parents who need to have perfect children to feel good about themselves are asking for misery. Your goodness as a human being or even as a parent has nothing to do with your son's grades. Your willingness to listen to him and to help him reach his goals and understand the obstacles has everything to do with being a good dad and a loving human being. The two of you can bond over his improved attitude, and he can vegetate in front of the VCR on the weekends while you sleep in.

FIND FAULT

*

We've been married for four years and have two kids but I usually feel like I have three children: If I don't constantly remind him, my husband forgets to call his mother, and then she's furious with me. He just ignores me when I tell him that if he doesn't call, she'll holler at me. I'm trying to be a good wife and mother, but he's just so childish. —ROBERTA, 29, EAU CLAIRE, WISCONSIN

Roberta, you've become the nagging mother that you hated as a kid. In your attempt to have the perfect marriage, house, kids, and lasagna, you've brought to life the horrifying stereotype of the nagging wife. It even starts before the wedding day with a woman deciding, as Adelaide is advised in the musical *Guys and Dolls,* to "marry the man today and change his ways tomorrow." (Of course, men buy into the opposite: marry her and she'll never change.) The idea of a man as a work in progress meant to be carefully molded by a woman who has nothing better to do with her time or her life (until her more malleable children come along) seems disrespectful. I'm not sure where the idea that loving someone was a license to criticize began. The idea of home being a place where you're constantly corrected goes a long way to explain why happy hour, when you can get really plastered before heading home, is such a popular American institution.

Pointing out the error of someone's ways implies that

+ They don't know any better.
+ You do.
+ You are morally superior to them.
+ Unless you constantly remind them, they will revert to their less moral ways.

This is not only the Warden Theory of Interaction but the Naggy, Whiny Warden Way of Life. The assumption that men in general and children in particular won't know the right thing to do unless you tell them repeatedly just gives someone who has little else to focus on something to do to make everyone miserable. This is a seriously bad idea!

Roberta, it's time to stop treating your husband like a moron. If you like his mom, you can send her a card. If not, simply remember that she's *his* mom, not yours. Treating people as if they're stupid encourages stupidity. Before I leave you snuggling with your honey, let me share a true story with you.

A journalist once asked a gorgeous, sexy, accomplished French financier why he had never married. He replied, "I was looking for the perfect woman." The journalist said, "Too bad you never found her." "But I did," the financier answered. "She was looking for the perfect man."

Since we all know our terrible little secret—that we're not perfect—looking for someone who *is* perfect is both daunting and self-defeating. Not only might we be judged by a harsh standard, but since perfect people can never make mistakes, anything that goes wrong has to be some else's fault because to admit error would make us . . . yep, less than perfect, so we set up a system of blame. Somebody has to pay. If you haven't already noticed, most people aren't crazy about being blamed for something, *especially* if they feel it's their fault. After all, we're living in a society that has raised perfectionism to cult status.

Accepting blame means you've got a crack in that perfect facade and it's only a matter of time before you're found out. It becomes frightfully important to get someone else to take the blame, so you've got a battle that no one wants to lose. These fights to the death with one person left standing are really hard on personal relations.

CONSTRUCTIVELY CRITICIZE

✳

My lady friend and I were playing cards with another couple three nights ago. We were sitting around the table and she mispronounced "Versailles." When I corrected her, she glared at me, didn't say another word to me all evening, and hasn't spoken to me since. I just didn't want her to embarrass herself in front of my friends. —IRVING, 64, CLEVELAND, OHIO

Irving, the notion of constructive criticism was invented by a know-it-all without friends or social graces. No one likes to be corrected and certainly not publicly. Saying, "But I was only trying to help" isn't going to make things any better. Are you sure your intention was to help, or might you have been trying to show how smart you were, so as not to feel embarrassed by her mistake? The next time you want to help, just ignore the mispronunciation. If you correct it reflexively, you can apologize by saying, "Sorry! I spoke without thinking."

Even if you think your motives are kind and loving, you're not helping unless people want to hear what you have to say. If they don't, you're just making it that much harder for them to take a step back and evaluate what *they* want to do, not what you want them to do. When you correct some-one, you take a position of intellectual and sometimes moral superiority, and that is often tough for the chastised person to swallow. Making some-one feel like a child isn't healthy for relationships, even parent-child rela-tionships.

The nastiest possibility here, Irving, is that you were somehow ashamed of your friend and felt that her goof reflected badly on you. Believing in a perfect universe means expecting other people to comple-ment (and compliment) us, which implies somehow that we're incom-plete. If adults don't feel self-reliant, we're talking serious trouble here. What if that other person is out of town, out of sorts, distracted, or depressed? By expecting other people to make us happy or whole we are placing a huge burden on others, and most people don't function all that well when they feel overburdened. This kind of emotional claustrophobia isn't a prescription for anything but panic. Other people can add to or detract from our happiness, but the job of being happy is your personal responsibility. So apologize to your friend, tell her if you correct her again in public, you'll give her $25 on the spot. Don't assume that since she loves you she knows you're sorry. Love isn't about mind reading; it's about feeling safe enough to be ourselves, even if that means scattering mispro-nunciations here and there.

ALWAYS DO YOUR BEST

✳

I tell my kids I don't care what their grades are as long as they do their best every day. My pa used to beat me when I got a D, and I remember feeling just awful for days. I swore I would never do that to my kids. —CECIL, 38, SPRINGFIELD, MASSACHUSETTS

Cecil, isn't it amazing how we can lose the point so easily? I know you're really trying to be a better parent, but in the effort, you've changed the words but not the tune. You hated the fact that no matter how hard you tried, your best wasn't good enough for your dad. He felt that if you failed at school, he had failed as a parent. You're certainly less threatening to your child on the face of it. But if your son thinks he's letting you down, he may feel just as awful as you did. We have good days, slack-off days, play-it-safe days, and go-for-it days. The notion that we should be at peak performance all the time is the Human Being as Robot Theory. None of us can do our best *every* day. What would "best" mean if it was so ordinary you *could* do it every day? By placing that burden on your children's shoulders, by saying, "I expect you to do your best," you're setting them up to fail, to disappoint you and themselves. Wow, *quelle* bummer.

Trying to be the perfect parent by doing the opposite of your parents is unrealistic and the stuff of which blame is made. Trying to live up to an unreachable goal will make you tired and testy and a pain in the neck to be around. And if you somehow manage to attain this mythical state of perfection, you may find that others are unwilling to play with you 'cause you're so intimidating. Which will make you a perfect lonely person or a pain in the neck.

Perfectionism also sets impossible standards for others. Can you imagine someone saying to Joan of Arc, "How about going out to dinner sometime?" and her saying, "I can't. I've got to save France tomorrow." How about a simple, "No, thank you?" This holier-than-thou stuff is hard to take. I'll bet no one ever asked her out more than once. And she wondered why her army deserted her. Her troops were probably thinking, "If she's so perfect, why does she need a nummy like me on the battlefield?"

So what's the alternative to believing in and expecting perfection? How can we cut each other some slack? What if we became willing to stifle the impulse to offer our opinion unless we were specifically asked for it? What if we treated kids—ours or everyone else's—with the same respect we accord a stranger who accidentally bumps into us? If you stop regarding other people's actions as personal affronts, you might allow yourself to enjoy your imperfect but lovely little self, and your shoulders may unhunch. Try the LERR approach: Loving, Evolving, Respectful, and Reasonable. It doesn't spell "perfection," but it may spell "happiness."

SHRINK-WRAPS

If you've been paying attention, you've probably noticed that the metaphor for perfection is often physical; the idea that a good person is a beautiful person is not unique to here and now. It has been just as treacherous and destructive for all its long history.

Pretty is as pretty does: No, pretty is as pretty looks. How people behave has little to do with how they look, although I do think we get the face we deserve as we get older—or, for some, the face they can afford.

Beauty is only skin deep: This is a confusing statement. It implies that there is more to beauty than skin and maybe hair and fingernails. Okay, so I too can figure out that the intent is to suggest that inner beauty, being kind or nice, is as valuable as good teeth and skin and bone structure. Duh, ever heard of beauty pageants? I'm not implying that beauty is crucial, but to suggest that being a good person will get you a screen test would be just plain delusional.

A thing of beauty is a joy forever: Check with your local plastic surgeon. Forever is a long time.

Misery loves company: Misery loves an audience. If you're trying to be company by saying, "I know how you feel" or "If you think that's bad, let me tell you what happened to me," you're about to find out that your company is not appreciated in the least.

FINE WHINES

- My daughter-in-law always gives me birthday presents that I hate. Why can't she be as thoughtful as I am?
- When I was your age . . .
- You always . . .
- You never . . .
- I'd never do something like that to you.

A PERFECTLY SILLY STORY

A perfect man and a perfect woman meet in a perfect place, have a perfect first date, and fall head over perfect heels in love. They have a perfect wedding with perfect in-laws and are well on their way to leading a perfectly wonderful life in a perfect house in the perfect suburb. They also have a perfectly adorable white picket fence and a cute cat and a lovely dog who get along—you guessed it—perfectly. One day the Perfects are out driving toward a perfect sunset in their perfect car, and they see Santa Claus beside the road. It turns out that his reindeer are on strike, so he's grounded. "How perfectly awful!" they exclaim. Being the perfect people we know them to be, they naturally stop, load Santa and all his gifts into their perfectly appropriate station wagon, and help him on his rounds. Alas, they hit an icy patch and bash into a tree, and only one person survives. Guess who that might be? Well, we know Santa Claus isn't real and there's no such thing as a perfect man . . . so . . . okay, you hate it. It's a joke, so don't blame me. And that's really the point about blaming someone when things don't go perfectly.

3

winning the lottery will free me

If money were the key to happiness, millionaires wouldn't have ulcers. They do and it's not.

Two *All-American* fantasies come crashing together to make the lottery fantasy: (1) "Money solves all problems," and (2) "Luck is better than hard work." This is the fast-food version of the can-do spirit that has fueled this country from its inception. And now the superlotteries have proven once and for all that bigger is not only better but a great deal more hysterical.

In our competitive capitalistic society, we have updated the Cinderella fairy tale from finding the prince and the glass slipper to a lottery ticket performing both magic wand and fairy godmother duties simultaneously. In that blinding flash, we leave the wicked family behind and take our rightful place among the chosen. Unfortunately this fantasy allows us to ignore the fact that adults have the power to make choices instead of passively lamenting our fate and awaiting the multimillion-to-one odds of being *chosen*.

The reality of winning the lottery is that it creates at least as many problems as it solves. The fantasy of winning the lottery can serve as a guide to what is important to us if we are willing to look seriously at how a windfall would affect our choices and priorities. The lottery fantasy can make reality more specific if we're willing to anchor it to a little hard work.

*

I'm always struggling to stay one step ahead of the bill collector. No matter how much I try, I'm always behind. Every week I buy a bunch of lottery tickets, even when I can't really afford them. I'm sure that one of these days I'm going to win the big one—like $40 million, at least, or even the jackpot that was almost $200 million. My wife says I'm a dreamer, but, hey, someone's gotta win, so why not me? We'd be fixed for life and we could relax and enjoy the good life. I'd buy a boat and a racing car, quit my job, and live the life of Riley. My wife would have furs and jewels. I'd build a bowling lane right in our new home—a mansion. —CHARLES, 39, PIEDMONT, CALIFORNIA

Charlie, you're not alone. Lottery-fueled fantasies raise untold zillions of dollars in all fifty states. Every week millions of otherwise rational, good-hearted, clear-headed people queue up, in the belief that there really is a chance that this time they could win. Somebody has to win, after all. Others believe that winning the lottery would be the answer to life's problems. As the sign says, all you need is a dollar and a dream.

The idea of getting something for nothing—or close to nothing—is the heart and soul of a country that seems to believe that dreams come true, whether it's flying to the moon, making images flicker on a screen, or giving everybody a shot at free education or a chance to own a car. We need to harness that ability to dream by focusing on our goals. My concern about lottery dreams is that there is no work involved; it's just a one-in-fifty-million long shot.

Look, far be it from me to bad-mouth a little innocent fun. I myself have been known to indulge in the gonzo dream from time to time while standing behind true believers in long lines to buy a ticket in the little soda store on the first floor of my building. I always promise to share my winnings with Abdul, the guy who sells me the ticket. He doesn't believe me for a minute, but he always smiles sweetly and promises that *this* time I'll win.

The first time I ever sidled into a place that sold lottery tickets, I felt daring and naughty. My daughter's first birthday was the day of the drawing, and I was a poor starving Ph.D. candidate writing my dissertation and working to put a husband through graduate school and living in Massachusetts. Buying the ticket was less about the money than about me being superstitious and sentimental. Interestingly, I had no dream when I bought that first ticket, just some ill-defined wish to test my luck, to not be so poor, to prove I was a good person who would be rewarded. When all this mojo failed to produce a winning number (I bought a ticket with my daughter's birth date, on her *birthday,* and I still didn't win), I became so skeptical of lotteries that it was another twelve years before I bought my second ticket.

Pennsylvania had the first lottery of over $40 million, nearly three times what any other lottery had been worth at the time. I was living in New York at the time and trying to figure out how I could get to Pennsylvania to buy a ticket, since I didn't own a car. It occurred to me in a flash that my radio program was heard there, so I went on the air and said if someone would buy me a lottery ticket, I would pay him back. A listener called and asked, "If you win, will you quit your job?" I said, "No way!" He then said he would buy the ticket.

I didn't win, and, yes, it did occur to me that if I *had* won, I'd have had an awful time negotiating my next contract. Which really brings me to my point: the *real*—albeit hidden—cost of the lottery fantasy is much more than the dollar spent on the ticket, or I would not have included winning the lottery as a dangerous fantasy. The real cost isn't the buck or two we spend on the ticket but the emotional price tag that is shouldered by all of us who

- ✦ Dream rather than problem-solve.
- ✦ Place our faith in a fifty-million-to-one long shot.
- ✦ Buy into the completely fanciful notion that money is the fountain from which all goodness flows.

That last notion is truly dangerous, passive, unlikely, and wrong-headed—the world according to the Church of *Lifestyles of the Rich and Famous,* with Robin Leach as its patron saint. Charlie, since you're a firm believer, pass the collection plate. Amen.

The dream of getting something for nothing is as old as human history. Fabulous lost cities, the gold of the Incas, and the treasure of the Sierra Madre, have long tempted people to abandon their families, their loyalties, and their sanity. The Bible, Hollywood, and Charles Dickens have all warned that the search for wealth is pointless. But it's easy to ignore these cautionary tales of punished greed when the rent is overdue, our kids want the latest expensive gizmo, or we're just too tired to count any more pennies or clip any more coupons. The daydream of unearned wealth allows our heart to escape our day-to-day feeling of failure.

All of us want respite from worry. Unfortunately, money is seldom the answer. In fact, a number of studies have shown that the opposite is true:

+ Marriages are often more solid when there is little rather than a lot of money.
+ Successful people seldom mention money as a primary motivation.
+ Lottery winners are almost universally less happy after winning than before they won.
+ Sudden wealth is actually slightly more stressful than sudden poverty.

So why and how did Charlie and the rest of us get this notion that winning the lottery would mean instant happiness? Well, part of it may be that poverty stinks. Worrying about survival is exhausting. But somewhere between survival and massive wealth is a healthy perspective on money and an emotionally balanced life, as opposed to a financially balanced checkbook.

I'm not going to try to sell you or anybody else the Mother Teresa theory of life, that poverty is holy. Worrying about money is a draining, joyless, and a miserable task. If you've got plenty of money, it's masturbatory. If you don't, focusing on your empty wallet is painful. Worrying about anything is counterproductive. Worrying eats up your time and energy without accomplishing squat, and it makes you feel victimized. The alternative to passivity is action. Get a job, get a budget, get a roomie, and get a good night's sleep. The thing to do is figure out how much you need for what you want; the difference between *need* and *want;* and what you can do to stop worrying.

But this chapter isn't a make-money seminar. It's a look at the seductive but mistaken notion that the important problems in life can be solved by money. The real seduction of the money-equals-happiness equation is that it diverts us from an analysis of the real problem. If you don't know the problem, you'll never get the answer. Money is seldom the problem; it's just the *symptom* of the problem. If money is always the answer, we'll never ask the real questions.

So where do we start, Charlie? We know four things about you:

- ◆ You live beyond your means.
- ◆ You're sad.
- ◆ You and your wife argue about money.
- ◆ You're not looking at what's really making you unhappy.

It's going to be hard for you to figure out what might make you feel better.

Charlie, let's start with the basics. Do you like your work? Are you paid the same as everyone else who does the same thing? If you learned some new skills either through training, an apprenticeship, or more schooling, would you get paid more money or enjoy other responsibilities? How do you and your wife spend your money? What do you and she consider luxuries and necessities? Do you eat out, buy lots of toys for the kids, go on expensive vacations? Do you have the same philosophy about saving and spending? Do you pay bills together? Does your wife work? And, Charlie, I know this is getting personal, but how's your sex life? Don't panic on me here. Lots of people have an easier time talking about their bedroom than their bank account, and to help you, I need to know about both.

If you're getting the feeling that money is more than inert green crinkly stuff, then you're well on your way to seeing the big picture—that money isn't anything. It's only symbolic, so it can't make you or anybody else happy. You've got to figure out what money represents to you. Is it freedom, status, or a chance to show your dad that you're successful?

In the early days of my radio program in Boston, I was inventing as I went along, since I had never intended to be on the air and I had no role models. I literally got called out of the blue to see if I wanted to do a talk show. I asked, "What's a talk show?" When I was in the car, I only listened to music. Once the radio folks explained what they wanted, I said, "No, thank you," and I've been doing the talk show ever since. I am easily convinced when somebody's really nice, so I decided to give it a try.

When I chose topics, I could get my listeners to call me to talk about seemingly difficult subjects—their shyness, adultery, never having kids. But when I suggested that people call in to talk about money, the phones went silent . . . and this was in the go-go eighties. Nobody wanted to talk about the psychology of money. I'm convinced that money is the last great taboo subject. We can talk about sex, politics, and religion, and we can even talk about how to *make* money, but when it comes to our *feelings* about money, we fall silent. As a topic, however, it is not only one of the most frequent subtext woo-woos on the program—a major preoccupation of American life—but also the stuff of which dreams are made. (In case you were wondering, "subtext woo-woo" is something hot and intense and important and sexy but completely unexamined. Don't worry if you didn't know, I made it up.)

MONEY AS CONTROL

✳

We fight about money all the time. Harold, my husband, just cusses a blue streak, pouts, or gets mad if I even bring it up. I've told him my folks will tide us over for a while, but it just makes him stomp out of the room. I admit, sometimes I want something nice for me or the kids and I'll just go ahead and buy it, even if I have to go through his pockets to get the money. I'm tired of depriving myself and my kids of the nice things in life. —ABIGAIL, 33, HOUSTON, TEXAS

Abigail, let's not get distracted here. Remember, money isn't just paper; it represents power, choice, and control. Money has become a big green tug-of-war in your marriage, where you are consciously or unconsciously pitting your husband's ability to take care of you against your parents'. Money is a symbolic swaddling blanket and umbilical cord. This is really dangerous stuff. You remind me of a woman who said she was caught between two lovers, one of whom was sexy and one of whom was rich. I asked her why she didn't figure out a way to support herself and date the man who appealed to her. I left her pondering the possibilities.

You've gotten yourself into a situation where you're partially willing to cede control to your husband; you say he gets mad if you bring up the subject of money. If he gets angry enough, you'll back down, but you know he's going to be angry to begin with. You taunt him, and he intimidates you. If I had to guess, I would bet this is how your mom and dad dealt with money. He would holler; then she would back down. Then she would tell him what a big, powerful man he was and what a silly little girl she was, and they would go and make love. The issues never got resolved, so today you are still willing to go to your parents, which means you're still being the good little girl who's obeying their rules. At the same time, you're forcing Harold to become a parental figure when you behave like a little girl. How many grown women in America are still on allowances?

The lottery fantasy is obscuring the power struggles that are going on between the two of you. It's really important to your marriage that you think through who you are and what you want. The two of you need to sit down and work out a budget. You don't want to feel as though you've taken each other hostage in a bank. And you, Abigail, may want to consider getting a job so you're not reduced to going through his pockets or asking your folks for an allowance.

✳

If I offer to pick up the check, my date gets either flustered or angry. If he lets me pay, I never hear from him again. Hey, I make good money and I'm willing to pay my way. How come when a guy picks up the check, it's sexy, but when I do it, he thinks I'm trying to bust his chops? Either that or I find guys who want me to be their sugar mommy. What gives here? —SHIRLEY, 42, CHICAGO, ILLINOIS

A woman having money does not ensure the same wide choice of men. This isn't surprising. Society changes slowly, and women who marry for money are still considered lucky, whereas men who marry for money are considered gigolos. Again, money means power and control. It has traditionally been what men had and fought for and what women wanted and married.

One of the secrets that many men have known and women are just beginning to learn is that many, if not most, financially successful men didn't necessarily start out to make a lot of money. They had a good idea, a better way of doing something, a passion, or a rich daddy whom they wanted to impress. They often enjoyed what they were doing, and they were willing to throw themselves into their work without the usual limitations of an eight-hour day or eight hours of sleep or a differentiation between workdays and weekends. Countless books have documented the passion that successful individuals bring to their work. In these situations, money is a by-product of their energy.

Shirley, I know you're feeling frustrated, but realistically, thirty years of men and women thinking differently about each other and their money cannot undo the thousands of years of conditioning that have molded men and their thoughts about power. Of course, as women begin to pay their way, men will feel appreciated for who they are rather than what they earn. Even God figured it was going to take the Israelites two generations, a full forty years, to change from slave to free mentality. Men, to a large extent, have been enslaved by the notion that their money, their ability to provide, was the most important attribute they could offer women. It's going to take a while for them to get used to the fact that you can pay your own way—and his too.

If you can be gentle but firm while you pay with a smile, you'll make him feel the warmth of your respect rather than the power of your gold card. Don't rub his nose in the fact that you've taken away something he thought was crucial to attracting you: his superior earning power. When both men and women are able to support themselves, this will be a brave new world where all of us will be valued for something other than our credit rating.

✳

Mom says it's just as easy to fall in love with a rich man as a poor man. I love Kenneth, but she's probably right. He wants to be a high school gym teacher. Hank is not nearly as cute, but he's a stockbroker and drives a Porsche. Mom says, "When the wolf's at the door, love flies out the window." I don't know whether to believe my heart or my mom. —MADELINE, 29, KANSAS CITY, KANSAS

Madeline, I could definitely use your mom on my program. She speaks in sound bites that Aesop, that wonderful old Greek teller of fables, would love. She's right to the extent that money is more than just money. But she's overlooked the notion that if women want to be treated as equals, they may have to assume more of the financial burdens of life. Incidentally, if I were a man, I'm not sure I'd be so crazy about folks assuming that my worth was based on my bank account. I'm reasonably sure that I'd want to be loved for myself.

Men and women have historically viewed money completely differently, undoubtedly because men could earn it and women had to seduce it. The only women who had their own resources were members of the royalty or the aristocracy, and even they were often controlled by men. For men, money means power, status, alliances—all those big-ticket items having to do with self-definition and self-worth.

To men, money is life's report card; for women, it's security. Men gamble with money because historically they've had access to it. They could earn it, find it, marry it, inherit it, or steal it. Men have for centuries been judged by the size of their wallets, and unfortunately for all concerned, this hasn't changed all that much. This fact has also made the risk-taking more exciting as well as crucial to their emotional well-being and standing in society. The more money a man could accumulate, the greater his power, which in turn increased his choice of women. Men gambled with money, whereas women gambled for love and took emotional risks. You can't gamble with what you don't have. It has only been recently, in the last several decades, that women have had access to their own money instead of just inheriting it upon the death of their husband or father.

✳

I don't really understand why my office manager is always harping about money. She's always telling me how hard she works, and if she threatened to quit, I'd probably have to come up with some extra money. She thinks she can guilt me into paying her more, but it just makes me take her less seriously. — LARRY, 54, BILLINGS, MONTANA

Larry, you've got to remember that you have been thinking about money and working since you were a Cub Scout. Women have come to the party a little later and are still sorting through the plan.

I can remember one Thanksgiving when I was seated at a large table with a bunch of men I didn't know. I was feeling particularly sorry for myself because I was far away from home and the guys who had promised me the moon at work hadn't paid me for months while treating me as if I didn't have the sense God gave a goldfish. I had just moved to a new city, was working long hours and scrounging to pay my rent. I was broke, lonesome, and questioning my judgment as well as my economic viability. I detailed my list of grievances to my dinner companions and added the final indignity, that the guys I worked for had really hurt my feelings. My dinner companion said, "Grow up. This is business. Their job is to get you to work for the least amount possible. It's just a game. If you're going to take the whole thing personally, you're not mature enough to be working." Wow, talk about your cold shower. In spite of his technique, he really was right. Taking work personally is a major mistake.

Larry, I'm not saying your office manager is quite as fragile as I was back then, but a lot of this business awareness is fairly new to women, even though we try to tough it out. Because women have been working for so much less of their history, we don't understand the rules, and we tend to take things personally. It's kind of like imagining what would happen if a Martian came down and played football for the first time. If he got tackled, the Martian would very likely be frightened and assume these weird Earthlings hated him. To the Earthlings, tackling is just part of the game.

So, Larry, don't tackle your office manager, but do tackle the problem by understanding her. That's what being a good manager is all about. And let's face it, as women, we're here, we're near, we try not to cry, and we work hard, so get used to it.

While we're at it, be aware that the office situation is a bit tricky for women managers as well. We're still learning the guy rules—for example, when men call each other rude names, it's usually camaraderie, but it can turn ugly: "s.o.b." is a term of endearment, but "bastard" is a grievous assault. Be patient, fella, not because we're powerless but because we're new to the game. Camaraderie—being one of the boys—is tricky.

Women in the workplace are still trying to learn the rules that you guys take for granted, whether they're about money or language or informal organization. As women in ever greater numbers begin making money in traditional male positions, everybody is having to learn new rules. The reason for the upheaval women have created in the workplace isn't related to the jobs or the money or the work; it's related to the fact that access to money is access to traditional male bastions—status, control, and choice.

Which brings us full circle—back to the lottery. The lottery fantasy is the shortcut to all the goodies that money can get you without any of the investment of hard work, time, and effort. Shortcuts are problematical, which is why most lottery winners end up miserable. I'm not trying to convince you that buying a lottery ticket is the first step to a wasted life. Heck, it's only a buck. I am trying to persuade you to scope out what money specifically symbolizes for you so you can figure out how to make your life richer without that winning lottery ticket. Once you know that money is only psychological and the only thing you can win in the lottery is money, you can ask yourself what *you* would do if you won the lottery. The answer is the meaning to your life. Money can't do anything. It can neither set you free nor enslave you. However, your ideas about money can enslave you. This is proved by lottery winners whose lives have been ruined, whose marriages have failed, whose kids have ended up suing them, and whose friends have left while the hangers-on have stayed. Sudden wealth is like sudden anything else; it's upsetting and disruptive. We think wealth is the goal, but it's only a tool to help you achieve that goal. Play the lottery game in your head. Play "what if . . ." and see what you'd do with the money to make your life better. Be richer for the understanding. And then, if you really want to, buy a ticket for a giggle. The lottery fantasy does have a terrific function as long as you *use* it instead of *believing* in it.

MONEY AS FREEDOM

*

He cheats on me, drinks away his paycheck, and yells at the kids, and we haven't had sex in a year. I'd leave him, but I love him. —CARLA, 44, SANTA ROSA, CALIFORNIA

Pretend for a moment that you have just won the lottery, Carla. Would you stay with him or would you go? You'd be out of there in a New York minute. Right? Anything you'd do if you had the money, you can likely do without the money if you put your mind to it and plan it. Honest. Don't kid yourself that you're staying in a lousy place for love. Tina Turner said it all when she said, "What's love got to do with it?" You've got to learn to love yourself first. Never, ever, ever let yourself be duped into thinking that love is money or money is love. And don't feel bad, Carla. You're not alone in this kind of thinking.

You may tell yourself that you stay in this rotten situation because you love him, but it's more likely because you hate yourself and are afraid you don't deserve better. Money won't buy you self-esteem, but a job will give you the emotional independence to find out who you are and what you want. For a moment, let yourself dream of what you thought he could give you and figure out how you can get it for yourself. Understand that money is only a key that unlocks the door—it's not the door, it's not the room, it's not the contents. Think for a minute. How can your lottery pipe dreams translate into laying a functional structure for real-life happiness? Maybe you can come up with a list that looks like this:

LOTTERY	REAL-LIFE SOLUTION
Travel	Work for a travel agent or on a cruise ship
Go to law school	Find a work-study program
Leave the stinker	Get a job and a lawyer

Get out of debt	Consolidate your loans, declare bankruptcy, and eat macaroni and cheese
Buy jewelry	Call the Home Shopping Network
Buy an island	You're right, you *do* need to win the lottery

Anything you can do if you win the lottery (except buy that mythical island), you can very likely do on a slightly smaller scale with hard work and perseverance. Most of us aren't going to win the lottery, but if we figure out what we'd do to make ourselves happy with that money we're well on our way to making ourselves happy, period.

If I've been able to convince you that money is almost always shorthand for something else—a greenwash, if you will, that can obscure the true problem and thus the true solution, you're well on your way to making your life work better. If you're not quite willing to completely give up the money angle, don't be embarrassed. People who aren't funny about anything else are funny about money. Folks who can rationally deal with a houseful of company, last-minute workloads, weepy friends, and ingrown toenails are a little squirrelly when it comes to money.

MONEY AS LOVE

✳

My mother just died. I've always taken care of her, since I was the one who didn't marry. Mom would wait for my sister, Sue, to call and then spend days telling me how special that phone call made her feel, when I was the one spending every day trying to make her comfortable. Mom left me her house and a little bit of money. My sister has always been jealous, and now she says that I've cheated her out of her birthright and turned Mom against her. I could give her some money, I guess, but I don't want to go against Mother's final wishes.
—STELLA, 64, ATLANTA, GEORGIA

Stella, let me say up front that it's your money and you can do anything you want with it. My concern isn't your inheritance of money but your mom's legacy of competition between you and your sister. If you had won the money in the lottery instead of inheriting it from Mom, would you give your sister something? I'll bet you would. Because this isn't about money per se; this is about your mother and what she gave or didn't give to the two of you. This is about sibling rivalry—that green-eyed envious ache that makes you resent your sister because you feel Mom loved her best when you were the one who did all the work. It's time for you and Sue to work it out. Maybe it's time to learn to share. It sounds like Mom's bequest has given you power that you didn't feel you had when she was alive. You are now vindicated: your mom *did* love you; maybe she even loved you best. You don't have to compete with your sister to win Mom's love. It sounds as if Sue is feeling a bit unloved at this particular moment. Rather than gloat (I know, it's tempting), remember how awful jealousy feels. You have the power to make *both* of you feel wonderful at neither's expense.

✳

He beats me, but afterward he always tells me that he loves me. I'd leave him, but there's nowhere for me to go. —JANE, 41, CARSON CITY, NEVADA

Jane, you're breaking my heart. Think lottery! If you won the lottery, would you stay or would you go? You could do anything you wanted. Think survival! I know it's hard to believe that you deserve attention if you've been around someone who used you as a punching bag. Go on welfare, get a job, find a friend, but get out! Use the lottery fantasy to save yourself. He beats you because he hates himself and he feels small. Making you cower makes him feel bigger. It's very likely his daddy felt the same way and did the same thing to his mama and to him. If you love him, leave him and give him a chance to save himself. But most important, save yourself. Use that fantasy of money as a way to get a new life. This isn't about money, honey, even though I know you think it is.

It might surprise you to know that rich women get battered too. Wives of doctors and lawyers and judges and ministers and rabbis and CEOs. Their husbands have money, but it's not the wives' money, and they feel that nobody in the community would believe such a fine upstanding man could hit a woman. They feel every bit as isolated and powerless as you do. Battering is about emotional power, not spending power. Women are conditioned to be passive, so even a wealthy woman will often go out of her way to appear submissive so her femininity won't be questioned. Few women covet the label "castrating," no matter how large their bank account. Jane, if you can't change your self-image, I'm terrified you will just exchange one thug in your life for another and continue to believe that you're second rate and don't deserve better.

MONEY AS CHOICE

✳

I just got offered a promotion, but it would mean moving away from my wife's folks, and my son would miss his senior year with his friends. My wife really doesn't want to move. She spends her days playing tennis, chatting with her friends, and working in her garden, which I think is great, but I feel if I turn down this promotion, I'm doomed with the company. —WALTER, 43, SOUTH BEND, INDIANA

Walter, try the lottery trick: if tomorrow you won millions of dollars, would you move or stay? If you're like most men, you like working, even though sometimes you wake up in the middle of the night worrying about supporting your family. Your work makes you feel important, and it should. Once you admit that to yourself, you can negotiate with the family about their needs as well. Can your son find someone to live with while he finishes high school with his friends? Is an unconscious tug-of-war going on between you and your in-laws for your wife's attention? Would she be willing to get a job so she could help support the family if you turn down the move? Is there something that would entice her to move? A larger house, to accommodate parental visits? More glamorous vacations? Going back to school? On the other hand, if you don't like your job, maybe this is an opportunity for you to think about your career in different terms.

Maybe the two of you are having marital problems, and taking a job in a new city is an unconscious way to force the issue? Perhaps this isn't really about money at all, but as long as both of you believe it is, you're stuck. Once you're willing to look at things together, your wife might choose to get a job herself. She might also opt to compromise by agreeing to stay in the new city for two years and return home if she didn't like it. The two of you might decide to have another child. Or maybe she's frightened about being in a new place or having to get a job. Whatever you decide together, as a family, will be better than anything you decide yourself. Consensus will remove this awful burden from your shoulders and make *everyone* feel powerful.

✳

I've been dating a widow for two years. She never offers to pay for anything, and when I hint about it, she says she's old-fashioned and her husband always paid for everything. Should I dump her? —GEORGE, 74, MIAMI BEACH, FLORIDA

George, you've got a really good point here, but you're bucking centuries of tradition. Men have access to power and money, and as such they have bartered for the favors of women. Is this a sexist practice? You bet your sweet bippy it is. Because something has existed for a long time doesn't mean it's right or appropriate or that it should be continued. I just want you to understand the magnitude of the historical precedent that your lady friend is consciously or unconsciously invoking. The man has traditionally courted the woman; each had something the other wanted. The man had money and power; the woman provided sex. We're talking the basic law of supply and demand here. Whether you're aware of it or not, that's actually part of what is going on with your lady friend. You're aware that the economics have shifted and that she too has wealth. She's aware that the demographics have shifted; there are a lot more women her age than available men. What's really interesting and a little difficult here is that you used to have the monopoly on money and she used to have the corner on sex. When one thing changes in society, especially in an economic model, everything changes.

Economics has gone through several shifts in the last century or so. Economic survival in developed countries is less of an issue, conspicuous consumption affects more people than ever before, and the emergence of a middle class has changed class structure forever. The rise of the middle class has changed how human beings do business because it has changed the way we think about money. For most of human history, what you were born into was what you got. If you were lucky enough to get rich parents, hurrah! And if you weren't, well, there was always the next life. (Where are you, Shirley MacLaine, when we really need you?) With the emergence of a middle class, the rigidity of the class system was dealt its first serious blow. The problem is that being in the middle is always a bit tricky and uncertain.

Being in the middle encourages people to aspire to have more while being aware of the danger of losing what they have. So, George, on a microcosmic level, you are reflecting a huge chunk of human economic history. You are feeling the pinch of being caught in the middle, between what you have and what you want. And you fear losing what you do have without the possibility of being able to regain it. All this can be challenging and fun when you're young, but it gets more and more treacherous as we get older and feel less able to make more or to make do.

George, are you still paying attention? If you remember the symbolic value of money, figure out what your fears are about money, control, and feeling taken advantage of. Sort out what you want and what you're willing to trade off in return. Try not to let yourself be too irritated or distracted by the fact that your friend has the ability but not the motivation to pay her own way. It's a weird new economic world out there. Don't panic, but don't try to have it both ways: the same old power without the need to take economic responsibility. The only real rule here is that there aren't many reliable rules left, especially regarding men, women, and money.

✳

We've only been married six months, but my wife complains when my office has a going-away party and my colleagues and I are supposed to divvy up the check for the honoree. She says she brown-bags it so we can keep to our budget, that she only spends money on us. She makes me feel guilty and selfish, but I'd feel like a real jerk not sharing the check with the other guys. What am I supposed to say: "We're really struggling here, so I'll buy my own lunch, but I'm not willing to contribute to the wine or my fair share of the meal for the guest of honor." My wife already makes me feel that I'm not living up to her expectation as a provider, and now this. I've gotten so I make up excuses not to go out with the gang at lunch 'cause I'm so worried. Either I look cheap to them or I'm a wastrel to her. —ALAN, 34, WASHINGTON, D.C.

Alan, you're right to be concerned here. The major cause of the breakup of marriages is money—not the lack of it as much as arguments about who spends how much on what and why. The issue of resources gets all caught up with dominance and submission, aggression and passivity, male and female. It's that old money-as-symbol thing again.

If everyone were rich, money wouldn't matter to anyone. It is a basic premise of human behavior that something is valued in direct proportion to its scarcity.

What we don't have always looms larger than what we do have. If I looked carefully at your situation, I would guess that what the two of you are fussing about here isn't money but how you *spend* your money. Your wife is saying she spends significant money only with you, but you spend money without her. If the two of you could each have a bit of cash of your own to do with as you wish, you might join the going-away party and she might splurge on herself—or even on you. It matters not. The point is that each of you would have some funds over which the other has no control. This might seriously lessen the antagonism between you and your wife, which has less to do with money than with how it's spent.

Sometimes it's easier to see the big picture if you're not looking in a mirror, so let me give you another example.

✳

My boyfriend and I are planning to get married. I don't get along very well with my father. He and my mom divorced when I was twelve. He's got lots of money, and I figure the least he can do is pay for my wedding. He says he'll split the cost with me. I told him if he doesn't pay for the whole thing he can forget about walking me down the aisle. —MIRIAM, 27, BOISE, IDAHO

Can you see that Miriam and her father are basically arguing about power and importance? Money is a way of paying homage. It can also be a way to punish people for past sins—war reparations, for example, are the revenge of the victor on the vanquished—or to get even for real or imagined slights. It is a way to control people.

Weddings are also about homage and power. Historically, a dowry was exchanged by men (the bride's father to groom) for the possession of a nubile female. Miriam, without even being aware of it, you're getting caught up in ancient issues. You're bartering with your father: "Pay my price and I will publicly acknowledge you as my father," wiping out your guilt. This is clearly big-league, expensive baggage attached to money, sentiment, status, and wedding cake.

Miriam, I hope you can see through all your various posturings to your heart which is poignantly asking your dad, "How much do you love me?" On some level, in all of these scenarios my callers were programmed to believe that love equals money.

✳

My friend and I go out a lot together, and she's always picking up the check. She's generous, and she has gobs more money than I do, but it makes me feel awful that I can't pay my own way. When I offer, she just tut-tuts me and says, "You can get it next time," but there's never a next time. —JOYCE, 58, HUNTSVILLE, ALABAMA

Joyce, this dilemma seems new and fresh and confusing to you because women have been doin' for themselves—economically, at least—only for the last twenty-five years or so, which is just the blink of an eye in human history. Ordinary everyday females are paying bills and buying cars, dinners, and jewelry with their own earned income. So don't panic. The phenomenon is new, but it isn't awful or all that dangerous. Explain to your friend that her largesse is making you feel small. You might offer to fix dinner for her at your house, baby-sit her grandkids or put together a photo album for her.

Before there was money, there was barter. Now that there's money, we barter love and respect without acknowledging the real issues. You might be able to explain to your friend that you understand that it gives her enormous pleasure to offer something of value to you, but you'd like to reciprocate rather than feel beholden to her. It's okay not to have much money; it's not okay to feel you have nothing to contribute.

The basis of any relationship is the assumption that everyone should bring something to the party. When we use that horrendous term "low self-esteem" we're talking about an absence of psychological and emotional money in the bank. The real question in every life, in every relationship, is whether each of us has enough to share. If you have a lot, the question is what can you prudently give up without changing the balance of power.

Make no mistake. Most people live by that other Golden Rule: He or she who has the gold rules. This explains why charity always feels terrific for the giver and uncomfortable and controlling for the receiver. It's an inherent statement of superiority that's often couched in moral terms.

Differences of any kind can cause problems, but when those differences are about money, logic flies out the window. In our heads we may understand that it's only money, but in our hearts we often believe that the rich are different, smarter, worthier, and freer. Even when all of the evidence

winning the lottery will free me   51

points to the contrary, we believe that rich folks are happier than poor folks, so why not aspire to be rich?

Money definitely does not make the world go around. It doesn't even stabilize its orbit. Feelings about money and all that surrounds it may make human beings behave in predictable ways. Believing in the power of money is like believing in the power of the flag, which is merely a piece of cloth that we salute in school or at a baseball game. It's not the cloth that has value, but what it represents.

Most things in life have very little to do with money. The only exception to this occurs when someone says, "I'm going to do something, and it has nothing to do with money." Don't believe it. In this case it's all about money.

Money can buy lots of trinkets—and sometimes even souls—but it has no value other than that with which we imbue it. Instead of believing that money will solve all your problems, figure out what your problems are and what you can do about them.

SHRINK-WRAPS

FALSE MONEY FANTASIES

Money is the root of all evil: Money is inert and doesn't move at all. Greed, envy, anger, and revenge are nasty, but money is just wrinkly paper.

Clothes make the man: Nope, but socks give you a fair hint.

Waste not, want not: Nah, even if you're frugal, something new and improved will catch your eye and inspire you to clean out your closet. And please don't think that dress will come back into style or that it has a few more good years left.

A fool and his money are soon parted: Where did the fool get the money to begin with? Besides, Wall Street brokers and comedians seem to me to be doing pretty darn well these days.

It's better to give than to receive: Well, it's certainly easier to give than to receive, since then you don't have to say thank you or pretend you like it. But it's sorta cool to get stuff, too. If all you do is give, you'll expect a huge amount of gratitude, which will make you wrinkly and cranky and bitter before your time and more than a little controlling.

MONEY SONGS TO BE AVOIDED LIKE THE PLAGUE

+ "Money makes the world go around."
+ "All I want is a man who is loaded with money." No, you don't. You just think you do.

SONGS TO MEMORIZE

+ "I'm Only a Bird in a Gilded Cage"—trapped by a rich man's wishes.
+ "Little Rock"—he thought he could buy me and he did . . . for a while.

SONGS TO TAKE WITH A HUGE GRAIN OF SALT

+ Nearly anything country.

MOVIES THAT PROVE MY POINT

+ *Two for the Road:* Audrey Hepburn and Albert Finney do fine until he gets rich.
+ *It's a Mad Mad Mad Mad World:* Everybody does fine until there's the possibility of everybody getting rich.
+ *It Could Happen to You:* Nicholas Cage shares a winning lottery ticket with Bridget Fonda, a waitress. The ticket ruins a marriage, a job, a friendship, and everybody's life
+ *Down and Out in Beverly Hills:* A homeless man, Nick Nolte, is far "wealthier" than his rich benefactors, Bette Midler and Richard Dreyfuss, who take him in and who are, in turn, taken in.
+ *The First Wives Club:* Goldie Hawn, Bette Midler, and Diane Keaton are all dumped when their hubbies get richer, older, and friskier. They seek revenge by taking their husbands to the cleaners, as they gleefully dance through Manhattan in an all-white wardrobe with matching pumps.

4

the truth will set you free

We each have to find our own truth.

W*e believe in* truth big-time. Well, actually we believe in truth as our own personal crusade. We know the truth, and we're going to make sure everyone else knows it. In this overbearing fantasy, there is only one version of the truth, and it will set everyone free.

This preoccupation with truth is based on two widely held and completely inaccurate assumptions: (1) that there is a secret to life, and (2) that mistakes should be confessed instantly.

In a three-dimensional world, different versions of reality exist, so finding the real truth is tricky. If the search for truth were simple, I wouldn't regard it as a dangerous fantasy, but the word "truth" itself reeks of a dangerous and sometimes hostile self-righteousness.

✳

My sister just got engaged to a real loser. One of the reasons I know he stinks is that I had an affair with him while he was dating her. I told her she could do better, and she said I was just jealous. So I told her the truth, that he was scummy enough to cheat on her with me. Now she's not speaking to me and she's going to marry him anyway. —AMELIA, 24, BATON ROUGE, LOUISIANA

Amelia, it's hard to feel terribly sorry for you at this moment, since your righteous indignation is based on a pretty scuzzy act. When Superman said he stood for truth, justice, and the American way, I'm not sure he was referring to doing your sister's boyfriend and then confessing. Even the Man of Steel might question your motives here.

I know that most Americans believe that truth and justice are the only way to go. Those values are part of our founding philosophy and our national psyche. Most of the rest of the world would consider this a hopelessly naive and romantic notion, but we persist in believing that truth is knowing not only what *is* (fact) but also what is *right* (truth). Justice is making truth work, making sure everybody acts the *right* way, the *American* way. We also believe that anybody (else) who doesn't tell the truth should be swiftly and summarily punished by a bolt of lightning or, at very least, a guilty conscience. In this comforting fantasy, doing right is easy and obvious.

Buying into this fantasy allows the self-righteous to view themselves as the instrument of destiny. No need to wait for *divine* retribution: "Hey, if the powers that be are busy, I'm willing to step in and punish you for your sins." So as long as we're telling the *truth*, we are not only blameless for any fallout but morally superior for being aware of the truth and courageous enough to speak out. Talk about self-serving . . . Admit it, how many times have you (yeah, you) said something wretched to someone and then responded to the person's anger by saying, "But I was only telling the truth." "Truth" and the resultant "justice" are surprisingly subjective terms. If this whole concept comes as a surprise, allow me to share the source of my perspective with you. Talk about shocking. . . .

Several years ago I had a phone system on my radio program that allowed my listeners to vote on any issue I could dream up. One day, when I was in a particularly feisty mood, I decided to hold a vote on cheating. I asked my listeners two questions:

1. If you knew you could get away with it, would you cheat on your income tax?
2. If you knew your neighbors were cheating, would you turn them in to the IRS?

I wasn't all that surprised that a full 75 percent of the respondents said they would cheat if they knew they would never get caught. But I must admit to being more than a little flabbergasted that 93 percent of the people who would cheat said that they would rat out their neighbor. Wow, what a dramatic example of "If I can't get away with it, I'm going to make sure you don't either." (I'm convinced that Mother Teresa must have called several times to keep the count at 93 percent rather than 100 percent.)

So what happened to truth, justice, and the American way? Sounds like the reality is much more about sneakiness, vengeance, and nailing the IRS. What gives here? Is Amelia really getting a bum rap from her sister? Are her motives as pure as the driven snow? Should she stick to her fantasy that as long as she's telling the truth, things will work out to her advantage in the long run?

Let's give Amelia the benefit of the doubt. She wants to believe in facts, truth, and a describable, logical, shared reality. The only problem is finding the *right* answer. Please forgive me if I refuse to play along with the notion of one absolute truth, which works fine only as long as the one truth is *my* truth. Most of us get a bit queasy when others think they know the truth and it's not our version.

Amelia, I haven't forgotten you, I'm just trying to figure out a way to help you without sending you to the corner with a dunce cap. It's perfectly okay for you to disapprove of your sister's boyfriend, and if she asks if you like him, it's okay to be tactfully and specifically honest. But frankly, my dear, you surrendered your right to be a fountain of truth when you had sex with him. Now you need to learn your lesson, clean up your act and hope your sister doesn't marry him. Family gatherings are going to be tough enough as it is. Stop trying to hurt your sister and focus on your own life instead.

TRUTH IS OBVIOUS

❋

My parents have been divorced since I was three. I always thought Dad abandoned us. I've recently gotten in touch with my dad, and he says Mom and her parents said they'd sic the law on him if he didn't clear out. I don't know who's telling the truth and who's lying. —JEB, 19, SALEM, OREGON

Jeb, somebody said a very long time ago that there are three sides to every story: my side, your side, and the truth. I think this person was overly optimistic. Most of us can figure out several "sensible" versions to support our perspective. You're trying to remember a situation that occurred when you were three years old, and sixteen-year-old memories can be a bit hazy. I'm not sure you will ever know the truth here, but does it really matter? You don't have to get caught between your mom's version of the truth and your dad's. Believe whatever comforts you the most. Even if there is such a thing as truth, how in heaven's name are we going to discover it? An impartial observer would be hard to come by; even if you can find someone who knew both your mom and your dad, that person's version isn't necessarily any more truthful than what you already know.

So is there such a thing as truth? Before you feel the bedrock of your existence shiver under your feet, take a deep breath and remember some of the things you believed with your heart and soul five years ago. You may have bought a watch that was guaranteed to last forever or believed that cellular phones were a passing fancy, or been wildly in love with someone whose name you've since forgotten. You may have thought your best friend would always be shorter than you, or perhaps you felt certain you would never try sushi or that Garth Brooks was a flash in the pan. It's not that you were deluded at the time, but you're now older and wiser, and what you believe is based on a wider perspective. I'm not trying to rock your world but to convince you that we all have to find our own truth, that truth is going to change, and that your personal truth won't necessarily be shared by anyone else.

Once you accept that truth is personal, you can relax and figure out your own rules. You can also stop looking for others to show you the way, and you can comfortably and happily give up the notion that you have to convince others that their truth is wrong and yours is right.

You don't have to worry if one of your folks is lying, Jeb. They could both be telling the truth—their version of the truth. If you look for your own version of the truth and leave them to do the same, you can save a whole lot of wear and tear on your head, heart, and internal organs. You won't have to sift through clues or dread family reunions anymore. Well . . . no more than the rest of us.

Think of all the energy you'll have available to live your life in a way that makes sense to you. Whew, what a relief to not be the keeper of any flame but your own. You can choose your truth, based on whatever criteria make sense to you. So if you're looking for the guru, someone to tell you how to run your life, look to your mirror rather than the mountaintop, and understand that the search is ongoing.

✳

I try to keep up, I really do. One day my doctor says my cholesterol is high, the next day I read in a magazine that the standards are changing. Is fat good or bad? What about eggs? And do I really have to give up chocolate? — HENRIETTA, 51, ELKHART, INDIANA

Henrietta, I would *never* make you or anyone else give up chocolate. (I do it every year for Lent, since I'm always asking my radio listeners to do hard stuff like stop drinking, smoking, gambling, or fooling around. The sacrifice does nothing for my disposition, so I promise, you can keep your chocolate.)

I fear you're looking for the truth, which is hard to come by. Just remember that ideas are for using, not believing. *Belief* in an ideal way to eat will lock you in, which is limiting in a world of change. What we allow ourselves and what we deny ourselves is based on our beliefs about what is good and important, and those beliefs are going to change. Knowing who you are and what is important to you will make your life easier to run on a day-to-day basis.

I know you were only asking about chocolate here, but the search for solid information affects every part of our life. Your body and your blood tests can tell you more about what's good for you than any magazine article or doctor, including me. You can sort out the truth for yourself. Just be careful that once you find it, your exuberance doesn't extend to convincing other people that yours is the truth with a capital *T.* Benighted souls that they are, they may feel that they also know the truth, and then you'll wind up in an arm-wrestling contest about whose truth is *really* the truth. That's why discussions of religion, politics, and tofu are taboo during family picnics, weddings, and first dates.

✳

Our son, age twenty-six, has been raised in a Reform Jewish household and has fallen in love with a twenty-five-year-old Fundamentalist Christian medical student who believes that anyone who hasn't taken Jesus Christ as savior is doomed to the fires of hell. We found all this out when he admitted he was going to convert. We pointed out that they didn't know each other very well and that he knew almost nothing about his own faith. That didn't convince him to change his mind, but he reluctantly agreed to study with a rabbi. Against our wishes, he visited his girlfriend's family at Christmas. He came home engaged, with the wedding planned for March at her family's house so he wouldn't be "sad when none of my family shows up." They plan to have a second ceremony on their first anniversary "once everyone has gotten used to the idea of us as a couple." We're heartbroken. —SAM AND SARAH, BOTH 49, SPOKANE, WASHINGTON (E-MAIL)

Folks, it's clear you have a fantasy of how your son's life should go, but that's your fantasy, not his life. If just for a moment, you could treat religion as if it were a choice of restaurants, most of the anguish could be resolved. Okay, you like French cuisine, I like Mexican, let's try Italian or order a pizza or Chinese or take turns. Not much heartache here. Heartburn, maybe, but no heartache.

Before you read me the riot act and point out that religion is more important than dinner, ask yourself why you're experiencing such an emotional response? Could it be because your religion is the *right* one, the *true* one and therefore it is crucial for you to convince the ones you love of its truth?

Sam, Sarah, if both of you can believe that the important aspects of your religion have been passed along to your son because of your reverence for your beliefs, would that comfort you? If you have bestowed an ethical code, a reverence for life, and a sense of spirituality on your son, does it make *that* much of a difference how he chooses to continue the tradition? If his character already reflects your love and teachings, could you see your way clear to allow him the flexibility to please both his family and his love?

Perhaps you two can relax and admit that there are different paths to follow and each of us has to find those paths on our own. This philosophy allows for more than one true path. If there can be multiple truths, there can be multiple paths and choices, all appropriate and right for the individual. When our truth doesn't allow for anyone else's vision, we can get into some nasty, unhappy conflicts.

Hey, I'll even allow you to reject my notion here. Think about it: just because something makes sense to you doesn't mean it will work for anyone else. Understand that when it comes to a choice between heritage and hormones, hormones will always win. I know your religious beliefs are important to you, but if you viewed them as choices rather than truths, you and your son would be a lot less anguished.

If it's any comfort to you, most of us find ourselves in a similar bind

the truth will set you free

sooner or later. Grappling with truth is not limited to theologians, philosophers, judges, and parents. It affects even the most rigid of all thinkers: four-year-olds.

One day when I was getting my daughter ready to go to preschool, she asked if we could play. I explained we would play tomorrow since today I had to play doctor. "You mean play nurse," she said. Gritting my teeth, but hiding my annoyance, I muttered, "No, Mommy's a doctor." My adorable kid, the love of my life, responded, "Girls have to be nurses, and you're a girl, so you have to be a nurse." Instantly forgetting the rules of Good Parenting 101, I bellowed, "I'm not a girl; I'm a woman, and I'm a doctor!"

I finally realized, when I calmed down, that I wasn't arguing with my angel but with the perspective of one of her four-year-old friends, a charmer named Christopher, whose mom was a nurse. I'm not sure that her buying his perspective rather than mine is a premature example of the sway of hormones over heritage, but it was clearly an opportunity to calmly explain multiple truths. It was also a good example of how important it can be to a parent for a child to accept the parent's worldview—and I thought I was so open-minded. I wanted my child to grow up knowing that women have the same opportunities as men and I was an example of that. She was comforted by a friend's view of the world, and because she liked the friend, she liked his world. *Sigh.*

RIGHT IS OBVIOUS

✳

My boss is a know-it-all. I tell him when he's wrong, but it only makes things worse. You'd think he'd be pleased that I catch his mistakes before anyone else notices. For some strange reason, I think I'm about to be fired. —RALPH, 32, HOPEWELL, VIRGINIA

Ralph, I'm afraid you're right about being fired. It sounds like you better update your résumé. Being right is a full-time occupation, and one that won't leave you much time for relaxing, loving, making friends, and blowing bubbles.

It sounds to me as if you're off on a truth tear; you're convinced that there's one and only one right path and you've got it scoped out. Ralph, viewing a difference of opinion as an error is going to cost you big time.

You'll find yourself spending most of your energy searching for the right answer and then trying to convince everyone that you're right and that they should be grateful to you for revealing the truth to them.

Most of life isn't true-false or multiple choice; we have to think about the short- and long-term consequences of our behavior. The easiest, quickest solution to any problem is to cut and run so that the problem disappears. You could spare yourself a fair amount of grief if there was no tomorrow. But as the song says, "There's got to be a morning after." And stale problems are much harder to deal with than fresh.

WE NEED ANSWERS

*

My wife is always testing me. She asks me questions and I know she has an answer in mind, but I'm damned if I can figure out what she wants. My mother did the same thing to my father. I'm convinced that's what finally killed him. — MICHAEL, 34, GREENVILLE, SOUTH CAROLINA

Mike, sounds like your marriage is in serious trouble. Always being under pressure to come up with the right answer is like taking a quiz you haven't studied for. If you look for the question rather than the answer, you may find yourself in fewer battles at home. You will undoubtedly be more relaxed, under less pressure, and much happier. Let me give you an example of how to think about questions rather than answers.

A year or so ago I was giving a speech in Portland, Maine, to four thousand people sitting on gym risers—the excruciating kind that will instantly paralyze the rear end of anyone over the age of fourteen. During the question-and-answer period, a man hesitantly approached the microphone and started telling me a woeful tale of his wife's dysfunctional family, their painful divorce, and the estrangement of his two sons.

Understanding how difficult this was for him in front of his friends and neighbors, and desperately wanting to help him, I calmly and quietly asked, "What's your question?" Without taking a breath, he continued his unhappy litany of his inadequate divorce lawyer and his problems at work and his dating difficulty. Undeterred, I asked again, "What's your question?" Completely untouched by my well-meaning efforts to get him focused on what was important to him rather than on less crucial details, he went on to explain that the kids had taken the dog, his wife had absconded with the furniture, and his heart was broken.

Feeling like a real rat, I persisted in asking him for a *question* so I could help. The crowd, much to my horror, was now chanting, *"What's your question?"* This went on for what seemed like hours but was most likely three or four minutes—which, let me tell you, is a loooong time. Then somebody clear up in the cheap seats hollered, "Do I take her back to court?" The crowd applauded wildly. Finally a question. Yeah, but it was someone else's question, not his. His might have been any one of the following:

+ How do I get the kids to call more often?
+ Do I need counseling?
+ What if they call their stepfather Dad?
+ Is it too soon for me to date?

Any one of a thousand questions might have focused on issues that were important to him. The audience, however, was lulled into a false sense of the rightness of the surrogate question, partially because they were so eager to escape their neighbor's discomfort and their own embarrassment witnessing it.

This rather painful example demonstrates how crucial the question is. You can't find the right answer if you haven't found the right question. Once you find a specific question, it is either on the mark or it isn't. If the question is on the money, the answer is either inherent or straightforward. Michael, if you ask your wife what she wants from you, perhaps you can determine either that she doesn't know or that she has a specific request.

Asking others for their question allows them to tell you what's important and true for them. It also has taught me to beware of really uncomfortable seating arrangements.

Often we don't ask the question because we're afraid to hear the answer, which may be part of what is going on in your marriage, Michael. The two of you are trying to ignore your fears. As much as we try to avoid it, discomfort is an inevitable and unavoidable part of life. We can sometimes be misled by our own wish to be comfortable.

SIMPLE IS BEST

My daughter is thirty-seven and not getting any younger. She's very successful at work, but she says she wants to get married and settle down. I tell her it's simple: find a man, get married, have babies, be happy. She says I'm nagging and I don't understand. —DAISY, 62, DANVILLE, ILLINOIS

Daisy, let's agree on a few of things:

+ *Nobody* is getting any younger.
+ You love your daughter.
+ Nagging never works.
+ Simple and easy aren't the same.

Your "simple" scenario might not be easy for your daughter for a multitude of reasons:

+ She may be working too much.
+ She has a different way of acting around men than you did at her age.
+ Many of the ways men and women relate have changed.
+ Men and women getting together has gotten more complicated.

What was true for your generation has likely changed for your daughter. What you want for your daughter is simple but not necessarily easy. Maybe I can show you what I mean if we look at something a little less emotional for you than your daughter's marital status.

A bunch of years ago I was asked to do a series of evaluations for the Commonwealth of Massachusetts to design living plans for retarded citizens. The idea was to hire psychologists to determine the specific requirements for daily living that would then be implemented by paraprofessionals at a much lower hourly rate. With my brand-new Ph.D. firmly in hand, I decided this was a way to make money while doing good. Armed with a buoyant optimism, I met with my first client, a nineteen-year-old man who was unable to feed or dress himself. I dutifully and enthusiastically filled out the paperwork, recommending, with great subtlety, that this person needed to become more self-sufficient.

the truth will set you free

"Be more specific," the letter from the state said.

Undaunted, I amended the goals to include the man learning to feed and clothe himself.

"Be more specific," the second letter admonished.

"Subject needs to be able to sit up in chair and feed self, using a spoon, three times a day in a communal setting and chew sufficiently not to choke," I replied.

Again the letter chided, "Be more specific."

By the time my evaluation was finally accepted, there were eighteen pages with forty specific behaviors per page. I could explain the angle at which a knee could be raised and a toe pointed to ensure a sock going over a big toe, eventually incorporating all five toes and a heel. The whole thing was an exercise in simplicity, but it sure wasn't easy.

Daisy, I'm trying to convince you of several things here with respect to your daughter. First, assuming she's really willing to listen to your advice, it's crucial to be very specific. Saying "You work too much" is not nearly as helpful as tactfully suggesting, "If you want to find a date, maybe you could take a boating course or a first aid course or rock-climbing lessons." Specificity shows that you're really trying to be helpful rather than critical and that you've thought about alternatives.

Even this level of simplicity isn't necessarily easy. Your daughter may be shy or unable to scale back on work commitments. What is easy for you may not be easy for her. Assuming that something is going to be easy is a blueprint for discouragement. Once you understand the difference between simple and easy, you may be able to help your daughter prepare for difficulty, which will increase not only her chances of success but also her willingness to listen to you. Simplicity reduces a problem to basics, but it won't solve the problem.

✳

I'm a happily married woman with three beautiful kids and a great guy for a husband. We married really young and it's been a struggle, but we've got a beautiful house and we really love each other. I went back to work about a year ago and my boss is really great and he's been really supportive. He asked me to go on a business trip, which was really flattering. The pitch went unbelievably well, and we went to the bar to celebrate, and, well, one thing led to another. This has never, ever happened to me before and I'm really ashamed. I know it would break my husband's heart, but I'm being eaten up with guilt. I feel like I've got to tell him, so I don't have to hide this terrible secret anymore. We've always told each other everything and this is just tearing me apart. Really. —GERALDINE, *42, SOUTH BEND, INDIANA*

Really, Geraldine, don't even think about it. Under the guise of telling the truth, you could inflict great damage on your husband as well as yourself. The momentary relief that you gain by confessing will hurt him forever and will place the responsibility for your transgression on his shoulders. Whenever people tell you they're just being honest, run, don't walk, away from them. They are about to bash you with impunity. If you object, they will put on a hurt face and whine, "Did you want me to lie?"

One of the easiest, simplest fantasies of all is that confession is good for the soul. The question is, whose soul? I have talked about confession when discussing the concept of tenacity and being right, but it is so dangerous and so seductive, it bears repeating.

One of the reasons not to do stupid things is so there's nothing to confess. Because if you do 'em, you've got to live with the consequences, including guilt and an undermining of intimacy and trust. The only reason to confess is if you're about to be found out. If the mistake is illegal, get a lawyer. If it's immoral, get a conscience. If you're confessing so you can be forgiven and absolved, realize, for most boo-boos, the tricky part is forgiving ourselves. Unloading makes the guilty feel better and the innocent feel worse, which is pretty tacky. It's not cool to compound error with manipulation.

✳

My best friend's wife told my wife that she's having an affair and not to tell. My wife told me, and now I'm in a real bind. If I tell, my wife will kill me, but this is my best friend, and if he finds out I knew and didn't tell him, he'll kill me. No matter what I do, I'm screwed. —JOHNNY-LEE, *32, HUNTSVILLE, ALABAMA*

Johnny, I agree the whole thing stinks. Tell your wife you don't want to hear any more secrets of this nature (she probably doesn't either by now). Hearing a secret confession is titillating until you think of the consequences of keeping a guilty secret. Letting someone unburden her conscience by burdening yours is a very expensive price tag to pay for gossip. The secrets people want to share seldom make anyone feel happier.

In this particular case, you can encourage your wife to tell her friend that it makes her uncomfortable to hear these kind of confessions because they undermine her respect for her friend. Your wife can lay it on pretty thick about how she's sure her friend will want to do the right thing and either work on her marriage or get out of it. If your wife stops listening, her friend won't feel the need to ease her conscience at your wife's expense, and if your buddy ever finds out, you can say that you heard a rumor, but you're confident that his wife is not that kind of person.

Wow, have we nearly averted disaster here or what? The moral of this story is not only "Don't ask, don't tell," but "Don't confess" and definitely "Don't listen to or encourage confessions." Hearing a friend's confession can compromise your integrity, your relationship, your respect, and a calm tummy. A confession can also encourage a person to offer advice, which will most likely be ignored.

SHRINK-WRAPS

TOXIC TRUTHS

There is only one true path: Unless you have a crystal ball, or a confessional, accepting that there are different paths to the truth will make you a happier human being, a better friend, and a nicer dinner companion. All of us need to have rules by which we guide our course, but they are personal and are not necessarily transferable to other people or other situations. All of us can learn much about ourselves and each other if we're willing to listen to ideas, not believe them, be willing to hold our own actions to a rigid standard and free everyone else to do likewise. Or not.

It's too good to be true: If it sounds too good to be true, it is.

Love at first sight: This is the world according to Hollywood. Committed romantics truly believe that they'll know—*they'll just know*—when their true love comes along. Even otherwise sensible people are willing to succumb to the rightness of love at first sight.

If it feels right, it must be right: All sorts of things can feel absolutely right at first. It feels right to pig out when you're hungry, for instance, and to soak up the rays, drink yourself silly when the booze is free, and hug strangers. Unfortunately, an action that feels right can result in nausea, sun poisoning, a hangover, or an assault charge. Impulse is a great initiator, but consequence has to be considered by all but the most infantile, who are assigned parents to keep them safe from the results of what feels right. It's okay to flirt with fantasy as long as the flirtation stops short of belief leading to action.

"TRUE" WORD WARNING SIGNS

Always: We've all said it, and we have certainly heard it: "You always put me down . . . forget my birthday . . . make me apologize . . . leave the seat up . . ." The problem with the word "always" is that most of us instantly start looking for counterexamples. The word becomes even more treacherous when it communicates bigotry—for example, "Men always have problems with commitment . . . like big breasts . . . eat with their fingers," or "Women always want to get married . . . worry about getting old . . . like to gossip . . . hate sex," or "Blacks always . . ." or "Jews always . . ." or "Accountants always . . ." Bigotry as a fantasy has the double-edged problem of victimizing both the group and the one who does the grouping. Generalities are not only false but irritating.

Lazy: All teenagers have this word leveled at them whenever they sleep late or do poor work in school. It's a statement of someone else's expectations about good behavior, and it has a distinctly moralistic undertone. We never call someone lazy for failing to go out for a hot fudge sundae; we just use that word when the lawn isn't cut, the table isn't cleared, or the taxes aren't done. If you're trying to motivate someone to behave in a way consistent with our wishes, try bribery rather than insult. Help the person to see what's in it for him to act in a way you favor. Shame undermines people's self-confidence, and in order to change, we have to feel that we can deal with the unknown. That comes from good feelings, not bad. The idea that shame is good motivation is a fantasy that didn't even work when Mom tried it when we were eight.

Never: "You never loved me . . . meant to help out . . . got the kids ready for Sunday school . . . were nice to my folks . . ." This is the same hyperbole as "always," but with a negative connotation. The tendency is again to think of counterexamples so that less dramatic statements that follow will be ignored.

Should: "You should have known . . . called . . . understood . . . stopped drinking . . . worn your seat belt . . . been a better father . . ." These are all statements about expectation, disappointment, and the past, which is a pretty unpalatable combination. "Should" applied to your own life means you've lost any control over what makes sense to you and are relying on somebody else's value system. I suggest you do something or refuse to do something because it makes sense to you, not because it's valuable or important to someone else. "Should" sets off warning bells and whistles that you've just taken a step back from responsibility for your own behavior. When someone else uses the word "should" on you, it's okay to ask "Why?" That question may lead you to what the other person's value system is all about. The "should" fantasy is supposed to work like the obviously widely held belief that honking a car horn will make obstacles magically disappear.

Stupid: This word is often paired with "lazy" when parents are lecturing teenagers, when bosses are hollering at employees, and when men are yelling at women. It almost always signals that a breakdown has occurred or a mistake has been made. It is another of those words uttered from a position of assumed moral superiority. Logically it is a nightmare since stupid people can *only* act stupidly, but it is part of the fantasy that if you catch someone doing something wrong and holler at her until she's sufficiently traumatized, she'll never do it again. If you're bound and determined to tell people when they're wrong, the word "wrongheaded" or "misguided" is more descriptive and slightly less insulting.

Victim: It's amazing how often we accuse others of making our lives miserable, as if in blaming them we are exonerated and set free. Actually, the opposite is true. When we explain a situation in terms of someone else's behavior—"He made me do it . . . She's really nasty . . . It wasn't my fault"—we give away our power to someone we already view as dangerous, which makes no sense. Unfortunately, we've become a nation of busybodies and crybabies who think that being blameless is the path to salvation. Being a victim is a terrific short-term solution to a problem, but it's a lousy long-term solution.

Why: Why me? Why did you do it? Why should I care? These questions are either self-serving, accusatory, or meaningless. To begin with, most questions are to be avoided like the plague. By definition, they're intrusive and this one tops the list, because "Why" asks for motive. Most of us are pretty unclear about our innermost workings, and we're often reluctant to reveal them when we are clear. Focusing on behavior rather than motive is a much easier way to do business. The only person it's okay to ask why of is yourself.

5

men and women are from different planets

While there are obvious anatomical differences between men and women, quite simply, we were all born on earth.

If you believe the popular press, the war between the sexes has been heating up ever since Billie Jean King whomped Bobby Riggs's butt at tennis in 1973. Ever since then men have feared that women had become the men they wanted to marry, had worked out enough to hold their own in arm wrestling, had become interested in only one thing—men's sperm.

Is it as bad as all that? No, but the changing roles of men and women have caused enough confusion for some very enterprising people to exploit the differences in communication styles and suggest that men and women have *nothing* in common. This is a ridiculous fantasy and I want it clearly understood that men and women are *not* from different planets. From my perspective as an anthropologist, psychologist, archaeologist, medical student, and engineer on the program that investigated the possibility of life on other planets, I assure you it just ain't so!

For most of human history, women were perceived as a sexual, anatomical, and economic threat.

+ **Sexual:** Women were believed to have mystical powers and were thought to be able to enslave men's minds. This fear was widespread—from Eden to Egypt to Salem, Massachusetts.

+ **Anatomical:** Besides the obvious, Eve didn't have the extra rib that Adam was alleged to have donated.
+ **Economic:** The idea that there was "men's work" and "women's work" was dispelled when men and women worked alongside each other in factories.

As social barriers fell, emotional ones seem to have taken their place, resulting today in the notion that men and women are from different planets. While the concept may be metaphorical, the notion has taken such a strong hold of our collective psyche that people now think men and women have galactic reasons for not getting along. This is the Typhoid Mary of fantasies: it should be avoided like the plague.

This fantasy is not only preposterous, but also downright dangerous because it cements the paranoid notion that the sexes can *never* understand each other. Fantasies that serve to divide, humiliate, and demean aren't worth embracing. Not only is this myth not true (the space station Mir has shown us irrefutably that there are no sperm pods on Mars), but it obscures the real differences in the ways that men and women are treated and behave. This difference has virtually nothing to do with biology and everything to do with economics. This is really good news, since the economy fluctuates, while the planet of origin does not.

※

We've been dating for eight months, and this is the fourth time in the last three years it's happening again. I just don't get what I'm supposed to do anymore. Everything I do seems to piss my girlfriend off. We never have sex, she never listens to me, and we fight all the time. I guess we're having a communication problem. I know that men are from Mars and women are from Venus, but . . .
—JEROME, 27, DES MOINES, IOWA

I know it's tough to figure out what's expected of you in a relationship. You sound to me as if you may be suffering from the widely held paranoid notion that as women get stronger, make more money, and become more independent, men are becoming obsolete. I can understand why you're so upset. As women have moved into the workplace, the government, and the boardroom, relationships in the bedroom have been disrupted. The power and authority that once belonged exclusively to men have been redistributed, and many men feel that women's gains have been made at their expense.

As women gained power in traditionally male bastions, they have often chosen to reflect that newfound power by going to the gym and changing their bodies so that they are now muscled in a way that suggests physical strength as opposed to the softness traditionally associated with femininity. And speaking of changing bodies, guys have a legitimate concern that the very biological basis of male-female interaction is shifting as women can now have babies without a man in their lives at all.

Men have not become obsolete, Jerome, but the rules have changed drastically. This conscious or unconscious fear—"Gee, do I even matter anymore? Do you need me or want me?"—goes a long way toward understanding the very real difficulties that men in general and you in particular are having getting along with the opposite sex these days. I know it's trendy to package these anxieties in unearthly terms: "Not only are we created different, but we will never understand one another because we come from different planets." This is a kind of hip version of boys being made up of puppy dogs' tails and girls being made of sugar and spice. Balderdash. Who needs a cute phrase that fosters only misunderstanding, hostility, and confusion?

Believing in this nonsense will only intensify the anger, antipathy, and alienation between you and a potential mate or even date. If it's any comfort, it's not only men who are feeling confused and unhappy about the changing roles of both men and women. Social transitions are hard on everyone.

Women feel that men are alien creatures who only want carefree sex while many men resent the absence of old-fashioned girls who put them on a pedestal. Some of these sentiments are as old as human history and some are the result of changing social and sexual mores, but none are the result of interplanetary travel.

If we agree that relationships between men and women are spicier than ever before, it makes sense to look for explanations of

+ The historical differences between men and women
+ The current cause of increased hostility between the sexes
+ An understanding or resolution of these conflicts

How did this preposterous and destructive Mars and Venus theory become a best-selling book and a series of cassettes and workshops? Okay, a great title is a great title, but we're talking a belief system here, not a bumper sticker. Describing people as completely foreign is usually an excuse to banish or belittle them. Unless men and women are willing to live lives completely isolated from one another, a search for similarities is much more profitable than labeling someone as foreign. So why has this idea created such emotional resonance? If we are tempted to take the path of least resistance, then walking away is always the best short-term solution to any problem. The problem with short-term solutions is tomorrow. Ignoring a problem is seldom a way of solving it.

We've all lived long enough to ignore fairy tales, to realize that there is no man in the moon, and to understand that men and women are not from different planets and not made of different materials—puppy dogs' tails, sugar and spice, or whatever.

In fact, even the most jaded observer would argue that both men and women need food, water, shelter, stimulation, and affection, which would certainly argue against the different-species fantasy. Furthermore, we both breathe air, metabolize food, and have skeletons that are indistinguishable once the flesh and muscle are peeled away. Why, then, would we want to believe that we are so different? What are the advantages in believing that we can't get along because we have nothing in common? If it's not biology, it must be sociology.

Jerome, in his frustration, offers a clue. When negotiations break down and you feel yourself losing ground, throwing in the towel appears to be a way of buying time or saving face.

Two hundred and fifty years ago, our forefathers regarded Africans as inferior, childlike, and stupid, basically a nonhuman species from another world. We now view this as an immoral perspective perpetuated by one race to justify enslaving another for economic gain. Whether you flash forward a couple of hundred years to the present or backward a couple of thousand years, it's the same situation: if a man can comfortably view women as essentially different, then there is no need to treat women equally or fairly.

Why, then, would *women* accept this incredibly destructive fantasy that men and women have nothing in common? Historically women may have had no alternative. They had limited ways of communicating outside their immediate circle since they weren't taught to read or write, so they couldn't form a sisterhood or relate to other women who weren't close by.

That social isolation is no longer an excuse, but a more powerful psychological isolation may be the basis of feelings of alienation. The underdog traditionally defers to the powerful because it is easier, safer, and sometimes necessary for survival. But it is one thing to go along with an enslaving idea, another to *believe* a notion that is both stupid and demeaning.

In a startling and dramatic demonstration of how pervasive and ingrained this unthinking deference is, I asked my listeners the following question: "If you found your best friend and your spouse were having an affair, who would you blame? Men blamed women (their wives) and women blamed women (their friends). If you believe you're powerless, you can't afford to antagonize someone who is powerful. We blame the disposable party, and we keep the valuable connection. Men and women both value men over women. And it is this issue—power—that has been and continues to be the true source of contention between men and women.

IT'S ORDAINED

✳

The Bible says that man is to rule over his dominion and woman is to be his helpmate. The problems in this country come from women not knowing their place and trying to wear the pants in the family. It's not natural: even animals know that the male should be in charge. —JESSE, 73, LAFAYETTE, LOUISIANA

Look, Jesse, I'm not stupid and neither are you: there are obvious anatomical and biological differences between males and females. The animal kingdom works sort of like the Bible; you can find reinforcement for any idea if you look hard enough. Do we really want to base our assumptions about human behavior on the actions of animals? I for one am not willing to assume that *all* females eat their young just because hamsters do. (Guess how I discovered this piece of biological reality? A female hamster was my daughter's sixth birthday party present from a well-meaning neighbor. It took her weeks to stop having nightmares. Hmm, Mom as a cannibal?) Most men don't hibernate like bears during the winter, and most kids don't follow a sock that smells like Mom, even if a duckling or a monkey will.

So let's forget about what animals do and move from biology to sociology. For a large part of human history, the primary legal, economic, and political bond between men and women has been marriage.

Marriage was the method by which children were protected and women were controlled. It was the glue that cemented the social order and strengthened political ties. Patrimony was the form in which wealth was passed down from one man to another. When a woman was given to a man of another tribe, money was exchanged in the form of a dowry so that her family was committed contractually to the man who would take care of her. From the very beginning, men exchanged money, and women went where they were told.

Women were bred for passivity; they were passed from father to husband to son. A woman whose family could not afford a dowry was forced into servitude or worse. As recently as the early 1800s, 80 percent of unmarried women in London were forced to make their living as prostitutes. Presumably, the other 20 percent were nannies or maids or cooks or in service to older sisters who had been married off. When Jane Austen wrote *Pride and Prejudice* and *Emma,* she was describing a world in which a woman had incredibly limited options if she could not conjure up a dowry. The situation makes for great drama in a movie or a novel but it's a lot more unpleasant if we're talking real life. The option of working as a nurse or teacher literally saved many women from selling their bodies, although early professional women were often considered no better than prostitutes.

A woman's concern about a man's commitment makes sense. A man's cavalier attitude toward sex is less about a biological imperative than about having the power to indulge himself without consequence.

Men fight to protect their assets. Historically, women haven't owned assets. Even today, in many states, a woman's assets become her husband's when she marries. The only assets women have historically owned were their own bodies, if that. Keeping that body in good shape was less vanity than economic necessity. In the bad old days a woman's asset was her body.

Today's man may shy away from commitment because for the first time in human history, commitment often means sharing their economic resources, which could be depleted by that very person who is twanging his heartstrings. Men have traditionally treated women as if they were worthless because historically, women have been without economic power. In a system based on economic power, the powerless will trade affability for access. If you can't be powerful, you'd better be nice. Crankiness is acceptable only from the king, not from the riff-raff.

Whoosh, Jesse, I hope I've given you a different way to think about you and your relationships with women. I know it's harder work than deciding that you are an inherently superior life form because of planetary or spiritual influences. Certainly the Bible is a valuable resource but you may want to increase your reading to include slightly more modern thoughts as well.

✴

I put myself through law school, I was on Law Review, and I'm really doing well in a firm of litigators. But it's hard to be a team player when I've overheard rumors that I'll be the first to be downsized if the crunch comes because the guys don't want to take a job away from a man with a family. These guys figure that I can stay home and let my husband take care of the family. —SALLY, 38, BOSTON, MASSACHUSETTS

Sally, in a capitalist society, you are what you can earn. A man without a job is called a bum and a woman without a job is called a wife. Even today, when a woman may work as a matter of economic as well as emotional necessity, her income is often considered less important than the "real" money her mate earns.

The point here is not to blame the guys at your law firm for being wicked enslavers of women, but to make the point that the traditional differences between how men and women behave are more economic than genetic. It takes time for behavior to catch up with history. Centuries of conditioning leave their mark on both men and women. Even women who work and plan to work are much less likely to own property in their own name than their male counterparts of the same age and income level; though many banks are acknowledging and attempting to change this practice by offering special rates for first-time female homeowners. (An awful lot of otherwise savvy women are waiting for a man to rescue them economically.)

I was once told that if the layoffs came, my boss would let me go before one of my fellow engineers, all of whom happened to be men, since I had a husband to support me, even though I was supporting *him* at the time. As it was, they waited until I went on maternity leave and then eliminated my position.

If you can calmly explain to the partners that you are not doing male or female work but just practicing law, you can spare yourself some anger toward both men and women.

IT'S GENETIC

✳

My boyfriend and I have been living together for a year, and I want to get married. I work for him because he's trying to get his business off the ground. We're living in his house, and I'm helping to fix it up and make it homey, but somehow, every time I bring up the m word, he changes the subject. —SAMANTHA, 29, STOCKTON, CALIFORNIA

Samantha, are you bewitched? Your boyfriend is unlikely to change his behavior because he's getting what's valuable to him. You write "welcome" on your forehead and then you're surprised when he steps on your face. This isn't him exploiting you; it's you exploiting you. Everything is in his name and you aren't even the hired help. By saying, "Please treat me as if I'm special while I act as if what I do has no value," you're making it astonishingly easy for him to do what you don't want him to do.

It's time to figure out what you want and how to get it. If you want him to marry you, set a deadline, tell him about it, and if he refuses, simply move out and get on with your life. No tears or cajolery, please, and don't even think about "accidentally" getting pregnant. If he really wants to spend the rest of his life with you, give him the opportunity to sort it out. If not, Habitat for Humanity or the local homeless shelter would really appreciate you donating your time to fixing up someone else's home and you won't have to worry about putting the seat down on the john. Give him a chance to appreciate your contributions, but in the meantime treat yourself as if you matter.

IT REALLY IS ECONOMIC

✳

I am trying to decide whether to buy a new couch. I have lots of money in the bank, but I'm not sure what my boyfriend wants to do. I make good money as a singer with the local opera company, but when my contract is up in three years, I'm not sure they'll renew. —HELENA, 48, SAN DIEGO, CALIFORNIA

Helena, you're allowing four virulent misperceptions about men and money to rule your life and your bankbook:

1. I can't make permanent decisions until a man comes along.
2. Sooner or later I'll quit work when a man comes along.
3. I can't spend important money on myself.
4. My life won't really begin until a man comes along.

I still don't know a single professional woman who doesn't have nightmares about becoming a bag lady. Helena is very much like a friend of mine (who was also a singer with a famous opera company), who lived in a single room occupancy hotel even though she had thousands of dollars in the bank. She was saving for a rainy day so she wouldn't have to live in a hovel. Somehow, it escaped her notice that she already was.

This syndrome isn't limited to women of a certain age in uncertain industries. I know young women with secure positions as secretaries who spend the equivalent of a mortgage down payment on cruise wear and cruises in the hope of attracting a wealthy man.

If we accept that the real behavioral differences between men and women have to do with money, then we can begin to negotiate with one another on a completely new, appropriate basis. We can begin to replace "I want you, I need you, I love you" with the much less claustrophobic "I want you" and "I love you." When need gets taken out of the equation, men may become less phobic about commitment. Women may also become a bit less willing to date someone whom they don't much like but who can upgrade their lifestyle.

What if women accepted that they were going to support themselves for a large part, if not all, of their lives and therefore planned to do just that? Many things would change. Little girls would plan careers rather than weddings as a priority. Both boys and girls would take home economics courses and learn to cook and sew for themselves. Maybe teenage pregnancy would decrease if the important goal was economic well-being, rather than attracting a man to take care of them. Not only would work be a priority for both sexes, but social ties would be based on genuine affection rather than economic necessity.

This sharing of the economic responsibility might also encourage those men who choose a woman primarily on her looks to expand their criteria.

If a man figures a woman has no economic viability, why not pick a cutie: "She might as well be decorative if she's going to be useless." The focus on looks might shift to finding a friend, someone interesting, or even a partner who could help shoulder money problems.

That's the real point isn't it: sharing? Maybe everyone could concentrate on the really important issues. Men and women might start relating to one another on the basis of mutual interest, self-sufficiency, and respect. Men might feel that they were being chosen for their personality, not their earning power. Men and women might remove the chips from their shoulders and think of actually trusting one another.

Think of it, there would be less antagonism, posturing, and defensiveness between males and females. Women could acknowledge their brains as well as their breasts, flaunt their degrees rather than their derrieres. For just a moment, think of any of the common complaints men have about women or women have with men and see if economics doesn't change everything:

- "She talks too much." This is actually two separate complaints about content not quantity. The complaint is more accurately: "She's talking about things that are not really important because they don't have to do with me or my world." Or secondly, "She talks so that I'll have to pay attention to her." Both issues change when both men and women value the work that each does.
- "He's never home." When you're sharing the economic burden, she's less likely to feel trapped at home because she's also out working and thus not asking him to be her lifeline. Plus, he doesn't have to work as many hours because of her economic support.
- "He never helps out around the house." Pay someone to do the stuff you both hate.
- "He doesn't spend time with the kids." You both view the kids as a shared pleasure and responsibility since both of you take financial responsibility for the family's welfare.
- "She's never interested in sex." Good sex is the hallmark of happy, productive people. Freud said we all need work and love and the love is easiest when the work feels productive.
- "He beats me and cheats on me, but I love him." If you won the lottery tomorrow, he'd be toast, so get a job, an education, and a sense of self-respect.

The differences between men and women aren't a result of different planets of origin, or any other catchy but whimsical misunderstandings of human behavior (like Eve popped out from Adam's rib). It's all about money, plain and simple. But please don't be misled into thinking that simple and easy are the same thing. When we're talking about changing economic realities, we're talking about changing the social order, and it's going to take all of us a couple of heartbeats to see what's in it for us. Men are understandably reluctant to give up the historical power and privilege that wealth has bestowed. Women's economic gains don't have to be at men's expense—but power shifts are seldom comfortable. That doesn't mean we all shouldn't start immediately—just don't be daunted by a bit of resistance here and there. Economic parity is simple and straightforward, but it means changing thousands of years of social conditioning.

The Golden Rule is the standard of all ages: he who has the gold rules, and it has been and continues to be *he* who has the gold, not *she*. Even with women gaining more access to money they earn rather than inherit, very little will change until we look honestly at this basic reality. Until then, men and women will continue to bristle over the definition of what it is to be truly male or female.

All our cuckoo ideals of how men and women *should* act, exist to soften the harsh realities about the power of the purse strings. As women become educated and are better able and willing to question the social order, they also become better able to function with some degree of financial and, hopefully, emotional independence.

Please, how many of us are still waiting for our knight in shining Armani armor to whisk us off to his place so we won't have to buy our own vine-covered cottage? More than you'd guess. I can remember feeling sorta blue one day and wishing for some guy to rescue me . . . until I started giggling and reminded myself that anybody who tried to take me away from anything in my life would likely get yelled at for his trouble.

✳

My husband and I haven't had sex for two years. I think he's having an affair, and I'm tempted to see if I can't find someone, too. I'm a stay-at-home mom with three kids, ages twelve, nine, and seven. I'm miserable, but I feel I should stay and work it out for the kids' sake. My husband won't go to counseling. Some days I don't know how I can go on. —MARTHA, 43, SCRANTON, PENNSYLVANIA

Martha, let's not take an unpleasant situation and make it intolerable. Why don't we start with the basics here: you're unhappy; that really is the place to start. Now answer some questions:

- The two of you haven't had sex for two years: is that the cause or the effect of your unhappiness?
- You suspect your husband of adultery? Why, other than your lack of sex life?
- How is your marriage outside the bedroom?
- With your children in school all day, are you using the stay-at-home-mom thing as an excuse to hide from the work world?

Let's start with the last point and work our way back to you. *Both* you and your husband are responsible for the kids, not just you. It's important to you, your marriage and the kids that child care not be regarded as women's work. Raising children is a crucial responsibility of adults of *both* sexes. We know that children are best served by two happy, healthy, adjusted, loving parents, not by a cranky, sad mom who clings to her children for dear life, since they are her only reason to stay in a loveless marriage. It does kids no good to be subjected to two unhappy adults who perpetuate their misery by indulging in the lie that they are staying together for the sake of the children.

So now that you're not hiding behind the kids, how is your marriage? Do the two of you talk about anything other than bills and the kids? When is the last time the two of you had a date? *Why* did the sex stop? What do *you* want? It's time for you to begin looking at the rest of your life. What do you plan to do with your time, your head, and your heart? I have no idea whether or not your marriage is viable, but I do know that you won't sort that out until you look honestly at who you are and what you want and how you're going to get it. If you plan to confront your husband and perhaps end your marriage, I suggest you get a job, not a lover.

Even if you don't plan to confront him, a job will do a lot more to improve your outlook and your prospects than a clandestine affair would. You'll also have a much easier time looking at yourself in the mirror, as well as facing your husband, your mom, and your kids. You may also find that men and women are surprisingly similar once the economic playing field is leveled. We can begin to relate to one another as beings who can enjoy the biological differences that make sex such a pleasure in the bedroom but still be able to leave it all behind when we meet in the boardroom.

And what about Jerome and his concern about what a woman could possibly want from any man? Are men becoming outmoded? Resoundingly the answer is *no*! Men won't ever be obsolete as long as there is still that urge to care and pair. Love and sex as a reason to get together makes sense; money as the exclusive or even primary basis of relationships between men and women is legitimately and appropriately doomed.

But "Sam" in *Casablanca* had it right: it is still the same old story; it's less a *fight* for love and glory, but the fundamental things do still apply, and money as a power base has gotten a lot less fundamental as time goes by.

SHRINK-WRAPS

LOVE SONGS TO BE AVOIDED LIKE THE PLAGUE

"The Most Beautiful Girl in the World": Come on, do you really want your whole relationship to be based on looks? What do you do about gravity, hair loss, and an extra pound here or there?

"Venus": Frankie Avalon made a bundle singing about his goddess girlfriend, which is a nice metaphor and good for bragging rights, but how about a really wonderful *mortal* who has about the same life span, housing, and food requirements and knows how to play Trivial Pursuit?

"You Are the Sunshine of My Life": Talk about dependency. You'd better learn how to be your own sunshine or there'll be too many dark days ahead. Find someone to sunbathe with.

"You Are the Wind Beneath My Wings": Talk about death wishes! Learn to stay aloft of your own.

If best-sellers dealt with reality rather than comforting platitudes that disguise rather than delineate and solve problems, what would their titles be?

FANTASY BEST-SELLING BOOKS
+ *Men Are from Solvency, Women Are from Vagrancy*
+ *Smart Women, Foolish Financial Choices*

- *Men Who Own Women and the Women Who Hate Them*
- *Ten Stupid Financial Things Women Do*
- *Women and the Depression*
- *Ova Nova on Venus; Testosterone Trees on Mars*

SEXIST FANTASY SAYING

"Boys will be boys": What else would they be—turnips? This seemingly innocuous phrase is sometimes offered as justification for men behaving badly.

6
ignorance is bliss

Knowledge is power.

Growing up is hard to do, and there is nothing more childish than being ignorant. "But I didn't know" is the great cop-out of the irresponsible. If you don't know, you think you can't be held responsible, so you can't be wrong. Whew, what a relief! Of course, the problem is, you also can't be right.

Deniability has become the mantra of modern life: you're safe as long as you don't admit to knowing, which is an incredibly shortsighted approach. Knowledge really is power, even if the price tag is a certain amount of anxious responsibility, and the only way to get smart is to learn. Learning implies intellectual inferiority, which feels both embarrassing and self-conscious but—whoopee!—the end result is actually knowing something.

Knowing is fun, and doing is even better. True adulthood is about taking responsibility, making choices, and getting on with it. The whole proposition is a lot more fun than I'm making it sound: a hidden, seldom discussed benefit of living in the land of the mature is the opportunity to eat Oreos *before* dinner, if you want to.

WHAT I DON'T KNOW WON'T HURT ME
✳

My husband and I have been married for thirty-five years. Last week he came home and out of the blue said he wasn't happy anymore and hadn't been for years. I thought we had the perfect marriage. He's still here, but I'm beside myself. I feel like I'm walking on eggshells, and I can't stop crying. I told him I'd do anything he wanted. Do you think this is a midlife crisis? What can I do to get him back? —BEATRICE, 54, TAOS, NEW MEXICO

Beatrice, I know this isn't a happy time in your life, but we still need to do a little reality check here. People don't just wake up one day and say, "Yesterday everything was peachy, but today I'm outta here," unless they're psychotic, and if you're married to someone who's psychotic, all bets are off anyhow. It's much more likely that, unless you're married to an Academy Award–caliber actor, you haven't been paying much attention. Bea, it's not that you're stupid or unobservant, but sometimes we make an unconscious deal with ourselves to remain ignorant.

This is the "what I don't know can't hurt me" school of life, also known as "I'm going to mimic the ostrich because keeping my head in the sand is the best way to go through life." This philosophy might actually make some sense if you didn't notice two things about an ostrich: (1) It's quaking because it's terrified; otherwise, why would the ostrich have its head in the ground? (2) Its hind quarters are really exposed.

"If I pretend I can't see it, smell it, hear it, or feel it, then it doesn't exist so I'm safe." If you choose this scenario, you're trading off imagined short-term comfort for long-term catastrophe. Even the shortest term comfort is based on the assumption that you can fool yourself while you're up to your ears in sand. This approach leaves both you and the ostrich stuck, scared, and vulnerable. Yech. This isn't the time to beat up on yourself or your unhappy missing-in-action husband, but it is precisely the time to figure out what has really been going on in your marriage. Look for the warning signs you previously ignored. If he wants to stay and love you (and you decide you still want the marriage) you'll have the necessary focus to begin to strengthen the relationship. Even if both of you decide you're better off separately, you'll feel less like you're at the whim of a perverse deity—or a husband who's taken leave of his senses.

This is definitely not the time to adopt Ollie the Ostrich as mascot: you don't have the luxury of big-time denial right now. The result of ignorance isn't bliss, but anxiety. Ignorance as a lifestyle is based on the fantasy that knowledge will hurt you and as long as you don't admit to knowing, you'll be safe. Both are patently false. But, Bea, speaking of animals, let me share an imaginary caller's story that relates directly to you:

ignorance is bliss

One day while eating shish kebab outside the Parthenon, sunning myself on the steps while putting the finishing touches on my tortoise-hare fable, I noticed two dogs sniffing each other out. One was mangy and skinny with that hangdog look about him. The other appeared well fed with a shiny coat. The first dog asked the second, "What's the story? How come you look so great and I look so lousy?" The sleek dog said, "Come live with me. You can have three square meals a day, a warm spot by the hearth, and someone to brush your coat." "Terrific," said the undernourished one. Off they trotted toward the healthy dog's house and were about to enter the gate when the mangy dog said, "Hey, why is there no fur on your neck?" "That's where they attach the leash," said the well-fed one. "I'm outta here," Mr. Mangy-but-Proud said. "My freedom is worth more to me than being well fed." —AESOP, ATHENS, GREECE

So, Aesop, what's your question? Just kidding. Obviously, a Greek fabulist from 580 B.C. did not call my program. However, the point is that even a dog in Aesop's world could understand how high the price of dependence is and that ignorance is the ultimate dependence. Opting to be taken care of means you're giving up control of your own life and assuming that someone else has your best interests at heart. For that situation to work out in your favor, you're going to have to count on being very lucky.

From the beginning, human babies struggle toward independence even when it means opposing the beloved parent. This fundamental push toward self-reliance is based on the ability to make choices. Choosing ignorance means an inability or unwillingness to see options. Counting on others to deal with all the available choices and to opt for your happiness before their own makes dependence a good deal riskier. The only time this dependence is necessary and relatively safe is in very early childhood, which is why adults mistakenly think of that time as blissful. This hindsight view of childhood ignores the terrible price tag of dependency.

If ignorance were so darn much fun, no one would ever grow up, independence would never be a choice, and only the neurotic would opt for information. The problem is that ignorance demands scads of trust, which is in pretty short supply after the first eighteen months of life.

EXPECT THE WORST

＊

All my brothers and sisters are mad at my parents. I guess we must have grown up in different families. I had a wonderful childhood. Everything was fun. I still feel my life is terrific. Okay, some days I'm really bummed, but, hey, life is great. If you look under rocks, sure you're going to find ugly, wiggly things, but why put yourself through all that? —JUDITH, 49, PETALUMA, CALIFORNIA

Judy, Judy, Judy . . . I'm not trying to make you unhappy, but I think you may be inadvertently doing it to yourself. If you look carefully at what you're saying, you really are expecting the worst. Your fantasy is that the world is an awful place (all those "ugly, wiggly things") and since you have no control over anything, you might as well pretend you're okay since it's just a matter of time till the goblins swallow you up. The risk is that your fantasy can become a self-fulfilling prophecy. By ignoring them, little problems can fester and become big problems, while your blinders keep you from seeing safer alternatives or being prepared to defend yourself when necessary.

When you decide not to look under the "rocks" or obstacles in your life, you're opting for ignorance. Not a good plan, so what does information buy you that ignorance doesn't? How about a sense of control over your own life and destiny? Information frees you from the fantasy that everyone else is looking out for you and gives you the tools to look out for yourself. Only a nincompoop would assume that there would never be a lack of conflict between your best interest and someone else's—if for no other reason than that you both want the last piece of pie.

Why would anyone ever opt to be powerless? Glad you asked. The problem about accepting responsibility is that the buck stops squarely with you, and what if you make the wrong choice? But if even a two-year-old is willing to risk making Mommy mad by saying no, then independence and self-interest must be a pretty basic human urge. Only a tired, insecure adult would choose to let someone else make decisions for her. The only logical reason to do this is that we so distrust our own ability to make good decisions that we're willing to assume everyone will make better choices. This means we've decided that being wrong is worse than making no choice at all. Bummer!

This assumption paints the world as doubly dangerous: evil and unknowable. The world as seen through the eyes of our ostrich friend is a short, brutish life, waiting for disaster to strike. Ignorance not only allows but reinforces irresponsibility: "I didn't know, so it's not my fault." Judy, my dear, blissful ignorance is a very expensive fantasy.

ASSUME IMMORTALITY

✳

My father is ill, and the doctors have told us it's unlikely he'll ever leave the hospital. Mom says we can't tell him, but I think we should, even though I don't want to upset Mom. —ISAIAH, 44, LA SALLE, ILLINOIS

Isaiah, I know this is a tough time for you and your family. Before we look at exactly what to tell your dad, let's look at some of the reasons you and your mom disagree here.

When we withhold information, we have control of that information. Once we've shared it, we lose some control. The informed person can confirm or deny assumptions, judge appropriateness of behavior, and pull rank by lobbing the grenade of superior knowledge at the troops. Isaiah, it's not surprising that this dilemma is causing a family schism, since it has to do with all the biggies: life, death, authority, responsibility, parent, child, loss, love, and respect. By sharing information, we level the playing field, leave ourselves open to judgment, and force ourselves to be responsible. You can see why we're tempted to withhold it.

The idea that information is bad or burdensome is left over from the power a parent holds over a child: "You're too young to understand or to deal with the burden of knowing." Parenting is admittedly a difficult task because making decisions is especially tricky when another's welfare is involved. It isn't that knowledge itself is burdensome. It's just that taking responsibility for another person is exhausting. Vigilance is hard, not knowledge. Knowledge can free you to make decisions. Keeping an eye on someone else can absorb so much time and energy that you are immobilized.

Isaiah, back to your question. Let's first make three assumptions:

1. Let's assume your motives in being honest with your dad are benign—in other words, you're not trying to punish him because once you were small and powerless and now the tables are turned.

2. We'll also assume that you've thought through the consequences of being the bearer of bad news. The temptation to withhold information is often based on an assumption of bad consequences: "If I tell Dad that he's dying, he'll hate me or be angry with me."

3. Let's also say you're worried about making your dad feel even worse than he already feels.

One of the best ways to decide whether or not to share information is to ask yourself if *you* would want to know, if the roles were reversed. Information doesn't necessarily imply a particular choice, it just means you don't feel that you're making a decision with your eyes closed. Sharing information is a sign of respect.

It sounds to me as if you've already decided to share this important information with your dad—and my guess is that he already knows. The question is really not what to tell him but how to prepare Mom to deal with his eventual death. She's thinking, "If I don't tell *him*, then *I* don't know, so I can pretend everything's okay." That won't work, and it will prevent all of you from helping each other say good-bye. Besides, who wants to spend this brief and important time pretending?

✳

A car hit our dog last night. I've told the kids he went to play in a neighbor's yard. The older boy looked at me funny, but I don't want to upset them. What do I say when they ask when he's coming back? I think they know something's wrong. —JOAN, 39, CUMBERLAND, MARYLAND

Joan, you've just put your finger on it: kids know when something is not quite right. We always know, don't we? Our suspicions don't have to be paranoid, as in "Life is awful, and it's only a matter of time before it all hits the fan." But pretending means everyone is always waiting for the other shoe to drop. Telling kids something other than the truth is always tempting. Hey, withholding bad news from *adults* is tempting. But whether it's Santa Claus, the Easter Bunny, or the end of Fido, are we really doing anyone a favor by pretending, even when the motive is benign? (I never told my daughter anything one way or the other about Mr. Claus, but one Christmas, I overheard her talking to her grandmother, who had obviously asked if Santa had visited. My daughter's response was "No, but he sent some stuff." Kids sort things out one way or the other.)

If you start with the premise that to *not know* is better than to *know*, you are assuming the world to be a bad and treacherous place. In this particular case, Joan, you're also pretending that death doesn't exist. Pretending not to know allows, at best, a fool's paradise—short-lived but happy while it lasts. At worst, ignorance doesn't even offer a short-term respite, but only a limbo full of worry and anxiety: it's only a matter of time. Until the worst happens, I can eat, drink, and be merry, but my happiness is going to be tinged with a sense of doom. Yikes, this is heads, I lose; tails, I really lose. Dying would be lousy, but if I don't die, I'm going to be overweight, hung over, and in debt from all that eating, drinking, and being merry.

As an eleven-year-old growing up in Denver, I was faced with a preteen version of this dilemma. I was supposed to be studying for a major math test the night of the Cuban missile crisis. (Remember Castro and Kennedy and Khrushchev squaring off about missiles ninety miles from Miami?) In those days we were all convinced that in the event of war, Denver would be a primary target because of the U.S. Mint, which makes pennies, nickels, dimes, and quarters, and NORAD, which housed the underground missile silos for North America. Even with no social life, scrawny ankles, and no chest to speak of, I didn't want to spend my last night on earth studying for a stupid math test. As I valiantly tried to convince my parents of my impeccable logic, they pointed out that if it wasn't my last night and I didn't study, I would *wish* it had been my last night.

Needless to say, I studied and we weren't blown off the face of the earth. Okay, my parents were right. Khrushchev backed down, and I passed geometry. The free world was saved because *I* studied. So there. To this day, I firmly believed that I single-handedly saved the world by knowing that the square sum of the two sides of a right triangle equals the square of the hypotenuse. (Can you believe I finally found some use for high school trig?) You may be asking yourself what this has to do with ignorance being blissful. Sometimes you have to be willing to look down the road and figure what is most or least likely to occur. Ignorance of consequences is seldom a credible defense. "But I didn't know . . . You didn't tell me . . . If only I'd known . . ." These are all statements that you're in over your head. Taking responsibility means looking at your options. Closing your eyes and choosing without having any information doesn't absolve anyone of responsibility; it just increases your reliance on luck, which is fraught with peril. Ignorance is intellectual baby fat. As adults, we view a lisp on a kid as cute and mispronunciations as adorable. As a child, feeling stupid, verbally inadequate, or powerless feels almost as bad as it will when you're an adult. Our love affair with ignorance is more a statement of the weight of adult life than any real value that being unaware possesses.

Joan, sit your kids down and calmly and quietly explain that the dog is dead. Don't be surprised if their reactions differ, from complete indifference to serious grief, depending on their age and temperament. As a family, you can plan a memorial service or a burial and decide whether to get another pet or not. The sense of foreboding created by the lie is more damaging than the reality of death.

My husband just died, and I found out last week that he had no insurance and he put our last vacation on our credit card. I never thought I'd have to worry about money. He always took care of me and said he always would. I can't believe he'd let me down this way. —HORTENSE, 84, BINGHAM FARMS, MICHIGAN

Hortense, you've gotten caught in a time warp here. The rules about how men and women deal with money have changed considerably in the last twenty years. When you were a bride, you likely felt that money was something a husband took care of, just as your dad took care of your mom. You, like many other women, have found out in a heartbreaking way how truly expensive *not knowing* can be. I'm not trying to make you feel worse than you already do, but as you've realized, a wife who knows nothing about the family finances is ceding all control to her husband. Viewing money as "man's work" means that the husband is left to determine how, why, and when money should be spent not only while he's alive but even after he's gone. That's too much power and responsibility for one adult to have over another.

Okay, what's past is past, so let's figure out what you can do now. What I don't want you to do is to ask your nephew or some other surrogate daddy figure to take over your finances. You definitely are going to need some help, but the help has to be along the lines of teaching you to take care of yourself, which means you've got to get real smart real quick. You don't have to get a Ph.D. in economics, but it's time to become informed about your mortgage, taxes, pensions, savings, Social Security, and life insurance.

Once you know what's going on, you can make some choices. Don't believe that you can't learn or that you're doomed to feel helpless and confused. Learning something new can make you feel a little overwhelmed at first, but that discomfort is much better than lying awake nights worrying about bill collectors and angry IRS agents. You know that *not knowing* is stressful, not restful, in the long run.

Women have historically not bothered their "pretty little heads" with facts and figures. Scarlett O'Hara has been our patron saint—"Oh, fiddle-dee-dee!" Her approach works reasonably well as long as she can trust the caretakers, but if those damn Yankees invade Tara, she'll be in serious trouble. Modern damsels are much more likely to be imperiled by a husband dying, divorcing, or filing for bankruptcy. The dynamic is always the same: "Take care of me and I won't ask questions."

Ignorance is truly a slave mentality. "Voluntary slavery" should be the ultimate oxymoron: why would anybody want to be enslaved? Slaves were kept enslaved by having no access to information, and kept ignorant by being prohibited from learning to read and write. What people are forbidden to learn has traditionally separated classes, castes, races, and sexes.

Historically, women have been educated only in the "gentle arts": embroidery, flower arranging, and pleasing a man. Perpetuating ignorance is a way of eliminating threats to the status quo. Not very nice, but understandable if you happen to be in power. For women to perpetuate their own ignorance is incredibly self-destructive. Why would you want to hold yourself back? The classic reason is fear—the mistaken belief that as long as you don't know, someone who does know will take care of you. Unfortunately, that isn't always the case, as Hortense has discovered.

Hortense, you are woman, let's hear you roar. You may discover that you have a real knack for money management, as well as a long-buried skill for self-reliance.

IF YOU LOVED ME . . .

✳

I don't know what women want. No matter what I do, it doesn't work out. I couldn't please my mother, my sisters hated me when we were growing up, and

*dating was agony. When I get the courage to go out on a date, it's pure torture.
I don't know what she's thinking or what she wants or how to please her. —JIM,
41, ATLANTIC CITY, NEW JERSEY*

Jim, be careful about this willingness to view women as completely different and unknowable. You're not alone in asking, "Does anyone ever know what a woman wants?" But you should know that this attitude is self-defeating. Human history is chock-full of examples of people doing horrible things to other people because they were "different"—whether the difference was based on religion, race, color, language, or sex. Once you define someone as unlike you, it's significantly easier to be mean to that person, intentionally or unintentionally. I know it's been the historical norm to assume that men and women are completely different. Even the father of modern sexuality, Sigmund Freud, pretended a certain frustrated, weary ignorance about women: "What do women want?"

Ahem, Dr. Freud: women want the same things as men: respect, fun, love, passion, attention, and intimacy. Men have never bothered to find out what makes a woman tick. But, Jim, it's a brave new world out there. You don't want to be continually angry, alone, or unable to deal with half the world's population. Turning a blind eye and a deaf ear on the humanity of females will brand you as chauvinistic or insensitive. Once you have defined someone as unknowable, you'll spend less time and effort in trying to understand who that person is and what she wants.

When you want to know what makes people tick, you will find them as flattered by your interest as you would be by theirs. Your willingness to be ignorant about women may actually be a statement of your uncertainty about who *you* are. If you don't know yourself, it becomes impossible to understand anyone else. It can also make you too defensive to let anyone close enough to know who you are. This is a powerful formula for loneliness, as I'm afraid you've discovered.

Don't be intimidated by what you don't know, but be challenged to learn what's important to you. None of us can know everything, but we can decide what's important to us and what's important to the people who are important to us. Knowing doesn't mean we have to have an opinion about it or be a world-class expert. Once we become defensive about what we don't know, we become brittle and frightened and act as if we're proud of our limitations. Being proud of ignorance is a costly attitude. Ignorance is blinding, isolating, and frightening. View yourself as a student willing to learn and you'll increase your fun, friends, and the probability of a good night's sleep (and maybe even a sleep-over).

You may think this is a tough assignment, but we're not talking brain surgery here. When in doubt, start with what you already know. For example, if you know how to woo a prospective employee, you know how to ask for a date. If you can explain what you need from an employee, you can explain chores to a reluctant teen. Ignorance in one part of our lives can be offset by the same technique we use in a more informed part of our life. Take an area of competence and let its principles guide you through something that seems foreign: selling a product is selling yourself, shopping is product analysis, seeing both sides is mediation. All of us know how to do more than we think we do. The basics are always the same, it's just the details that change, so don't get hung up on the details. Don't be afraid; just be aware.

WHAT YOU ALREADY KNOW . . .

✳

I work as a sales executive and I'm the top producer for the firm. I'm attractive and smart and I get a lot of dates, but I don't seem to get any follow-up dates. If I had the same problem in my professional life, I'd starve. I can get my foot in the door personally, but somehow I just can't seem to make the sale and get the second date. —LISA, 32, SAINT CLOUD, MINNESOTA

Lisa, as a salesperson you're aware of what can happen when you try too hard and oversell. If you're good at sales, you've learned to let buyers come to you and tell you what they want or need. As a good salesperson you know you have to believe in the product. You would never undercut yourself, sell at an unreasonable price, or appear too eager for the sale.

Why not take what you know in this successful area of your life and apply it to an area that doesn't work so well? Then you will be operating from a position of authority, even if it turns out to need some fine-tuning. Realizing that you know nothing about an area that's important to you can leave you helpless and confused, but you should be willing to learn and find a good teacher. Believing you'll never know is a dead end. Knowing what you don't know is the first step to learning.

✳

I have a really successful supermarket supply business that I've built from the ground up. I'm really good with people until it's time to go home. Then I feel like a doofus. I have no idea how to make my wife happy. No matter what I do or say, she sounds angry and sullen. I tell her I love her, but it doesn't seem to do any good. —SOLOMON, 49, ATHENS, GEORGIA

Solly, what would you do if you had a valued employee who seemed about ready to quit? You'd call her in, tell her how valuable you considered her, and ask her what it would take to convince her to stay. You might further inquire if there's something outside of work that's distracting her or if something has changed in her work environment to cause problems. Applying this same approach to your wife is likely to be much more productive than saying, "Is anything the matter?" or, even more disastrously, assuming there's nothing you can do.

If you were being interviewed for a job and your prospective employer said, "Hey, you're going to get paid the same amount of money and do the same thing every day with the same people for the next thirty years," most people would run screaming to the hills. During an interview, we ask about opportunities for advancement, when the next raise is likely to occur, and what skills we need to acquire to reach the next level; yet in personal relationships we are offended by the idea that we may actually need to learn new things, work at it, or change. If we were as sloppy and unwilling to work at our jobs as we are reluctant to improve our relationships, unemployment would be at an all-time high.

✳

We've been together since sixth grade. I really love him and I know he loves me. We're talking about getting engaged, but for Christmas he gave me wading boots, and I got a Miami Dolphins T-shirt for Valentine's Day—and the only thing I hate worse than football is fishing. I don't know if I can spend my life with a guy who's so clueless. My sister says if he really loved me, he'd know better. —ANNABELLE, 19, JACKSONVILLE, MISSISSIPPI

The final cry of ignorance in relationships is the "if you loved me, you'd know" lament. Annabelle, I don't want you to ask this guy or any guy to read your mind in order to prove his love. It's *your* job to figure out who you are and what you want. Then, sweetcakes, *tell* him. I guarantee you'll both be much happier. You don't want to play this game because what you're really saying to him is this: "If you truly love me, I can continue to be ignorant of my own feelings and desires and completely irresponsible about conveying them to you. Loving me will give you the secrets to what makes me tick. That way, you will know me better than I know myself, and I can remain ignorant because you will be so knowledgeable."

I know this sounds preposterous, but it's amazing how often this mind-reading notion comes into play into otherwise sane relationships. One person throws out another's beloved ancient robe because it's ratty, seeing only the worn spots, not understanding the beloved part. Getting to know someone takes times and effort, especially when *we're* the person we want to know better. Ignorance is passivity at its most virulent and dangerous. Denial is just ignorance with attitude.

"Hear nothing, see nothing, say nothing" is the ultimate act of hostility toward a loved one. It always comes attached to "You're a louse for expecting anything of me." This is not exactly the stuff of loving, caring, and nurturing involvement. Involvement means wanting to know and being willing to share in return. Interest is truly the currency of involvement. "I have a secret" is a fun party game; it even worked as a television show for a while, but it is a lousy relationship mode. Withholding information from another person perpetuates ignorance for the student and power for the teacher. Withholding information from yourself is a way of diminishing yourself and your options.

SHRINK-WRAPS

The most positive use of a fantasy is to point out the discrepancy between what we have and what we want. These particular fantasies perpetuate the idea that ignorance is bliss. It isn't, it's just plain old dumb-as-dirt ignorance.

FALSE IGNORANT FANTASIES

Blondes have more fun: Are we talking natural or bottle here? If it was fun to be considered stupid and sexually available, there would be no sexual harassment suits.

Look before you leap: It's always sensible to do a bit of reconnaissance but, look, if you're leaping, you've already got the momentum going and you're committed with all that energy. Once you're of a mind to leap, even an empty swimming pool isn't enough to slow your forward trajectory. Well, okay, there is that nasty splat against the concrete bottom. You look before you cross the street and investigate before you invest. You may even call your mom before you get engaged. Leaping is an act of faith and courage and risk. People suggest that you look before leaping only after you've already shared your passion and commitment. They're most likely worried because you've convinced yourself and may persuade them to go along for the thrill.

Silence is golden: Silence is manipulative, withholding, and often passive-aggressive.

7
stick to your guns

A ferocious commitment to being right is an expensive lifestyle choice. People are going to fight back.

T*he idea that* your view is always right has a long and bloody history. Whether the "right" comes from a higher being or an internal voice, tenacity in the face of all opposition is viewed as crucial for success. Wimping out is the ultimate failure, a result of cowardice in the face of adversity.

Yeah, well, who's right is often determined only in retrospect, and in a world of increasing complexity, the ability to negotiate and empathize is more valuable than ever. It's simplest to see the world as black-and-white, good and evil, right and wrong, friend or enemy. It's just that what seems simple is a very costly perspective.

Sticking to your guns means there will be dead bodies littering the landscape, some of which might belong to friends and potential allies. If differences can be understood and appreciated, nobody has to go to war over who's right. This is a chapter about giving up the simplistic idea that a friend is someone who always agrees with me and a foe is someone who always disagrees with me.

WHEN YOU'RE RIGHT, YOU'RE RIGHT
✳

Whenever I get into an argument with my wife, she takes a completely illogical position, and when I point out the error of her ways, she hollers and cries and says I'm just being domineering. I now figure it's easier to just shut up and go along, but then she says I'm pouting. No matter what I do, she finds fault with me. It's kind of like heads she wins, tails she wins. —KEVIN, 47, SIOUX CITY, IOWA

Kevin, sometimes it's not a matter of who's right but of who's left. I'm talking survival, not victory here. I'm talking about looking at the bigger picture. The ability to see beyond the obvious and immediate is what learning is all about. Almost everything psychologists know about how humans learn we have gleaned from either rats or college undergraduates—two cheap and available resources on which graduate students and professors can perform experiments.

Let me tell you why rats are the preferred resource: If you put a rat in a maze, sooner or later the critter will find the cheese. Once the rat knows the location of the cheese (lots of consistent trips down the right path), you then move the cheese and find out how long it takes for the rat to consistently head in the right direction again. Learning theory is based on how long it takes the rodent to locate and remember the cheese placement.

Undergraduates are much more difficult to use in this kind of experiment since they have to be "right." They're going to continue to go down a maze that they know is the *right* one, either because it worked before or because someone once told them a left turn is always the quickest way out. Humans are the only creatures who are convinced that they know the true path, the right way, and will consistently ignore any evidence to the contrary (like the absence of cheese).

Kevin, I know you are convinced of the value of your opinion, but you've lost sight of the larger goal here, which is not to be right, but to be convincing, impressive, or charming. Unfortunately, even if you're right in this situation, there's no cheese and no payoff. And even worse, you've boxed yourself in: your wife is mad, you're frustrated, and everybody loses.

If you're arguing about a past event, you'll find that people have very different memories. One famous study focused on the differing opinions of spectators at the Harvard-Yale football game. The Yalies thought the game was well played, well officiated, and a wonderful example of skill and sportsmanship. The Harvard fans thought it was a dirty, underhanded, stupid contest in which cheating was allowed by incompetent officials. Guess who won the football game? You're right if you said Yale. Obviously *truth* depends on whether you're winning or losing. You and your wife haven't evolved a style of communicating that allows for a difference of opinion, only for winning or losing. If every argument is a fight to the death, the tension level will continue to rise while your ability to communicate honestly and truthfully will plummet. What if both of you became better listeners and more polite in your disagreements? What if each of you pretended you were disagreeing with your boss and you didn't want to lose your job, but did sincerely want to contribute to making your job more effective? My guess is that not only your communication skills would improve, but your marriage would as well.

Being right can be relative. When I was growing up in Denver, my father tried to make that point to me early on, after I'd cleaned the bathroom. I'd say I'd cleaned it; he'd holler that it wasn't clean. We were both stubborn and adamant and sure we were right. His point was to *get it clean*, not *to have cleaned* it. I was right, I had cleaned it (swished a cloth around the sink, sprinkled cleanser hither and yon, flushed a couple of times), but it just wasn't *clean*. You can see here that the issue isn't blame but effectiveness, so sometimes when you're right, you're right, and sometimes being right is really wrong and a cold comfort. I'm not arguing for a morally ambiguous universe, but I'd rather have you be effective, moral, and caring, even if you're not necessarily right. If you're right, someone else has to be wrong and most of us like being right, but we really *hate* being wrong. If you're going to insist on being right, you've likely got a fight to the death on your hands. If you're just looking for an effective joint solution, and not interested in wrestling over who's right and who's wrong, you'll have a chance to look for a path that pleases both of you.

In your mind, being right may consist of what worked in the past, what your parents did, or what you've always believed. Slavery, applying leeches, and drowning witches were all considered not only right but virtuous and moral in the past. Wars have been fought and perfectly nice people slaughtered in the name of being right. Most of us adopt a surprisingly similar attitude in our dealings with one another, especially if that other happens to be a child, a member of the opposite sex, or anybody else who brings out the latent bully in us. The desire always to be right is dangerously close to the assumption of a nation with inherent moral superiority. So, Kevin, how about if you practice being effective instead of being right? Leave being right to someone who is loaded for bear, filled with anger, and just itching for a fight.

✳

I work really, really hard at school and my mom and dad say I'm really smart.
The other day, Tiffany asked if she could borrow my homework. I told her no,
and I told the teacher. Now Tiffany won't talk to me, and everybody at school
says I'm a tattletale, but it's her fault. She shouldn't have asked to copy my stuff.
—SERENA, 14, FLINT, MICHIGAN

Serena, you're right, but it sure is costing you a lot. You're learning the
hard way that there's a big difference between doing what you think is
right and trying to convince someone else that what you're doing is right.
We're a country that feels really confused about blowing the whistle on
other people. Whistle-blowers are almost always right, but they're very
seldom well liked. You may want to ask yourself why you told on Tiffany.
Were you mad at her? Did you want to protect your grade? Did you feel
that you had to beat her? Or maybe it's just really important to you, as it
is to most of us, not to lose and not to be wrong. I'm not saying you should
have let her copy your paper, but it might have worked out better for you
if you'd just said no to her and not told the teacher. Being right can sometimes be very lonely, especially if you've pointed out that someone else is
wrong. Being wrong feels so painful and scary that we will fight not only
to be right but to prove that we're right, *especially* when we're wrong.

You're really not alone in this dilemma, Serena. You or your mom may
have even seen me in an episode of *The Oprah Winfrey Show* entitled
"Whistle-Blowers." I was invited to give some advice to three self-
righteous guests: an angry receptionist who snitched to the boss's wife
about their affair, a woman who'd been fired who then bad-mouthed her
ex-friend to personnel, and a disgruntled man who told his partner's ex-
wife the number of the partner's Swiss bank account.

We're talking major anger here, and as the "expert" called in to tame the
chaos, I tried in vain to convince the audience and guests that minding
someone else's business is very, very risky and seldom appreciated. What
at first glance looks like righteous behavior is often just judgmental or vin-
dictive and is usually a diversion we create so we don't have to take responsibility for what is going on in our own lives.

The audience was not only not buying what I had to say, they were
more than a little hostile. "What's right is right," an audience member
hollered. I finally was able to persuade even the most vocal dissenters to

rethink their position when I gently pointed out that, not surprisingly, all the self-righteous folks who tattled had an ax to grind. Without exception, these seeming paragons of virtue had gotten into some kind of beef with the company or individuals involved *prior* to the event that so touched their consciences they felt obligated to snitch. This isn't all that surprising: minding one's own business is not nearly as much fun as being righteously indignant over someone else's behavior.

I'm not suggesting that there aren't legitimate times, places, and situations where righteous indignation is an appropriate and moral response, but we have to be aware of our own motives. When I tattle on my sister for having an extra helping of ice cream, am I blowing the whistle because in a righteous world each of us should only get our fair share? Or am I doing it because she'd tell on me or because she got an A in algebra or because I'm convinced that Mommy loves her more?

Serena, just for fun you might want to rent the movie *Broadcast News,* in which Holly Hunter plays a woman who always has to be right. Everybody's always mad at her, not because she's wrong, but because she *is* right. Holly believes, as you do, that right is might and being right will make everyone love and respect you. But she finds out, to her chagrin, that she just intimidates people and they turn ugly!

Since you were even younger than you are now, you've sensed how dangerous it is to be wrong. When we do something wrong, even as young children, parents get mad and holler and we get afraid that they won't love us anymore, which is why, as kids, we learn to lie so quickly and so well. Even grown-ups think it's so important to be right all the time that they will argue, deny, and even lie in order to make people think they're right. Sometimes we get so caught up in being right that it feels as if it's not just about saving face but about survival.

Most of us are not intentional liars; we say something because we believe it to be true. The more emotional the topic, the more certain we are that we're right. We see the world through our own eyes, and while we think we're open-minded and capable of learning, most of the time when we know we're right, we stick to what we believe is the truth. To do any less when we know we are right would be cowardly.

This is something we obstinately and passionately believe because it has been a part of our upbringing. But the world would be a whole lot better if each of us would decide what is right and why it is right and when it is right for us and let everybody else do the same thing. We get into trouble when we decide that our right is right for everybody. How about if you find your truth and let everybody else do the same?

TRUTH IS CONVINCING

✳

My younger sister and I have always been great friends, but recently no matter what I say, she gets angry. I think it all began when I told her that the guy she was dating was two-timing her. She told me to mind my own business, but then she found out I was right. You'd think she'd be grateful. After all, I was only watching out for her best interests. —FIONA, 34, MONTREAL, CANADA

Fiona, ask yourself how pleased you would have been with her if the roles had been reversed. You are indulging in one of the fatal truth fantasies: that people will be grateful if you tell them the truth. If that were the case, "I told you so" would be the four most popular words in the English language and heaven knows they aren't.

I once got thrown out of a grad school class, Psychotherapy 101, when the professor said it was the therapist's job to orient the patient to reality. I said, "Whose reality?" I mean there's the therapist's, the patient's, society's, and the insurance company's reality, like, duh, telling someone the truth is only giving him your view of reality.

Even the most "objective" of us have to filter the world through our own experiences and understanding. It's not that truth is relative, just that it's open to interpretation over time. Each of us must find our own truth. Most of us are pretty resistant to someone else telling us what to believe, and it's logical to assume that everyone else feels pretty much the same way. Be aware that "truth" has an aggravating tendency to change over time. Today a doctor who bled his patient would probably lose his license, but a hundred years ago bloodletting was to doctors what penicillin is today. Fortunately, most of us aren't going to be the subject of future medical or historical scrutiny. Nevertheless, so as not to be caught in the funhouse mirror of history (even our own), we should keep our thoughts both private and flexible.

This flexibility is facilitated by repeating this statement at least three times a day: "Ideas are for using, not believing." *Believing* implies not only being right but being *divinely* right, which limits critical evaluation.

Evaluating an idea based on its effectiveness allows field-testing and change without embarrassment. Believe what works for you and let everyone else do the same. Imagine the saved time and energy you can then apply to your own life. You can afford to be curious rather than judgmental about everyone else's life.

CONFESSION IS GOOD FOR THE SOUL

✳

I've been dating this woman for a little more than two months. Last night we got intimate, and she told me that she'd had an affair with another woman when she was in college. I guess I must have looked shocked, because she asked me if I was okay. I told her sure, and pretended it was fine with me, that I was cool. Still, I can't get it out of my head. When I asked her why she told me, she said she was just being honest. —LOUIS, 38, DALLAS, TEXAS

Louis, your unwise friend is laboring under the delusion that confession is good for the soul. Actually, it's good only for the soul of the confessor. The person who has to listen to the confession is burdened. She feels better; you feel worse. One should confess only to priests (why do you think the confessional is dark and anonymous?) or therapists. Even confessing to Mom can be tricky. She might tell Dad, Sis, or Aunt Julia.

Once you've confessed to someone, you've made him your accomplice. First, he is duty-bound to keep your confidences to himself lest he appear untrustworthy. Second, he must either forgive you—which means you're home free and if he ever brings it up again, he's a lowlife—or berate you, in which case you can say you were only being honest, so he becomes the bad guy again.

That's the hypothetical downside. The practical downside is even slipperier: Somebody's got the goods on you, which makes conscious or unconscious blackmail a very real possibility. You've now put yourself at this person's mercy. If you've wounded him or her by your confession, you're stupid, and if you haven't, you've still painted yourself as unsavory and vulnerable, which is very tempting for someone to exploit.

I hope you're now convinced that confession is a very expensive indulgence. Let me also add that if anyone approaches you with the tempting words, "Can you keep a secret?" you should exclaim lustily and at the top of your lungs: *"No,* I'm the blabbermouth of the known universe!" Believe me, you will spare yourself untold heartache.

✳

I've been married for sixty-two years. My wife found out last week that I'd been having an affair with her best friend for the last forty years. She said she'd finally had enough and she left. She won't talk to me, and I need to tell her that it was only about sex. I have never loved anybody but her. —HOWARD, 83, ARVADA, COLORADO

Howard, you may be auditioning to be the Viagra poster boy. I'm not sure that even a note from your pharmacist would help here. Wouldn't the world be an easy place if all we had to do was explain and everything would be hunky-dory? All differences of opinion would disappear once we explained our perspective, since most of us are convinced that we know and speak the Truth with a capital *T.* Howard, things are bad enough here. Don't succumb to the fantasy that an explanation will make everything okay. What could you possibly say that would help?

Admittedly, communication is frustrating and once we've gotten on the righteous path, we want everyone to follow—if for no other reason than to confirm our belief that it is the true path. When some benighted soul dares to argue or try to persuade us to follow their path, we often launch ourselves into the sorrowful assumption that they just don't understand. (I'm still not sure how the assumption "If you loved me, you'd understand" got to be the ultimate "if . . . then" statement of the universe. The only person who can reasonably be expected to understand you is your mom and I'm not so sure you want to go there.)

Okay, so we all agree that it's unwise to assume that everyone will understand us all the time. It also is silly to assume that just because we're "right," reiterating the point will win us instant support. The notion that if you can just explain your logic, someone will agree with you is charming in its naïveté, but completely impractical. It rests on the assumption that the only thing keeping people from agreeing with you wholeheartedly is their ignorance. This may be true occasionally, but more often than not the idea is both self-serving and inaccurate. Howard, I'm afraid your fantasy falls into that damning category. You've cheated and betrayed your wife. It is egotistical and delusional of you to assume that all you have to do is explain yourself and everything will be hunky-dory. Perfectly nice,

stick to your guns

sincere people can have widely divergent opinions on everything from politics to eating meat to whether chocolate should be a controlled substance, but your behavior certainly hasn't been "perfectly nice." Surely, you're not trying to convince either me or your wife that adultery is just about a difference of opinion. It's wrong, and it's a nasty way of showing "love." You're fantasizing that explaining away your wife's complaints will save your marriage.

RIGHT IS MIGHT

✳

I always try to do the right thing. Nobody appreciates me. Last week I baked two dozen brownies for my bridge club. Nobody said thank you, and three women said they were on diets and why wasn't I more considerate. —QUEENIE, 42, YUMA, ARIZONA

Darlin', send those brownies to me. Asking other people to be grateful is asking for trouble. All of us need to do what we think is the right thing and if other people applaud, terrific. If they boo, reevaluate your plan, and if you still think it's right, do it because you think it's right.

All societies have rules that govern behavior, and those rules, about what's okay and what's not, are initially passed along at the mother's knee. Kids listen because Mom and Dad are bigger and more powerful and the source of food and love. Adults continue this socialized behavior because they've internalized these values and view them as their own or because they're scared silly that someone will put them in jail if they break the rules. Once kids get big enough to wander away—or when societies are so large that there are more people to break the rules than there are policemen to catch them, somebody has to invent ways of increasing the probability that individuals will do the right thing. This process is called socialization, or internalizing societal norms. I would call it believing that someone will reward you if you do good and destroy you if you don't.

Whether we're talking about a two-year-old who will pause a moment before reaching into the cookie jar when Mommy's in the other room or a grown-up returning that extra dollar that the cashier miscounted, we act on the fundamental assumption that not only will good be rewarded but that naughtiness will be punished. We further expand this notion to believe that there are good and bad people. There are two inherent problems with this theory both in the specific and in the abstract. First, who determines what's good and what's evil? And second, what is the reward? Are you saying, "Well, as long as your heart is pure, if you're doing it for the *right* reason . . ."? Heaven protect us from folks who are only trying to

+ Help
+ Be honest
+ Be kind
+ Do the right thing

This moral certitude is clumsy and dangerous when it masks ulterior motives. If you don't believe me, read on.

✳

I saw my brother-in-law coming out of an apartment building at 6:00 A.M. How can I tell my sister without her being mad at me? —DEREK, 39, BURLINGTON, VERMONT

Derek, you may have hit the ruinous fantasy jackpot here. Your assumptions are a genuine disaster six-pack. You've covered all the major goof groups without even working up a sweat:

+ Being right
+ Whistle-blowing
+ Explanations will set you free
+ Expecting gratitude
+ Purging by confession
+ Potential reward for doing good

Deep doo-doo, Derek. Deep, deep doo-doo.

What's your motive here? I know you're legitimately concerned, but do you view yourself as a loving brother trying to protect your sister, or might something else be going on here?

Do you like your sneaky brother-in-law—or even your sister, for that matter? Could you be getting even with the dude for making more money than you do? Are you remembering last week's golf game where he slaughtered you, or are you acting out some unresolved sibling rivalry? Is your dad always asking, "Why can't you be more like your sister and your brother-in-law?"

Derek, if you feel morally bound to talk to someone, why not tell your brother-in-law what you saw and see what he says? Sometimes under the banner of truth and justice and doing the right thing, we are whitewashing a less lofty motive. Lying to others about our motives is not acceptable; lying to ourselves is poisonous.

These are the same issues raised when twelve-year-old Joanna called to complain that she got in trouble for telling her parents about her brother's copy of *Playboy*. She asked me if I agreed that looking at naked women was a nasty thing for her brother to be doing? I said, "Joanna, let's not try to manipulate the doctor." My questions concerned her motives. Was she trying to protect her brother from evil influences, save his soul and his innocence? Or was she currying favor with Mom by being the perfect child? Could her motive be revenge for the time he wouldn't let her borrow his bike or for the day he teased her unmercifully about her weight? I suggested that Joanna mind her own business, which included searching a bit deeper for her own motives.

Derek, you can see by even a twelve-year-old's example that self-righteousness is hard for others to swallow. Tattling also calls your trustworthiness into question: "If you'll rat out someone else, will I be next?"

At least people who admit that they're not playing by the rules or who are overly self-involved are easier to get along with if for no other reason than that they don't ask you to like them when they do something awful to you. As that great psychologist William Shakespeare said, "One may smile, and smile and be a villain."

✳

I'm only doing the best for my family. They don't always appreciate my attitude, but I always have their best interest at heart. I really do know what's best, and I just hate it when they argue with me. —MELVIN, 37, DULUTH, MINNESOTA

Melvin, I've got to tell you, given a choice between someone who says she's looking out for my best interest and someone who admits she's watching out for herself, I'll take the latter every time. You aren't even given the room to be angry with the former because they tell you it's for your own good. All of us have to learn to watch out for ourselves, which doesn't mean that we're selfish or nasty. We all need to practice what Elvis

Presley preached: TCB, or "Taking Care of Business," which is our basic responsibility. I know you feel you're selflessly taking care of your family but each of us—you and every member of your family—has to know what they want and how to get it. This doesn't mean aggressively taking from someone, but asserting who we are and where we stand. Being assertive means standing up for yourself. Being aggressive means standing on someone else's toes. We only have to be right for ourselves and allow everyone else the same privilege and respect. Melvin, if you can leave your martyr hat at home, you're going to get invited out more and have a much better time. You may even find the energy to be the kind of guy I know you want to be: a hero, a man who can be counted on. Don't we all?

It's tricky to be a stand-up person when doing what's right for you means helping an enemy. All of us want not only to win but also to vanquish our enemies. This is quite human and understandable, but what's a guy to do when winning an award means your exploitive boss gets praised? Does it diminish your enjoyment of the award? Are you tempted to sabotage your own reward so at least the fink doesn't benefit? Do you allow your kid to visit your ex even though your ex cheated on you? The real test of character is not doing the right thing but doing the right thing even when it means that your enemy wins. Revenge is understandable and common, but a waste of time and occasionally really misleading.

One of the hardest lessons of adult life is that sometimes by doing what you know to be the moral and sensible thing, you help the bad guys win. If you're a single parent who hates your ex, you still have to encourage your child to be pleasant to the fink because you realize that as a parent, your priority has to be your child's welfare, not your wish for revenge. Sharing your kid for the child's sake even when the financial support is overdue is tough, but being "right" in punishing your ex by withholding the child is childish. Yeah, I know it's hard to do the right thing and watch the dreaded ex profit from your good heart, but as long as you don't *lose* anything by doing good, don't sweat it. It's a comfort to believe that there is some cosmic scorekeeper who will give you extra credit for being wonderful and generous. Believing that karma is a boomerang—what goes around comes around—is a Band-Aid for those ouchies where we realize that the reward isn't arriving anytime soon and someone whom we dislike is gonna win.

Melvin, beware also of the Magoo theory of life, which allows for those strange and inexplicable moments when completely wrongheaded, self-involved behavior turns out to be exactly and improbably right: the basketball haphazardly thrown whooshes through the net in the final second, the wild guess turns out to be right on the money, the random act of folly turns out to be the right thing at the right moment.

If being right is always effective and being wrong is sometimes right, you may believe that life is chaotic and unpredictable. The superior alternative, which I highly recommend, is to run our lives by rules that seem reasonable to us and let everyone else do the same. The time and energy saved by not arguing is a handsome benefit, and the lack of smugness might even open your pores. And once you've figured out that you're wrong, it's perfectly okay to just keep still and regroup, not argue or sulk.

The more focused you are on *your* life and *your* problems, the more likely you are to have a positive effect on your path. We need to plan each day as if we were going to die tomorrow and conduct ourselves each day as if we were going to live forever. If our lives are *only* about ourselves, what's the point? Being on this planet and taking up space without enriching our lives and the lives of others seems a terrible waste. But the only way to matter to someone else, let alone do all that fun, honest, worthwhile stuff, is to be straight with ourselves so we always know who we are, what we want, and where we stand. Sticking to your guns is messy and violent. Knowing who you are and what you want is neat and serene.

SHRINK-WRAPS

FALSE RIGHTEOUS FANTASIES

Pride goeth before a fall: Oh, pooh. Pride is what allows you to stand tall for what you want and be your best self. Arrogance and self-righteousness may go before a fall, but not pride.

The meek will inherit the earth: All together now—"Just the dirt." If you expect people to appreciate you because you're passive or right, you have completely misunderstood human behavior. If you write "Welcome" on your forehead, don't complain when someone steps on your face.

It's not whether you win or lose: Of course it is. That doesn't mean it's okay to cheat, but if it didn't matter, there would not be two words: winner and loser. Everybody wants to be one and doesn't want to be the other; therefore it is logical to assume that it matters a lot whether you win or lose and if you don't believe me, tell me who lost to last year's Super Bowl champ.

Grin and bear it: This is not only masochistic but bad communication as well. How is anybody supposed to know what you're feeling if you've got a silly smile pasted on your face all the time. If something hurts, say "Ouch." Martyrs are a pain in the neck to be around on a daily basis.

Right makes might: No, large armies, nuclear warheads, baseball bats, large-caliber rifles, and compromising photos make might.

You can't teach an old dog new tricks: If you have enough doggy biscuits, I'll bet you can.

Statistics lie: No, people who use statistics lie. Statistics are just numbers in a certain order.

God is on my side: This idea is one on which I've expended considerable thought since I went to school in the Southwest Conference, where football is king and every game began with a prayer that the good guys would win. I could never quite figure out, first of all, how someone who created the galaxies could spend all that time assessing who should win college football games and, second, how the losing team could ever hope to win against anybody. If it's true that sometimes the bad guys seem to win, maybe that Cosmic Counter will tote things up and it will all even out in the long run. Perhaps sanity lies in believing that.

8

good always triumphs

Life isn't fair. Get used to it. Do the best with what you've got. And no whining.

Human beings crave structure. The idea of randomness is truly terrifying, so we invest in rules and regulations and trust in a simple world where good is rewarded and wrongdoing is punished. Without this basic structure, people wouldn't stop for red lights, control their tempers, or pick up litter. We further insist that certain values—like fairness, love, and comfort—are forever good.

I'm not suggesting that these values are bad, but they can be misleading fantasies that make us embittered and haggard when we realize that life may not be fair, love may not be unconditional or eternal, and comfort isn't necessarily a good thing. Even expressing these sentiments aloud sounds preachy, but once we accept the reality that different people are going to believe in a different standard of fairness and goodness, we can preach less and focus on leading our own ethical life.

LIFE IS FAIR

✳

I always try to do the right thing. I'm nice to my mother, take in stray cats, never cheat on my income tax, and give blood. I write to my aunt Gertrude once a month and floss after eating. I have no friends, I have no dates, and I just got fired again. Why do nice guys always finish last? —RUPERT, 29, KEENE, NEW HAMPSHIRE

Rupert, lighten up! Having a pity party is not a good use of your time and energy. One of the reasons you're feeling so bummed is that you're buying into the fantasy that good will always be rewarded and that the wicked will always be punished. Unfortunately, these are equally inaccurate assumptions. I hope you are being good not because you're looking for a reward or because you fear punishment but because your behavior makes sense to you. If you are doing the right thing only because you're waiting for the applause, you're bound to be disappointed.

Don't berate yourself; you're not alone. The fantasy that the good guys always win is fundamental to the maintenance of human society. It keeps most of us from flinging bricks when we're angry, and in the long run, it may even be true, but only in the really, *really* long run. Counting on a fair system of punishment and reward is going to make us embittered, suspicious, and cranky.

The word "fair" is seldom used unless we are defending ourselves or attacking someone else. All may be fair in love and war, but fighting fair is aggressive rather than reasonable. In a marriage, the one who is fighting "fair" often creates a compromise and then offers it as his or her position. As a result, the partner can give in and feel like a wimp or argue and feel foolish. Even being fair isn't always fair. And it sure won't win you any popularity contests.

Hey, listen up, Rupert. Once you buy into this fair scenario, you've got to ask the follow-up question: "Fair by whose standards?" It certainly isn't fair that kids get cancer or that the guy who cheats on the math test doesn't get caught or the nicest person you know is also the homeliest. War, poverty, illness, and cellulite are definitely unfair. There may be some order to the universe, but if there is, it seems beyond our ability to understand. If you're looking for fairness, you're going to be angry or bewildered a great deal of the time, not to mention envious and irrational.

Most adults, knowing that a thunderbolt isn't going to knock over income tax cheats, adopt a more personal code of ethics. Those of us who have a Rupertesque view of the world believe if our division wins the Good Guy Award, then our sales force was inspired, our campaign brilliant, our customers wise, and the outcome historic. If our team loses, however, we believe the other guys cheated, the bookkeeping was shoddy, the office was understaffed, and the contest was unfair. A problem arises, however, when someone else's rules don't jibe with ours, because most of us are willing to play by the rules as long as the rules are ours. The majority of us aren't that crazy about being told what to do by someone whose belief system is different from ours, whether the difference is religious, political, or culinary (should we include meat in chili, for example). How many adults do you know who adore being lectured about right versus wrong? When in doubt, ask yourself how you'd feel or behave if the roles were reversed. That usually works like a charm.

Once you can accept the possibility of more than one "right" answer, you can do what's right for yourself and let everyone else do likewise. Think of all the extra time you'll have to polish your own act. Oh, the luxury of having no one's business to mind but one's own.

Rupert, life is neither fair nor unfair. It just is. It is the responsibility of an adult to develop an ethical sense of right and wrong and to make our lives work within society. If you expect society will give you hugs for good behavior, you're going to set yourself up for disappointment. Leading a life that makes ethical sense to you should be reward enough.

LOVE IS UNCONDITIONAL

✷

My wife and I are expecting our first child. We want to raise a child who will be a good person in this rather confusing world. My parents say all you have to do is love your kids and it will all work out. I'm not so sure. I'm easygoing, but my wife says kids need discipline. The baby isn't even here yet, and we're already worrying about doing the right thing. —ALVIN, 31, ALLENTOWN, PENNSYLVANIA

Parenting is the hardest job any of us ever undertake, Alvin, and the one for which we all feel dreadfully ill-equipped. If our folks did a great job, their parenting seems effortless; if we hated our upbringing, we don't want to adopt the same policies. Doing exactly the opposite doesn't seem all that wise. So either way, whether our parents were great or horrible, as parents, we're clueless. As kids, we want our parents to love us, no matter what. As adults, we realize that we weren't always so lovable, which makes us nervous about being able to love our own kids unconditionally—especially if they act like we did.

Most of our parents did the best they could with what they had, but the rules change with every generation. Before you beat the daylights out of yourself, let's look at this unconditional love that every parent is supposed to have for every child. As any parent will tell you, you can love the child without loving the behavior, so the question becomes how to socialize, not love, your offspring. Even the most docile children will occasionally be stubborn—that is, they'll have their own sense of what is right and fair. Is it fair to assume that, just because you're bigger, you're right and your child is wrong? Nah. I'm going to let you in on one of the most valuable secrets of really good parenting: you need to *listen* to your kid, whether we're talking about an infant's cry, a six-year-old's whine, or a teen's rationalization. I don't mean you should *obey* your cherub (you *are* the parent, after all), but if you listen, you will acquire really good information.

Asking children what they want or why they're doing something will give you information while offering the kids a chance to explain, as well as making them feel that their opinion actually matters. This technique doesn't allow you to abdicate your parental responsibility, but it does offer you some insight into the soul of that mini-person. If as parents we viewed ourselves more as teachers and less as wardens, our kids would have to assume more responsibility for their lives, which might result in fewer ulcers and gray hairs for us. Everybody would win.

Al, before you and your wife decide you have incompatible parenting styles, remember that your parents didn't always agree and you turned out okay. Just adopt the basic rule: whoever gets there first rules until the next crisis; if you catch the kid misbehaving, it's your choice of punishment and ditto for your wife. Don't undermine each other in front of the child and never use the "Wait till your father comes home" technique.

＊

I know I'm supposed to love my kids unconditionally, but one of my sons is a drug addict. He stole from his father and me, never held a job, and broke our hearts. I've got high blood pressure, and his father worries himself sick. I try to love my son, but I'm afraid if I don't cut him loose, I'll end up hating him. — ELMIRA, 63, BEAUMONT, TEXAS

The fantasy of unconditional love is truly one of the most destructive notions about goodness and love—the area where we're most vulnerable. We all assume that truly "good" people love unconditionally and that is what makes them so darned "good." This notion demeans the concept of love, not to mention intelligence.

For nearly five years of my life, every Monday afternoon after I finished my radio program, I'd put on flat-heeled shoes and hike on down to one of the toughest neighborhoods in Manhattan to work with young runaways and street kids at a shelter. The organization loudly and proudly proclaimed in their advertising that their credo was "unconditional love." I'm not sure exactly how this concept works when it's applied to family, let alone to imperfect strangers. My on-site observations suggested that this philosophy translated into "I have rules that I will not share with you. If and when you let me down by breaking these unspoken rules, I will toss you out, because you will have shown yourself to be unworthy of my unconditional love." Whoa.

This fantasy served to solidify the caretakers' sense of innate and holier than thou superiority while making the kids unbalanced and terrorized. After all, if the youngsters could be rejected by such spiritual and saintly people who loved unconditionally, the kids must, in fact, be truly evil and the scum of the earth. If love is unconditional it can't be earned or deserved.

These kids, who had been beaten up or raped or were just lost souls, were looking for the impossible: strangers who would love them. A more humane system would have taught these sad teens self-reliance instead of making them dependent on an illusion of love and acceptance. I was eventually frustrated by a system that was both hypocritical and destructive, so I left.

Elmira, you've bought into the unconditional love philosophy, and it's breaking your heart. Of course you love your son, but love doesn't have to be blind and deaf. You will always love him. But there are always conditions on behavior or there would be no sense of self-preservation. There is no such human thing as unconditional love when we're talking actual behavior. What could love possibly mean if we behave exactly the same way toward someone whether they're hugging and kissing us or lobbing grenades in our general direction? Talk about confusing—who would want to live in such a world?

Survival depends on knowing the difference between a friend and an enemy. Would you let them both in your house, introduce 'em to your dog, share your secrets? Of course not. A friend who tries to destroy you is an enemy.

You love your son, Elmira, but he needs to find his own way in this world. It may be time to set some limits, not on how much you love him but on how you show your love. Are you helping him or hurting him? Think of it this way: if you see someone drowning and you can't swim, should you go in after him? Of course not. You're not going to save him, and if someone else comes along who *can* swim, they'll have to decide whom to save—you or him. Don't drown yourself. Your son is flailing around in the water. You can't save him. It's time for him to learn to swim.

LOVE IS ETERNAL

✳

She was my first love, and even though she's married to someone else, I know she still loves me. If I could only see her alone for a week or two, I know she would feel the same way. There will never be another girl for me; I'll love her to the day I die, no matter what. —JACKSON, 27, HAMILTON, OHIO

Jackson, if I've told you once, I've told you a thousand times, you've got to lay off that country-western music. I'm sure you're a good guy, but love doesn't conquer all. People change, and love changes, but you've embedded your love in amber like some hapless beetle. Love is eternal only if you're mindless, indiscriminate, and somewhat self-destructive.

We would probably all be happier if we dispensed with the word "love" altogether and focused on conditional affection, which is flexible and open: "If you do something I like that makes me feel good, I'll do the same back to you. If and when one of us runs afoul of the other, whether it's in the next hour or the next decade, we can discuss the behavior and the alternatives and decide what each of us wants to do at that moment." With "affection" we could stop using the word "love" as an assault weapon.

EASY IS BEST

✳

I'm really lonely. I live at home, and every time I want to buy some stylish clothes to attract the opposite sex, my mother says any quality woman will see

through all that window dressing to the real me. —CARL, 31, UTICA, NEW
YORK

Carl, I know you love and respect your mom, but we've got to get you
out of the house occasionally. Inner beauty is great, but it never hurts to
look clean, neat, and up-to-date. What's going to catch your eye first: a
rusty old clunker or a car with a sleek paint job? Sure, you're going to look
under the hood, but which is going to grab your attention? There's nothing wrong with being attracted to attractive people. That's human and
understandable. It's only when appearances are your *sole* criterion that
you're being superficial. I'm not suggesting that you spend your next three
paychecks on a makeover, but people are influenced by how you present
yourself, in the same way you are influenced by how others appear. You can
be loved for your inner self and still have a neat and clean outer self.

But you're a big boy now, Carl. You've lived enough years to begin to
evaluate what seems sensible and what doesn't. I know it's a temptation to
cling to those simple statements of childhood. I'm not trying to make your
mom look stupid, but I'm suggesting that some of the things we accepted
as gospel when we were kids have no real value in adulthood. Make sure
you're not adopting your mother's perspective just because it's easy.

If you view comfort as a measure of rightness, you're going to get stuck.
Any change is going to provoke a certain amount of anxiety just because
it is unfamiliar. It's time for you to deal with the shadow your upbringing
casts over your sense of fun and pleasure. You don't need to holler at your
mama, but you can think back to your childhood and reevaluate some of
those rules in the light of who you've become. Believe in the worthiness of
pleasure as opposed to the value of pain.

✳

*I'll know when my love comes along. It'll be just like in the movies. It will feel
right, and that will be that. If you have to work at it, what's the point?
Everybody tries to make things so complicated these days.* —BOB, 37, VER-
MILLION, SOUTH DAKOTA

Bob, you have the philosophy of a lifelong bachelor. Falling in love is
easy but seldom simple. Complications can occur if one of you is already
married, living far away, or underage. Falling in love is easy; staying in love

requires courage and patience. If ease is the criterion, you may find your-self in a situation that is not only complicated but wrongheaded.

EFFORT IS REWARDED

*

I really worked at this relationship. I tried like I never tried before to be posi-tive, giving, and loving. No matter what I do, it never seems to be enough. I tell him I try, but it only seems to make him mad. —YVONNE, 44, OSHKOSH, WISCONSIN

Yvonne, sweetcakes, there is only *doing* and *not doing*. Don't even think about *trying*. It sounds as if you stopped being yourself and tried to please someone who may not be pleasable. Some people believe that if it comes easily, it's meant to be. But that's just as pointless as investing in the idea that if you work really hard you can overcome *all* obstacles and be rewarded for your dedication. The one and only time this will ever be true is in kindergarten, where the teacher gives out gold stars for effort. My uncle actually won a prize for being the best sneezer in preschool.

Unfortunately, a more permanent and unsavory consequence of this fantasy is the notion that if you try hard enough, people won't much care about your effectiveness. The bad news is that drudgery stinks. The good news is that if you succeed and are smart enough to keep your mouth closed about how easy it was for you, you'll be rewarded. If you blab about how little effort you had to expend, you'll get nailed by people who are envious or less talented. If you can do the job easily and well, good on ya. Just don't be smug; it'll show. It's tacky to brag, and people resent it.

Yvonne, I know you work hard at everything you do, but sometimes your hard work isn't enough. It doesn't sound like he's working very hard, but even if he is, the relationship just isn't cooking. If no matter what you do, it's not enough, maybe the answer isn't to work harder, but to take a good look and make sure this guy hasn't become a project or even an obsession. Make sure he's worth the effort you're investing.

While it is important to work hard at our lives, if we have to bring our efforts to someone else's attention, we're likely in trouble. If you say, "Look, I've really worked hard at this relationship," you'll sound desperate. It sounds whiny and self-serving. If you're reduced to asking for gratitude in order to maintain someone's tie to you, something is already very wrong. Hard work makes us feel connected and alive, but asking others to reward the effort rather than the results is asking for charity.

✳

I'm afraid to let anyone get close because I've been hurt so many times. I know the right person will understand this and keep trying and be patient. In the meantime, I've sure kissed a lot of frogs while looking for that handsome, understanding prince. I'm a really good person and I don't understand why I'm still alone. —FLO, 44, FORT PIERCE, FLORIDA

Flo, everyone over the age of sixteen feels like at some point someone's done 'em wrong and they're probably right. You may have exacted some damage on that cute little third grader to whom you neglected to send a Valentine or that shy kid in eighth grade whose stutter you laughed at. This doesn't mean you're a rotten person, and you're not being punished now for youthful insensitivity. This is not a time to wallow in self-pity but to take some emotional risks. I'm not suggesting you march down to the harbor and pick up the first sailor you meet. I am suggesting that it's time for you to get out of your own way and stop assuming that if you play it safe your goodness will be rewarded one of these days.

I would love to persuade you to try the "life is a daring risk or it's nothing at all" blueprint for a month or two. I'm not talking about selling your condo or your wardrobe or your body, but coming out of your shell a bit. This may mean taking tango lessons or flirting at the bus stop or knocking that chip off your shoulder.

Self-pity is never pretty. Henry Ford said a mouthful when he said, "Never complain, never explain." I would add, "Don't explain how you tried." Suck it up, do the best you can, and don't ask for sympathy. Most folks are pretty unwilling to offer it, and when they do, they view you differently forever.

Also refrain from self-justification: "I'm really a nice person. . . . I try really hard. . . . It's not easy for me. . . . It's how I was raised." Effort isn't rewarded; results are. Think about it: you're not going to applaud your surgeon for trying to save your life, you're going to pay her if she gets that infected appendix out in time. Trying is just trying and is almost routinely offered as an excuse when the desired result was not achieved.

Flo, you're making all those inattentive men the bad guys. If you're a bristly ball of anger, both men and women will stay away in droves. We all move toward pleasure and away from pain. *Lighten up.*

✳

I'm a good person, but every place I go, people always ask me to compromise my standards. I'm out of work for the second time this year, although I know I'm reliable and hardworking. My résumé is beginning to look really spotty. How do I convince someone that if I could just find the right boss, I'd be a great worker? —RENÉ, 58, HARRISBURG, PENNSYLVANIA

Don't walk away, René. Unfortunately, marketability has very little to do with goodness, and more to do with applicability, usefulness, style, and audience. This means how *you* come across. Hoping for the "right" boss is a dangerous and time-consuming fantasy. It sounds as if you believe, as I did, that all you had to do was finish school, be a good person, and the world would beat a path to your door. Imagine how many people who didn't wake up and smell the coffee are sitting around muttering quietly under their breath, "Yeah, but I'm a really nice person and I'm ready to do good." Waiting for someone to notice your inner goodness is making your well-being dependent on someone else's perception of you. What if they're nearsighted or shortsighted? Stop believing in some abstract, faintly self-serving concept of good and evil. Run your life in an ethical and moral manner, let everybody else do the same and have some fun. Smile, giggle, get tickled.

NOTHING CHANGES

✳

I saw this really attractive woman at the club last night. She was alone and smiled at me, but I figured she'd probably come again one of these days. I was tired last night and wanted to get home and didn't have my good-luck tie on. Besides, I read in some women's magazine that it's never a good idea to appear too eager. Next time I'll get up the courage to ask her to dance. —CYRIL, 68, SAG HARBOR, NEW YORK

Cyril, you've succumbed to the "If they asked you once, they'll ask you again" philosophy. I know that, technically, you could have done the asking, but her eyes were asking, so you blithely assumed they'd ask again. It's okay for you to be shy, but please don't assume the universe is aware of your plan or your tie wardrobe.

Unfortunately, once we believe in fair and easy and obvious, it's tempting to believe in a universe of absolutes that doesn't change very much. If you're good and feel you'll be rewarded, then it's only a matter of time before you'll be "discovered" by the right lover, the right boss, or the right friend.

The second-chance theory can make you really unhappy. If Sharon Stone asks you to go dancing, there's no sense playing coy and suggesting that you've got to wash your car on the assumption that she'll ask again. Be aware of your priorities. If it's important to you, rearrange, renegotiate, renege, but never assume that you'll get the same opportunity again. Everything changes.

✳

I just got a call from an executive search firm. They're looking for a director of personnel, and they said I had to let them know this afternoon, yes or no. I hate being rushed. My boss is out of town for two more days. I don't know what to do. —ALICE, 37, FALLS CHURCH, VIRGINIA

Alice, you and Cyril must have gone to the same "If they asked you once, they'll ask you again" seminar. If you're not careful, I'm afraid you'll end up sitting by the phone until cobwebs appear. Don't assume your convenience is crucial to others, even if they happen to be aware of it. Conversely, their convenience doesn't have to be your priority, either. If they want you today, they will most likely want you tomorrow, too, though maybe not next week or next month. Meanwhile, unless you can figure out why the situation would change in twenty-four hours, maybe you should wonder if they're fooling with you. So ask yourself if you really want to do business with people who would fool with you.

However, if the offer has to do with concert tickets, a charter flight, or a TV appearance, and if it's something you really want to do, put yourself out and go for it.

LUCK IS A REWARD

✳

If it weren't for bad, I'd have no luck at all. My wife left me, my kids hate me, I just lost my job, my dog bit me, the transmission dropped outta my pickup, and the roof leaks. My brother got all the luck in the family. When the good Lord passed out luck, I thought he said "duck" and shot mine. —BARNEY, 39, BATTLE CREEK, MICHIGAN

Gotta love your sense of humor, Barney. Before we leave the land of good and evil, absolutes and superheroes, let us dally for a moment at the altar of luck. The notion that only good people have good luck is a burden that should be laid to rest once and for all. Luck is a condition that the envious and the lazy attribute those who seem fortunate. If you want to believe in luck, please realize that it's a random force rather than a reward. That way you won't get distracted from working on your life, and envy of other people's good luck won't be such a thorn in your side.

As Mae West was heard to mutter, "Goodness has nothing to do with it." If you're going to worry about why Cindy Crawford has those cheekbones or why your sneaky friend gets all the girls, you're likely the obstacle in your own path. If you're going to believe in luck, you've got to believe in both good and bad.

Barney, instead of continuing to envy your brother, take a deeper look at why your relationships aren't working. Could it be that your passivity in waiting for luck to hit you upside the head is the same attitude that leaves you a spectator in your own life? This is it, buddy—your life. Start treating it as a project worth your time and effort and see how lucky you get.

As a personal credo, it is important to live a good life while understanding that having goodness and mercy follow you all the days of your life is a personal wish list, not a societal directive from you. In the final analysis, only you can determine what goodness and mercy are for you. Enjoy the task; resist the misery that comes from convincing others of your worth or their unworthiness.

SHRINK-WRAPS

Longing for the simplicity of childhood is a way to feel safe. The easy childhood world of right and wrong offered comfort. A life based on absolute rules that you can write on a T-shirt is a comfort. It's simple and easy. If only it were real. Let's play a game to show you what I mean. I'll give you a simple statement from your childhood, and then let's see what it looks like from an adult perspective:

CHILDHOOD MYTHS OF GOOD AND BAD BEHAVIOR

If you step on a crack, you'll break your mother's back: You might twist your ankle, but if your mom is taking her calcium, she's probably safe.

If you lie, your nose will grow: Perjury is a no-no and there are plastic surgeons to take care of your nose, but an awful lot of people are really convincing liars.

If you kiss a boy, you'll get pregnant: If you're old enough to read, I'm sure you've sorted this out for yourself. The underlying notion here is that sex is really dangerous and not to be dabbled with.

If you cross your eyes, they'll get stuck: Making faces really aggravates adults, but crossed eyes are inherent and they can be corrected.

If you crack your knuckles, you'll get arthritis: Making noise is irritating, but arthritis is an inflammation of the joint, not a punishment for being boisterous.

If you lie, I'll know: Not if you're pathological or keep it simple or tell me something I want to believe anyhow.

If you leave, I'll die: Only if we're Siamese twins; otherwise my heart beats separately from yours and my lungs are my own too.

9

somewhere i have a
soul mate

*Believing you have a mirror image who will love you
gives mirrors a bad name.*

Choice is scary, so the idea of destiny is relaxing. Since the scariest part of your life is your love life, the idea of a soul mate is truly seductive. The idea that someone out there is searching for you is a comfort when a blind date is breathtakingly lousy, Saturday night is lonely, and even nerds seem to have found true love. If we believe that somewhere our other half is awaiting reunion, then all we have to do is keep breathing and keep looking. No effort is required and the only real necessity is to dump the pretenders who turn out to be frogs in soul mates' clothing.

One of the pitfalls of this charming but basically lamebrained philosophy is that no matter how long the relationship or how cunning the disguise, at the first hint of incompatibility, we are going to be tempted to bail out. In this scenario, it's crucial not to waste time and effort on someone who isn't the one. Hey, if this fantasy were either uncommon or simply loony, okay, but it's not. It can undermine perfectly viable relationships that just need some effort. Compromises and negotiations are the hallmark of reality-based interactions, the problem is that they require work and commitment.

Sleeping with a slice of wedding cake under the pillow so that we'll dream of our intended is okay when we're young, but as adults, we should eat the cake, check out the receiving line, and go into relationships with our eyes wide open. Besides, who needs a crumby bed?

IT'S A NOAH'S ARK WORLD

✳

I've got a great life with one glitch: I love my job, I have a great apartment, but I'm so lonesome I could die. I've tried all the singles organizations. I've even written a personal ad. Everything seems to go really well at first. My friends tell me I'm good-looking. But if I don't find the right guy soon, I'll probably never find him. You know that thing they say about women over thirty-five: "finding a guy once you're forty is about as likely as being taken hostage by a terrorist." I know there's a perfect guy out there for me, if we could only find each other. —PATSY, 33, NASHVILLE, TENNESSEE

Patsy darlin', calm down. Panic isn't a useful dating mode. That article you're referring to about a woman over the age of forty having a hard time finding a mate made headlines, but the findings were almost immediately disputed. You're a smart, successful woman. Let's figure out why you're in such a hurry and what you can do about it.

For most of human history the lone woman was at risk. A single male might find life more difficult without a mate, but he could still hunt or forage; a female was helpless. A lone pregnant female could seldom survive without the group feeding her and her young and protecting both of them from predators. We've come a long way, baby—sorta. We can now heat our caves, light our way, move away from danger, cook our food, gather at the local shopping mall, and raise kids alone. But for many women and some men, the fantasy persists that you're not going to be able to survive without a partner. This Noah's Ark theory of life warns that when the floods come, Noah will only allow male-female couples on the cruise. The fear is that if we don't hurry up and find a mate, the rains will come and we'll be left behind to drown.

Patsy, the weather forecast isn't bad, and if the rain comes, you can learn to swim or find a rowboat. You're not going to perish if you don't get paired off. If you can face your terror of being alone, you can choose to make rational, personal choices rather than being pulled down by the dark fear of drowning alone. You're fine just being you. Honest.

*

I've known this woman for three months. The first two and a half months were fabulous. We have everything in common. We laugh at the same jokes, love hot fudge and butterscotch mixed together, Rollerblading, and Toni Morrison. It's like we've been together in another life, and the sex is like two souls communing. But all of a sudden, all we do is argue. The last two weeks have been sheer hell. Her mom is great and I love her dog, but everything else seems to be coming apart at the seams. —JONATHAN, 28, NEWARK, NEW JERSEY

A belief in the Noah's Ark theory of life leads directly to the need for a mate, and since we are loath to describe ourselves as primarily hormonal, we clean up the response by saying that what we really want is a soul mate. Jonathan, I'm afraid you're suffering from a nasty case of the soul-mate blues. You've taken an initial attraction, based primarily on lust, chemistry, and need, and parlayed it into a full-blown Macy's Thanksgiving Day Parade balloon that's full of overheated air and very vulnerable. If it's any comfort, you're not unique here, either. (I know what you folks are thinking, but Jonathan and Patsy would loathe each other on sight. They're both too needy.)

Jonathan's assumption that he and his girlfriend have everything in common is based on too little information and too much intensity. All of us want to be loved and appreciated for what we are and how we think— because of our warts, not in spite of them. The shortcut to all this acceptance seems to be finding someone exactly like us. Yeah, right, like that's really gonna happen. Especially when the other person is a stranger and our perceptions of each other are being filtered through hormones. Gotta love the clarity that sex appeal offers . . . not!

Most people aren't completely delusional. The assumption of sameness obviously isn't based on physical appearance, so we jump directly into the spiritual. Jonathan can believe that he and his beloved are a single soul that has been split in two and only when the two are together can the soul be reunited. Spirituality and dependence are neatly combined in this seductive, illogical fantasy. Adding a little past life regression analysis ("we've been together in another life") allows even sensible people to hurry through the getting-to-know-you phase and get right to the forever-and-ever phase. I certainly like a romantic movie as well as the next person, but I hope none of us confuse this goo with reality.

Even if this illusion were true, the danger here is that these soul-mate assumptions make both parties move at the speed of light past things that they shouldn't be moving past at all, let alone at warp speed. Things like the following:

+ Are you a morning person or a night person?
+ Are you a saver or a spender?
+ Do you love or hate PBS?
+ How do you feel about cremation?
+ What do you do on Sunday morning—read the funnies or go to church?
+ How do you feel about family vacations?
+ Do you like chunky or smooth peanut butter?

Somehow, these topics never come up between soul mates. Instead, even a trivial similarity can trigger the thrill of recognition: "You mean you like the first year of *Star Trek* better than the third year, too?" Also, much more dangerously, even major differences are ignored, especially in the beginning. Both Jonathan and his beloved are vigorously and feverishly dedicated to the mission of demonstrating how much alike they are.

ALL YOU NEED IS LOVE

✳

I love him, but I'm not in love with him. I used to love the way his neck smelled. Now it seems like a nasty case of ring-around-the-collar. He was dependable and solid and crazy about me. These days, all he does is work. —JENNIFER, 43, AKRON, OHIO

Unfortunately, being a soul mate is a short-term occupation. How long can a relationship exist based on who you'd like that person to be rather than who he is? How long can either of you ignore the differences that make each of you unique? Sooner or later the discrepancies begin to emerge. Jennifer, I'm afraid you're confusing love with lust and unfamiliarity with passion. The same things you once admired about him are the things that are now making you testy. That dependability is what made you sure he'd be a good provider, which is what he's trying to do when he spends so much time at work. Let's worry less about his neck and more about necking. What if you decided that, for a month, you were going to treat him the same way you did when you were focusing on who you wanted him to be. You may find that you really appreciate who he is, and he may feel the same way about you, once he doesn't have to measure up to the fantasy.

✴

We've been seeing each other for six months. He used to love my friends and hang out with me at my mom's. Now all he wants to do is chill with his friends and drink beer. —MARY, 19, JACKSONVILLE, FLORIDA

If the similarities have been inflated to near mythical proportions, the differences will feel uncomfortable and threatening to the illusion of compatibility you've got going. You have to ignore these differences, or their very existence will become scarier and scarier. Big stuff and little stuff—not liking the same movie or restaurant, being grumpy or cheerful in the morning—will take on the proportions of a gigantic, terrifying needle ready to pierce that over-inflated Macy's parade balloon of your soul-matedness.

Mary, you're in the same bind as Jennifer. Realistically, it takes six to nine months, minimum, to figure out whether there is enough between the two of you to make a relationship. At this point, it's hard to tell if the fantasy has worn off and the reality is pretty tepid so you're both ready to move on or just that the fantasy has worn off and the reality is just slightly less exciting. Are the two of you spending too much time together? Are you too needy? Has he neglected his friends to be with you, and is he now feeling the loss of their company? What characteristics do you really *like* about each other, and how much of your attraction is just a basic hormonal surge? Don't despair, just look at what's really going on here and what you both want.

✴

My best friend since first grade and I started a health food store together eight months ago, but she's not doing her share of the work. When we originally talked about doing this, it seemed like we wanted exactly the same thing, but now we seem to argue about what vitamins to stock, whether to expand to include soy-bean take-out, who gets the weekend off, who closed up yesterday, and whether

somewhere i have a soul mate   129

it's okay to take a lunch break. The partnership just isn't working for me any-more, but I don't want to lose a friend. —DAVID, 37, COLORADO SPRINGS

The assumption of sameness leaves both parties incapable of negotiating the differences that will inevitably occur between two people. This happens with friends as well as lovers. David, just because you've known your friend in one context doesn't mean you know how she'll react in all situations. You're confusing quantity of information with quality of information. First grade compatibility may have very little to do with what it takes to run a business together. Sharing secrets, homework assignments, and cootie catchers says you have the same sense of humor and willingness to share, but it doesn't look at grown-up issues like division of labor, monetary styles, work ethic, or long-term goals.

This assumption of a shared soul looks at one point of reference and generalizes everything else. The platonic soul-mate approach encourages the same maximum emotional involvement based on the minimum amount of data as the romantic soul-mate assumption. Neither approach works because there is absolutely no structure here; you're flying without a net. Liking someone is lovely, but it's not a basis for going into business together without more investigation. "Wouldn't it be fun to work together?" is a fantasy. You need a sane reality-based approach that says, "Here's what's true for me. Now tell me what's true for you." In this case, David, sitting down with an accountant or someone from the Small Business Association may help both of you clarify your goals and salvage both the business and the friendship.

Women in particular often have a difficult time with adult friendships. Twelve-year-old girls, on the other hand, can easily form intense bonds with one another—the best friend phenomenon. Two incomplete personality structures are interwoven based on an incredible communality of interests that never occurs again: boys, growing breasts, braces, nasty Mr. Carruthers in homeroom, cheerleading practice, and the geek who dared to ask you to dance. That overwhelming commonality won't occur again till both of you are old, if it ever reoccurs. (We are more alike at the beginning and end of life because we have less physical mobility and fewer responsibilities at those times.) Many women go through life longing for that closeness with a friend—the soul mate fantasy applied to a nonsexual relationship. Being aware of the longing to feel intimately connected can help protect us against rushing into emotional minefields. Shortcuts through minefields need to be avoided.

The younger we are, the less formed we are in terms of personality and interests. For this reason women often spend their whole lives searching for that perfect friendship they had when they were twelve, and men may fondly recall elementary school days before girls became the "enemy" and "icky." Adults, however, have much more fully developed personality structures and lifestyles. Longing for that intimacy is unrealistic since personalities will never again be so unformed and flexible.

David, this is part of your problem. You're longing for the earlier relationship you had with your best friend, and you're working on the memory of who both of you were, not are. Faced with anything other than perfect mutuality, you're at a loss. If you can be brave enough to look at who both of you are, you may be able to start the business relationship on firmer footing. If you persist in the fantasy, I'm afraid that both the business and the personal relationship are doomed. One of the reasons David has been able to keep his soul mate fantasy going for so long is that in platonic friendships, intimacy is based on hearts and heads, not genitals. Heads and hearts seem to get somewhat less bruised when genitals aren't involved.

✳

We've had a few dates, and he's really nice and a good listener, which is important since I'm in sales and I like to talk, but I'd like someone a bit more charismatic, with more get-up-and-go. He seems to really like me, but he sure doesn't say much. —EILEEN, 29, FLINT, MICHIGAN

Opposites tend to attract at first and then aggravate the daylights out of each other later on. Eileen, I'm worried that you're going to be much less willing to get involved with someone who seems different from you if you decide you need your mirror image to feel whole. Your initial attraction to this man seems based on the fact that he's *not* like you: he's a good listener, nice, low-key. But as you begin to feel closer, it sounds like your own inadequacies are surfacing and you're shutting down. Make sure you're not looking for someone who validates who you are by being you. Don't be looking for, yeah, you guessed it . . . a soul mate.

Let me emphasize for a moment that it's not a bad idea to wish to be with someone who is like you. Similar is okay; identical, however, is really tricky and dangerous. The idea of a soul mate doesn't deal with similarity. It deals with exactly-the-same. All of us have to be aware of and comfortable with our own identity.

Realistically, if Eileen or anyone else doesn't feel whole, it's time for therapy, not a date. Another person cannot complete us. Relationships can't be the Spackle to our emotional drywall. Eileen has to stand alone, comfortably and happily, before she can look to be with someone else. That other person then has a manageable task: to merely add pleasure to her already functional and meaningful life.

✳

He still lives at home, he doesn't work, he yells a lot and spends more time with his mom than with me, but he's my soul mate. I love him, and I want to be with him forever. —SHARON, 36, SAN FRANCISCO

Sharon, slow down, chickie. As Diana Ross sings, "You can't hurry love." I know you're in your thirties and you want to get this whole mating shebang over and done with, but it sounds to me like you've got a notion in your head, or more likely your heart, that's preempting your usual sensible self. It is seductive fun to assume that someone you don't know is just like you, especially when this assumption allows you to completely ignore the time-consuming, tedious, and potentially disappointing process of actually discovering who that person is. Sharon, it's possible that without being aware, you're tempted to shortcut the process so you don't have to show him who you really are, either. By assuming that you've found Mr. Right, you can convince yourself that you're looking in the mirror at a familiar face. This is very risky and shortsighted business.

So what's the alternative, you ask? How about going slowly? What about believing that a stranger can't accept or reject you because he doesn't really know you nor you him? Getting there is not only half the fun but also a necessary part of the process. Taking shortcuts in relationships is as dangerous as skipping bricks in construction. You get finished earlier and with less cost, but the structure is unsound and the whole thing is likely to come crashing down. Shortcuts don't make a lot of sense when you don't know where you're going or who you're with or even where you want to go.

This soul-mate business is really, really seductive because it is a chance to love ourselves while seeming to love someone else. We can simultaneously affirm that we are worthy of love while seeming to love another who—golly—is just like us. Unfortunately the price of this twofer is turning a blind eye, a deaf ear, and an ignorant heart to reality. Sooner or later . . . yeah, think fragile bubble.

AFTER THE FALL

✳

I fell in love with him on the Internet. He's everything my husband isn't: kind, considerate, willing to talk about his feelings and spend hours with me. I just don't understand what's going on now. We finally met face-to-face, had the world's most romantic weekend, and I haven't heard from him for a week. Every time I call him I get his machine, and he hasn't answered my E-mail. I finally tracked him down at work. He said he'd get back to me, but he hasn't. — SOPHIE, 52, GREEN BAY, WISCONSIN

If I said the word "fall," you would very likely say "down" or "off." If I asked you to tell me about falling experiences, you might talk about slipping on the ice or falling on your tailbone.

Sophie, I'm willing to bet that you always wear your seat belt, check the stove twice before leaving the house, and floss after meals. You're a relatively sane adult, like the rest of us, so how did we all come to view falling in love as a positive experience? Falling in any other context means being out of control, fearful, and in danger. It may be that this romantic notion has been used to cover up the very real fears about intimacy, dependence, and rejection that are inherent in learning to love someone and allowing that person to figure out who we are. It may also cover up a superstitious reluctance to look a gift horse in the mouth. If we look too carefully at someone, we may not like what we see—or the other person may look back and not like what he sees.

You can see how this unwillingness to look closely is first cousin to a soul-mate attitude. It's only when our heart is at risk that we are so frivolous and daring. No one ever talks about falling in love with a job or a vacation without doing any research whatsoever. Even when we fall in love with a car, we have the mechanic check it out before we buy. If it's a house, we wait for the bank appraisal before committing ourselves. Only when it comes to love, the most important of all areas, do we embrace the notion of letting go and falling over the cliff.

ALL YOU REALLY NEED IS LOVE

✴

We've been together three years. He was my first true love, but he's cheated on me a lot. Every time I take him back, because he says he really loves me and wants us to be together forever. Then again, he almost never tells me he loves me unless he wants sex, and he ignores our child. I know I should leave him, but I really, really love him and I know he really, really loves me. —CHERYL, 19, NAPLES, FLORIDA

Cheryl, I know you're young and scared and unhappy, but I really need you to listen here. Admittedly, love is nice, but there are much more important commodities, like respect, communication, give-and-take, and self-respect. You met this dude when you were a baby, and now you have a baby. Ready or not, it's grown-up time. If you have a child, you can't be a child anymore, no matter how young you are. In adult relationships, the *balance* of give-and-take is much more complicated than either simply giving or taking. In a sensible universe the only way most people are willing to give on any sort of long-term basis is if we're getting something back. In order to get back something of value, we've got to work out what each of us wants and is willing to offer to get it. This concept gets sticky for a soul-mate junkie. After all, if you're soul mates, each of you knows exactly what the other desires. To actually have to communicate your wants and needs smacks more of negotiation than romance.

I don't want to hurt your feelings, Cheryl, but I'm concerned that you're confusing love and sexual attraction. Don't misunderstand me, there's absolutely nothing wrong with sexual attraction, but to sugar-coat it with notions of forever is asking for trouble. Attraction is terrific and can certainly make the world go 'round and our hearts beat faster. It's a great reason to look farther, take risks, and stick around. Love at first sight is lust with potential. There is certainly nothing wrong with lust or potential, but neither should be confused with reality or knowledge.

You've got some hard work to do here. If you truly love this guy, it's time to set some limits. You can be his woman, his mate, or his wife, but you've got to figure out specifically what you want from him. You really can get along without him, even though you think you can't. It's time to worry less about who he is and more about who you are. Don't allow sex to blind you. Know who you are first. Then begin looking at how he behaves and who he really is. At that point, decide whether or not you want him.

We've been together six months now, and we couldn't keep our hands off each other from the very first time we met. It's not that I don't think she's hot, but I wonder if she's really the one for me. I know she loves me, and I guess I love her, but I don't know. I feel like something's missing. —EDGAR, 41, MINNEAPOLIS, MINNESOTA

Yeah, Edgar, like a sense of who the two of you are. Maybe the sex is still good, or maybe the novelty's worn off a bit and the lust has ebbed and sex has gotten a little ordinary. It seems to me that you have both neglected to really get to know each other. Having some information about each other—how you think, what happens when you have a cold, and whether your parents are alive—allows the two of you to trust each other enough to show what you really feel and who you actually are.

After a while, everybody gets tired of pretending. "I love him, but I'm not in love with him" is shorthand for "I want the fun but no work. I want the romance, not the reality, I want the fireworks without the smell of gunpowder."

Hey, don't we all? The problem is unless you have a lobotomy and date people with the IQ of an eggplant, sooner or later—usually sooner—real personalities and wishes and desires emerge. Making sure there is enough information in place will minimize unpleasant surprises and increase the probability of having a healthy, long-term relationship.

There was this guy that I went out with and he was really hot and everybody liked him, but he liked me, even though I'm not very pretty and I'm not too smart. My father hated him, but he hates everybody and would hit me when he found out I was seeing Dwayne after he told me not to. I really loved Dwayne, but once he hit me. I loved him a lot, but I had to love me better, so I stopped seeing him. —STEPHANIE, 15, NEEDHAM, MASSACHUSETTS

somewhere i have a soul mate

Stephanie, you've said it all. It takes some people a lifetime to learn that lesson, and some never learn. You've had to learn it the hard way, sweetie, which breaks my heart, but you've learned it and you're only fifteen. Bless you.

TRUE LOVE LASTS FOREVER

✳

She was everything I was looking for in a wife. She was loving to me and deferred to whatever I thought. But now, after five years, she's gotten bossy and short-tempered. Where is the little girl I married, and how can I get her back?
—JOE, 38, CINCINNATI, OHIO

Joe, I'm not sure how little your "little girl" was when you married, but it takes a certain number of years to form an adult personality. Even if she was ninety-four when you married, you better believe that if love does last forever, it's going to change form. This shape-shifting can confuse us. I am convinced that women choose men thinking they can change them and men choose women assuming they will never change. How can we expect these relationships to work? First of all, they need a firm basis in reality that will allow for change without catastrophe. Fantasy is resistant to change.

Implicit in our fantasies about the eternal nature of true love are three heartfelt beliefs that:

1. Nothing will ever change.
2. If there is change, both people will change in the same direction.
3. Only the things you dislike will be changed.

As you may recall from high school biology, every cell in our bodies is replaced in a seven-year cycle. If our bodies change that much, the likelihood of our feelings remaining constant is unlikely. Not only is the little girl you married all grown up, but so is the fresh-faced guy she married. You've both changed. I'm not saying people will fall out of love or stop loving, just that feelings, bodies, perspective, and expectations change. Sex may very well change a relationship, but sex isn't love—even though in our charmingly benighted way, we pretend it is. Change is movement, and when you're dealing with sex and expectation, movement is seldom predictable. While it is undoubtedly true that people change, the direction of that change is often hard to predict. The assumption that two people will change in the same direction is therefore even less likely, and the assumption that only the irritating stuff will change is definitely not logical. The reasons people change are often hard to ascertain, difficult to understand, and surprisingly personal. The behavior we are most likely to change is our own. The behavior we are most likely to want to change is someone else's.

BODIES DON'T LIE

✳

My girlfriend is really crazy about me, but there's this other woman, and she's so wonderful, that I get turned on just by looking at her. My girlfriend is okay, but this other woman has convinced me to keep looking. I guess my girlfriend isn't the one or I wouldn't have gone gaga over the new one. After all, I trust my instincts. —STEVEN, 37, TUCSON, ARIZONA

The soul-mate notion gains strength from the idea that if your body is responding, then all is right with the world, your head, and your heart. This makes about as much sense as believing that having damp palms means you're scared. It might . . . but then again, it might mean you're in an overheated room, you've been holding a drippy glass, or you couldn't find a towel to dry your hands. Any given body response may have more than one explanation. Lust isn't love, and anticipation isn't desire. When your heart is telling you to hit the sheets or go into business or buy a dog or a motorcycle, your head is actually interpreting data in a way that pleases you. It is the ultimate form of rationalization—taking unrelated data and superimposing upon it a system of logic that makes sense to you. In science it's called cooking your data. Bodies lie, cheat, whine, mislead, and distract. But bodies aren't the problem—it's the interpretation of bodily data that is to blame. We need to overcome our tendency to act upon casually and occasionally catastrophically misinterpreted data.

✳

I had been working with this guy for a while, and at his going-away party I said, "I'd like to get to know you better." He said, "Look, I'm sure you're a lovely

person, but you're too old for me and I'm not sexually attracted to you." I laughed, which really surprised him. We talked for a while, and he asked if he could give me a lift home. I said, "Well, I guess so." At my door, he asked if he could kiss me good night. I asked, "What kind of kiss? You said I was too old and I didn't turn you on." We dated for a year and a half and got married eight months ago. — DINA, 53, SAN DIEGO, CALIFORNIA

You go, girl! You've resisted the dangerous notion that there is one perfect person in the world who's there just for us and we'll both know when our love comes along. Even if we have a soul mate, the signs may be confusing enough to warrant caution, time, and the courage to be the unique person you are. Whoosh, what a relief, Dina! Your self-reliance and sanity offer the cure to the soul-mate blues.

The urge to merge is a basic instinct, but because we have these big fat brains on top of all of our other organs, we have learned to be somewhat careful about who we let into our lives, our hearts, our heads, and our beds. Still, the urge remains. Nowhere is the conflict between head and heart more evident than in a country that believes with equal fervor in efficiency and passion. Love at first sight is the McDonald's of relationships, but most of us are looking for a little more nourishment.

SHRINK-WRAPS

Avoid renting these videos when you're feeling blue or after a first date.

HOLLYWOOD SOUL-MATE FANTASIES

On a Clear Day You Can See Forever: Barbra Streisand discovers through her psychiatrist, Yves Montand, that she has lived before, but can she find love this time around?

Sleepless in Seattle: Tom Hanks is a lonely widower whose son calls a talk show trying to get Dad a date. Meg Ryan hears him and decides to find him. They keep crossing the country, just missing each other until the last minutes of the film, which find them on the top of the Empire State Building, where they discover what we've known all along: they're destined to be together.

Dead Again: Kenneth Branagh and Emma Thompson play a couple united by her memory loss (clearly big in soul-mate scenarios), finding that in a previous life they were both connected to a forty-year-old murder. The confusing plot got even murkier, since the stars were married to each other in real life when the movie was made. Reality has since intruded.

FOOD FOR SOUL MATES

These foods are pretty, sugary, appealing, and without real value.

+ **Falling in love is wonderful.** The wine—a heady, intoxicating bouquet.
+ **All you really need is love.** The appetizer—a gorgeous ethereal presentation.
+ **True love lasts forever.** The entrée—palatable but without nourishment.
+ **Bodies don't lie.** The dessert—a sweet, decadent confection.

realities

G et real" has become the new and belligerent way to express disappointment, frustration, or simple anger without actually calling someone a liar. Personally, I like reality. You might even call me a reality junkie, and I'd love to convince you to share my preoccupation with the here and now. Being real is a way to get involved, to be focused and alert. The problem is that getting real takes a certain amount of thought and concentration. Fantasies are fun because they require only imagination. These rambunctious realities demand work and consistency, plus you actually have to think about what you're doing. Bummer. But the payoff on these grubby, sweaty realities is real pleasure, not this virtual reality stuff, but actual, honest-to-goodness, living, breathing rewards that don't disappear when you close your eyes or turn off the computer.

Reality is genuine, authentic, and actual. Trust me, you want real experiences in the same way you want real money, real love, and real flowers. Living your life in a real way by real rules means that your time, thoughts, and energy matter. *You* matter.

I'm not trying to persuade you to give up romance novels or sentimental greeting cards, but I would like you to give up the notion that real life is like those larger-than-life plots and characters. Take an occasional vacation from your life by indulging in a moment or two of fantasy, but don't confuse the vacation with your life plan. If I can convince you to embrace the eight realities discussed here, your life will improve so much that you won't have to retreat into fantasies to be happy. If you escape only temporarily, at least the reentry into your real world won't be so jarring.

If you can focus on yourself and what you want, you can give up destructive daydreams, expectations, shame about your feelings, and the urge to tell other people what you think they need to know. You will gain a sense of serenity and well-being by feeling more comfortable in your own skin, without having to compare pelts.

When you do decide to decipher, not change, someone else's actions, you can be guided by the same straight line you use to understand your own behavior. Once you understand that you do things for reasons, you can accept that others do, too. This approach allows you to be more curious than condemning, more accepting than accusatory. Not only will your complexion improve, but those "four o'clock in the morning, who am I" blues will be minimized, and your popularity will greatly increase.

Fantasies are an instant escape from problems that won't go away. Once you accept that you're better served by spending minimal time on short-term benefits and maximum time on longer-term payoffs, you'll think about options in a new and cheerier light.

Hey, I know reality is sometimes blemished, but it's also excitingly alive and important and the spot where all of us have to learn to live our lives.

1

never tell someone something they already know

Compliment people sincerely and keep nasty thoughts to yourself.

T*he subtitle of* this section should be "The Truth Trap." It is the antidote to the fantasy that the truth will set you free and that honesty is the best policy. In order to be social, living things have to communicate, and for humans, this communication is tricky stuff. Most animals have to be close enough to smell, touch, see, and hear each other to interact effectively. One of the niftier but trickier things about being human is that the feedback loop has gotten wider. The distance between one organism doing something and the other noting it and sending back a signal has really widened. If we aren't close enough to see each other, we can use the phone or a videotape, and hearing isn't crucial if we can use E-mail or snail mail. AT&T has allowed us to reach out and touch someone not only over the phone but also through instantaneous messaging on-line, and it's only going to get easier, cheaper, and better. We've even gotten so far away from using our sense of smell that we think we have to use Obsession, Opium, or White Shoulders to make sure we're fresh.

As the first of the realities, this chapter focuses on communication that is uniquely human: what to say and what not to say, plus how to say it effectively, not irritatingly. To be able to communicate well, we must first understand ourselves so we can honestly express what we are feeling. As the computer guys say, garbage in, garbage out. If we're clueless, truth can't be communicated. Self-delusion (being clueless about ourselves) is the essence of really bad communication.

Free speech doesn't mean anybody has to listen; it just means everybody gets to talk. In our society we believe that things are worth what you pay for them, so other people's unsolicited advice is often considered worthless by everyone except the speaker. Been there, felt that. . . .

I make my living telling people what they *don't* want to hear. Most people who call my program want to hear not only that they are totally blameless and exemplary but that whoever is bedeviling them is a louse. My task is to gently focus the caller's attention on what specific things he or she can do differently to improve the situation, whether that means adopting a different tone, perspective, or behavior. I get gobs of practice trying to find new ways to solve problems but I never (well, almost never) offer unsolicited advice in my private life. Most of us know what we're doing wrong, but rather than face the reality head on and do something constructive, we flail about looking for someone to blame in the futile hope that that person will change so we don't have to. The preferred strategy here is to attack the person you're blaming, based on the time-honored tradition that the best defense is a good offense. Trust me—not only will it not work, but it will make your partner in the dilemma feel hostile or guilty or both.

❋

My younger brother and I have never gotten along, but I love his daughter, my fourteen-year-old niece, even though I don't see her that often, since they all live in Florida. She says that her parents are druggies and they hit her and have punched her in front of her friends at school. I want to tell my brother about his drug problem in a tactful way. —MERYL, 43, MANCHESTER, NEW HAMPSHIRE

If you and your brother haven't gotten along in the past, Meryl, telling him that he's got a drug problem isn't going to improve the relationship. If you haven't seen him lately, I'd think about doing so. Fourteen-year-olds are not often praised for their accurate and objective reporting. If your brother has a drug problem, it may be news to you, but I assure you that *he* is aware of it.

If your focus is on your niece, figure out what you can offer her that might help her: maybe a summer at your home or even a school year there. Make sure you tell her that she will have to follow your rules, so she doesn't think she's checking into the Meryl Marriott and will be able to come and go as she pleases, now that her parents are elsewhere.

But, Auntie Meryl, we never, ever tell people something they already know, *especially* when it's negative. My guess is that, if you are honest, you'll admit that you don't view your brother fairly and objectively. If your next-door neighbor's child said she was living in a crack den, you'd at least observe the neighbors for a few days before calling the cops.

Knowing your own agenda is a good beginning. Are you trying to punish your brother or help him? Do you want to kidnap your niece or help her solve her problems? If you don't know your own motives, you're going to be on the defensive in an already inflammatory situation. So let's chill for a moment and figure out the goal here.

Once you are clear about motive, it's even more important to focus on *what* you're trying to communicate. The *how* of communication is incredibly sophisticated, but usually we're tempted to blurt out our feelings without thinking about what we're trying to say and why. We've all gotten a bit careless about the real purpose of communication, which isn't just to let our lips flap or our E-mail circulate but actually to interact with other people. Meryl, don't be tempted to fire off an angry letter or leave a nasty message on your brother's answering machine and wait for the explosion. Good communication is a two-way street that has to be carefully paved and even resurfaced from time to time.

Our willingness to mind other people's business because we want to seem helpful or caring is uniquely and dangerously human. My favorite horrible example is the so-called intervention. The idea that a person actually might not *know* that, because of his drinking or shooting up or snorting, he is disrupting other people's lives is dangerously naive. The idea that a group of family and friends telling him how awful he is will result in a tearful renunciation of booze and drugs is wishful thinking. It is more likely that he will run shrieking from the room hollering, "I always knew everyone was out to get me."

Alcohol has been, is, and will continue to be, the major drug of abuse in this country, and intervention is a nasty outgrowth of the disruption that alcohol causes to relationships. The willingness, even with the best of intentions, to tell people wretched things about themselves reflects a desire to focus on what's easy (someone else's problems) and ignore what's difficult (our own shortcomings). You can do almost nothing about someone else's problems, even when they're not drug-related, but *especially* when they are. You can do quite a lot, however, about your own shortcomings. Ganging up on someone else to get her to change her behavior has to be seen for what it is: a dangerous last resort. This isn't to say that people can't discuss difficult personal issues together, but it is a warning to beware of motive.

Meryl, I know you want to do something helpful here, so let's look at the *exact purpose* of the communication—which isn't all that obvious. We often state the obvious or irrelevant:

+ It's a nice day today,
+ It's Monday already,
+ Wow, it's cold out.

These natterings establish the social fabric onto which more elaborate and meaningful patterns can be woven. Okay, so we can agree that some communications are more significant than others. Between the nearly irrelevant remark you might make to your brother ("How's the weather?") and the truly meaningful comment ("Who are you and what do you care about most?") lie messages that are often hidden, judgmental, and lethal. Here are two of the most popular messages:

+ An insult disguised as an honest comment.
+ Hostility masquerading as truth-telling.

Hostility and insults are both hurtful and counterproductive, and they can be surprisingly hard to identify when they are camouflaged as honest comments. We get into patterns of behaving and are unaware of how callous our style is. All of us have made hurtful remarks on purpose. We apologize, feel chagrined and go on. My purpose here is to highlight the subtler ways we unwittingly harm each other with words, so that we can be more aware in crucial situations. I have organized these all too human, ubiquitous tendencies into six categories: buried barb, eager expert, clever communicator, written warrior, apt aper, and curious quester.

If you find your own style of manipulation here, don't be surprised or ashamed. Just be aware that it will limit your effectiveness, popularity, and chance of having a date for New Year's Eve, so cut it out. Okay?

THE BURIED BARB

*

I don't know how to respond when someone tells me I have a pretty face and I would be really attractive if I'd just lose a few pounds. The other day I ran into a former neighbor whom I hadn't seen for years, and he said, "Wow, you've really put on weight." I couldn't decide whether to punch him or cry, but I couldn't get angry, 'cause then he said, "I'm worried about you." —AIMEE, 54, PINE BLUFF, ARKANSAS

I wish I could give you a hug, Aimee. I agree that you're entitled to feel really angry. It was a hurtful thing to say and whitewashing it by saying, "I'm really worried" doesn't offset the thoughtlessness. All of us have made dumb comments that we might have viewed as well-meaning before we noticed the decided lack of enthusiasm with which they were met. I can't think of very many folks (other than people recovering from a debilitating illness) who would appreciate being told that they'd put on weight. Just as a drunk knows that she drinks too much, most of us are completely aware of every pound we gain, unless we're completely blind and stupid—like "Silly me! I didn't know I'd put on weight because I've been in a gravity-free environment until just this moment."

In our weight-conscious society, telling someone she's put on a few pounds borders on the sadistic. This doesn't mean that your ex-neighbor is wicked, just that he's a bit thoughtless. If it's any comfort, he'd likely not be thrilled if you commented on his hairy ears or love handles. It's amazing, isn't it, that we comment on weight and size from the beginning of our lives. Moms in the park comment on the size of newborns. I've even heard myself say, "Wow, she's huge and wonderful," about an unusually robust two-month-old. Unfortunately this tendency to comment on an infant's body doesn't necessarily abate as the child grows. Even folks who would never comment on another adult's weight or zits or bad hair day feel no compunction about commenting on a kid's baby fat, complexion, or growth spurt: "Gee, you're growing like a weed." The poor kid isn't even allowed to defend himself without getting sent to his room for talking back. Childhood and adolescence are difficult enough without an adult commenting on a kid's physical awkwardness. They either don't care or are painfully aware without hearing about it from you. Even the snottiest kid can get hurt feelings from careless comments like "That purple hair is really weird," or "What possessed you to pierce your lip?" Either way, calling attention to what you consider a physical abnormality isn't likely to be seen as anything other than antagonistic.

As adults, we forget the torment and the helplessness of not being able to talk back to our elders. My mother, whom I love dearly, is the queen of "I liked your hair the way you had it last time." Yikes, Mom! I know sometimes you think of me as a hopelessly dorky eight-year-old, but I'll respond much better to a positive comment than to a critical remark.

If you find yourself tempted to comment on your kid's Mohawk, punk, or pink hair, multiple piercings, or cornrows, just whip out your junior high yearbook and look at what you once considered cool. Hairstyles are as political as anything else about our appearance, and everyone is allowed to make her own statement.

The only behavior we need to evaluate is our own. Saying "When I was your age" is a dreadful mistake, but *thinking* "What did I do when I was her age?" is not a bad idea—as long as you don't *say* anything.

In general, when you tell someone you don't like his hair, her outfit, her weight, or his height, you're commenting on something the person is already aware of. If he too hates the haircut, you've only compounded his misery. If he actually likes it, you've hurt his feelings for no reason.

Is there a right way to comment negatively on someone's appearance? Aimee, I know you're voting no. When asked, "Do you like my new glasses?" and you *definitely* don't, how about a smile and comment on nifty new shoes, the weather, or "hey, why ask my opinion? My hair looks like the circus just blew into town." It's the basic rule: When in doubt, say nothing at all. Thumper the rabbit from *Bambi* gets my vote: "If you don't have sumpin' nice to say, don't say nuffin' at all." When you're cornered, general positive statements are a worthwhile substitute for specific criticism. And if you're feeling gracious and complimentary, aim for specificity rather than making it a blanket statement.

GENERAL STATEMENTS

+ You've lost weight.
+ You got a haircut.
+ That's a new shirt.

SPECIFIC COMPLIMENTS

+ You look great in that color.
+ Your new haircut is fabulous.
+ That style suits you.

A final thought here: even when the hair grows out, the weight is lost, the puce tie is discarded, *never* be tempted to say, "I didn't want to tell you then, but I really hated your hair that way" or "You looked like one of the elephants from *Fantasia*" or "I assumed that shirt was a gift from a color-blind friend." Insults after the fact are still insulting.

THE EAGER EXPERT

✳

My girlfriend is beautiful, but she's got awful teeth. I keep telling her not to laugh without putting her hand over her mouth because it really wrecks the picture. When I mimic her gesture to remind her, she goes postal. You'd think she'd understand that I'm just trying to make her look better. —LANCE, 31, HOLLYWOOD, CALIFORNIA

I'm surprised she hasn't gestured *you*, Lance. Let's take a meeting here. Think how you'd feel if she constantly harped on your bald spot or the fact that your knees are knobby. In these situations, gratitude, even if deserved, is not our first impulse. Even if you think you know how she feels about her teeth, it's a much better idea to gently ask if she's interested in your suggestions. Be willing to hear "Thanks, anyway." If you feel you know more about her feelings than she does, it's still best to pose your assertion in the form of a question: "Gee, I have an idea that might make you less worried about your teeth. Would you like to hear it?" If she says no, believe her and back off. Lance, insulting her isn't going to increase her confidence.

Most folks are understandably sensitive about being lectured to about their own lives. Even when it's their field of expertise, know-it-alls are seldom loved. Trying to remake your friend into an image that suits you is most likely futile, frustrating, and unpleasant for you both. You're adults.

never tell someone something they already know   151

Accept who both of you are and either like it or leave each other alone with dignity and self-respect intact.

THE CLEVER COMMUNICATOR

＊

I tell my daughter that her dating strategy (doing nothing but working all the time and hoping someone will find her at a Weight Watchers meeting) will leave her an old maid. She's not getting any younger. I'm only doing this for her own good. I really want her to be happy, and she seems so sad. —ADELE, 61, WILMINGTON, DELAWARE

You might be sending a very different message to your daughter than your care, love, and concern. It's very likely she hears you saying that she's a failure. It's never appropriate to tell people what they already know; it demeans their intelligence and hurts their feelings. (Have you noticed that we seldom tell anyone something positive for their own good?)

It's just as important to evaluate whether it makes sense to tell someone something negative that they may *not* already know. Just because we know, doesn't mean we have to tell. Ask yourself what good could come of knowing and whether it is really your place to convey the information. If the only reason you can find to spill the beans is "I'm just being honest" or "He has the right to know," maybe you should keep quiet. Knowledge is power, and all of us like to feel powerful, but at what cost to another person's well-being and serenity? Seriously consider whether what you are about to say has any real value to the listener. Information is sort of like your bank account: it's nice to have it, but you don't have to show it to everyone. Adele, it's okay to keep what you know and think private if no good can come of sharing except to make you feel powerful at your daughter's expense.

To effectively communicate, you've got to

+ Know what you're feeling.
+ Conceptualize it.
+ Find words to express it.
+ Verbalize it so that the other person can understand you. It does no good to be incredibly articulate in Swahili if the other person only speaks French.

The other person then has to

- Hear what you say.
- Figure out what she's feeling or thinking.
- Begin the whole process in reverse for herself—figuring out her feelings, conceptualizing them, and expressing them.

And so it goes and we're only at the first round of information-gathering. Few of us are so constantly self-aware that we can lead off with what's really important. Usually we either don't know or can't admit it to ourselves, so the ball has to go back and forth numerous times until we get to the heart of the matter. If the whole thing sounds time-consuming, complicated, and a bit tedious . . . bingo! If you don't devote the time to being patient and self-aware while the other person sorts it all out, you're going to assume too much and understand too little.

One of the cleverer, more productive ways of communicating is inward rather than outward communication. Up to this point, communication has meant giving and receiving information from someone else. We can also communicate with ourselves. For example, if something about someone else's behavior bothers you, it is very likely something that bothers you about yourself. Adele, could it be you feel that you've failed as a mom or that you see something of yourself in your daughter's loneliness? Conversely, is her self-reliance disconcerting to you? If you think your daughter is kidding herself by ignoring the problem and putting her energies into her job, it may anger you more if avoidance is a tendency you both share. Someone lying to you is more enraging if you hate your own tendency to bend the truth.

I once had a weekly client who needed therapy for some problems at work. He was normally quite placid, but came in furious one day because his wife had called him a drunk. I asked him what he would have felt if she'd called him fat. "I would have laughed," he said, "'cause I'm not fat at all."

"Yes . . . so why did it bother you when she called you a drunk?"

My method of communication wasn't particularly effective in achieving any sort of dialogue, but it did strike a painful chord with my client. How we communicate with ourselves is even more crucial than how we communicate with others. Sending out wrong signals to other people can be confusing, sending them inward can be devastating.

THE WRITTEN WARRIOR

✳

My boyfriend of three years cheated on me. When I found out, I told him to take a hike. I've written him a letter telling him how hurt I am and asking him to explain how he could treat me so badly. I'm trying to decide whether to mail it or not. —PEARL, 22, SHAKER HEIGHTS, OHIO

Pearl, don't do it. I know you're hurt and angry and you want some sense of closure. But you really don't want to beg him, which is how he will view that letter. Keep your wounded pride intact, and don't give him the satisfaction or the ammunition. Who knows where that paper might end up? Never put anything in a letter that you wouldn't want to defend in court. I know you're not going to court, but it's unwise to send insulting or inflammatory missives—in other words, don't leave a paper trail.

For a society that seems to have lost the ability to maintain written social correspondence (I swear my aunt is the last living soul who would rather write a note than pick up the phone), we seem to *love* to put really nasty things in writing. Whether the letter is to the boss, a parent, a child, a lover, a spouse, or a neighbor, we seem willing to unload hurt and anger under the guise of just being honest. Face-to-face interaction is tougher and requires more courage, but it also offers the reward of immediate feedback and possible resolution. There is a lot of value in telling someone how you feel if it can foster understanding, but a twelve-page single-spaced diatribe is dangerous. My lawyer won't let me put *anything* in writing until he's okayed it. So let me play lawyer here, and counsel you to flush it, burn it, or bury it, but don't send it. Write it, reread it, memorize it, then vaporize it. Find another way of expressing your displeasure in person and maybe pondering whether that unhappiness actually has to be voiced at all.

Please don't misunderstand me. I'm in favor of communicating your feelings and thoughts. Words aren't always perfect, but they're the best we have for conveying meaning. Face-to-face is better than over-the-phone, but over-the-phone is better than a letter. A letter allows minimum feedback and maximum risk, and a letter is forever.

Pearl, if you're absolutely convinced that your motives are pure, your heart is unblemished, and your conscience is clear, at least ask yourself how you would feel if someone said the same thing to you. Hear those words directed to you and figure out a kind, specific statement that doesn't make you cringe. Then write it out, and if it still looks okay, convince yourself for the third time it really needs to be said, take a deep breath, sleep on it, and if you're still certain, reread this chapter.

THE APT APER

✳

My wife says she hates birthdays and anniversaries and Mother's Day, and I can understand why. We're a little pressed for money these days, but I knew the dishwasher was on its last legs, so I thought I'd surprise her with a new Maytag. She pretended to like it, but we haven't had sex since I gave it to her three and a half weeks ago. —PHILIP, 48, AUSTIN, TEXAS

Philip, I don't know what your sexual frequency pattern has been in the past, but I can tell you that a dishwasher doesn't get all that many women hot and bothered. I agree she's giving you a mixed message here, but my fear is that you're mirroring behavior. Not only are we bothered by behavior in others that we loathe in ourselves, but we also often unconsciously do for others what we wish they would do for us—mirroring. You were thinking practically, which is probably what you wish she'd do, but practical is not really what she wants.

Let me give you another example: women are notorious for throwing surprise parties for their men even though the guys insist that they *hate* birthday parties. Men tend to gloss over (from ignoring to minimizing to, God forbid . . . forgetting) their women's birthdays because they don't consider birthdays a big deal. (This whole problem arises in elementary school when little girls all throw surprise parties for each other while boys of the same age take one friend bowling.) Once we all grow up and get married, the pattern continues to haunt both men and women. When women say, "Ignore my birthday," they mean "Don't tell anyone how old I am, but do something lavish and wonderful."

In your current pickle, Philip, I would suggest flowers, candy, and a down-and-dirty discussion about honesty.

THE CURIOUS QUESTER

✳

There's a new guy at work, and I'm dying to know all about him. Every time I ask him about his wife and kids (does he have either?), he smiles sweetly and walks away. I'm trying to decide if it would be okay to stay late and go through his desk. —CRYSTAL, 44, ABILENE, KANSAS

Crystal, get a grip. It is normal and natural to be curious, but our curiosity is best served by looking inward and being aware of our own strengths and weaknesses. Going through his desk will give you information you can't use and a reputation as a sneak if you're caught. Figure out what you're looking for—not a marriage license or pictures of wee ones who look like his offspring. Be willing to look in that personal mirror. No, not the one that shows zits and that pesky chin hair but the one that focuses on your soul. The more aware you are of who you are and what you want, the better you can compensate for or clarify or avoid pitfalls. Being curious about someone else is tricky. Being open and tolerant is a way to *invite* confidences rather than just asking questions, which are always intrusive.

This guy is either shy or coy, so, Crystal, why not be who you are and see what happens? You don't want to be involved with a turtle, but at this point your curiosity about him is making him uncomfortable. He's not going to share anything with you until he knows a bit more about who you are and what you want.

I know you're dying to get the truth from him and he wants the same from you. This truth stuff is a bit tricky when we're applying it to anyone other than ourselves. Whenever we think we're telling someone the truth, we're very likely telling them something unpleasant about something they already know. No one ever says, "Can I tell you the truth?" followed by "You've lost weight, you look great, and you have never seemed happier." The truth is much more likely to be "You've gotten fat, you have a drinking problem, and I saw you with your secretary." In the name of truth, we often say rude, ugly things that wound people and that ought not to be said. Resist the temptation to tell the truth—especially if you'd likely rip someone's lips off if he unloaded the same truth on you.

Asking for the truth is often shorthand for "'Fess up before I expose you." Know your own truth by keeping tabs on yourself. Instead of deciding to be the truth patrol, look for consistency and pleasure in others and then you won't have to go snooping around. Before you say, "I'm only being honest," make sure that you're honest with yourself about your own motives. Between honesty and duplicity is silence—a truly adult choice, especially if it's neither sulky nor sullen. Truth is very often self-serving.

✳

This chapter started with the admonition never to tell people something that they already know, especially when it's negative, and ended with the idea that people are allowed to not tell you what you're panting to know. Silence is most easily and appropriately broached slowly and carefully with trust and time.

Know yourself and give everyone else the time and space to know who you are and to share themselves with you.

SHRINK-WRAPS

REALITIES THAT SHOULD NEVER BE SAID ALOUD

Life is hard: Few things are easy. A task may look easy if someone else is doing it well, but this doesn't mean the task is easy for her or for you.

No one gets out of here alive: Living is a terminal experience, although most of us earnestly want to believe that we're the exception. We're not, but then, you knew that.

Learn to compromise: We all need to feel that we won a little and lost a little. The tricky part is figuring out when to compromise and when to stand our ground. Usually the person urging compromise means, "Compromise by doing it my way."

Know when to hold and when to fold: On the face of it, knowing when to cut your losses is a valuable skill. This is also known as the Kenny Rogers school of life, which promises you'll look great with gray hair and a beard but be unable to stay married.

Whatever will be will be. Wow . . . talk about pithy! The New Age version is "It is what it is." What would it mean if it wasn't what it wasn't or wasn't what it is? *In vino veritas.* Or, if your classical education is a bit dusty, "In wine lies truth." Anything in Latin is surely true, but people never do anything drunk that they don't wish they could do sober.

THE ONLIES

The only two things you never need to worry about are yesterday and tomorrow: While this is undoubtedly true, if you show me someone who lives by this tenet, I'll show you someone whose medication needs serious adjustment.

The only thing to fear is fear itself: And the IRS, which is just a specialized form of fear.

The only sure things are death and taxes: I would add . . . and wrinkles.

2

expectation is the death of serenity

Expectations say a lot about you and nothing about the other person, which is a sure recipe for disappointment.

We have a long and varied list of expectations. We expect

+ gravity to work
+ the sun to rise
+ cars to stop at red lights
+ wrongdoers to be punished
+ good to be rewarded
+ taxes to rise
+ politicians to lie

None of these expectations can get us into much trouble, and they do allow us to keep on truckin' on a day-to-day basis. As you might guess, these are not the unpleasant expectations I want to warn you about. I'm talking about the unspoken, barely acknowledged but powerful urges that make us *want* things from others without being willing to ask. These thwarted expectations result in disappointment and disagreement, hurt and hostility. I plan to teach you to exorcise those nasty little demons from your life and I promise that you will be a happier, calmer person as a result.

TIES THAT BIND

✳

My kids have really let me down. I spent my whole life scrimping and saving so they'd have a better life than I did. And what do I have now, a bunch of ungrateful, lazy, unmotivated losers who never call and never visit unless they want something. They can't hold jobs or keep their marriages together. If I'd known they'd turn out like this, I don't know that I'd have chosen to have kids at all. —HANK, 54, PORTLAND, OREGON

Wow, Hank, sounds like you're having a really rotten day. I hope some of these feelings will pass, but it sounds as if they've been simmering for a while. I know it's not much comfort, but in a poll conducted a decade ago, parents were asked if they would have children again if they had known then what they know now. A whopping 75 percent said they would not have children. Blimey, does this mean that kids are an endangered species? Are children this horrible, or are our *expectations* for our children too grandiose?

When we expect something of someone, we are really focused on *our* needs and wants, which is understandable but shortsighted. Expectations are always about us, the attempt to superimpose a template of what we want onto someone else. What if our expectations don't jibe with that person's? That's where the trouble begins. I'm going to try to convince you that if you can let go of your expectations, or at least examine them, you'll have a calmer stomach, a better relationship with your kids, and a chance to reduce your Bufferin budget by half.

When we intensely expect something, we are anxiously waiting for someone to act in a certain manner, often without their knowledge. The object of this expectation can meet your expectation, surpass it, or fail to meet it. The other person loses no matter what. If she surpasses your expectations, your opinion of her was too low. If she fails, your expectations were too high, and you're both disappointed. Even if she meets your expectations, she only breaks even, since you *expected* no less. This is an unpleasant way to run a relationship: it's heads you lose, tails you lose. A game in which everybody always loses is a really bad game.

If all this weren't wretched enough, expectations have the added liability of causing you to focus on a future event instead of enjoying and savoring the present moment. When you tell a child that you expect her to do her best, you have just robbed her of the initiative to do well. It's perfectly okay to say, "You're smart. What do you think you can do?" and then applaud the child when she reaches *her* goal, not yours.

Hank, my guess is that for years you've been disappointed not only in your kids but also in yourself, your life, your friends, your parents, and your marriage. Maybe it's time to take a look at who *you* are and what *you* want. You can then *ask* for what you want and hear what others—your kids included—would like from you in return.

Instead of all those blue meanies circulating in your head, you could be specific and clear and much happier. A life without any expectations would be tedious and unproductive, random and disconnected. This chapter is about the expectations that get us into trouble, like trusting others to know who we are, live up to our ideals, and consider our wishes before their own.

Expectations rob people of the potential for pride, surprise, and victory. When you expect something of another person, that person is left with only two options: pleasing you or rebelling. Either way, both of you stand to lose and neither gains very much at all. Expectation can clobber optimism, initiative, and creativity. It's sort of the elephant gun of human behavior. All nuances and small, delicate life-forms are obliterated. *Bang.*

Hank, I want to explain how your expectations may be preventing the loving behavior you want from your children. I'll tell you a little story about myself. As a Rice University undergraduate, running all those learning experiments on rats and fellow students, I found that studying sometimes got a bit tedious, so I would wander across the street to the Hermann Park Zoo. Visiting my favorite creature—a very old, partially blind, clearly sad African elephant—would allow me to submerge my misery in what I guessed was his. Francis, this huge, lumbering, majestic beast, was chained to what had previously been a railroad tie that was sunk probably six feet into the ground by a steel anklet that allowed him only about seven or eight feet of movement in any direction.

My girlish and overly sentimental heart went out to this creature who could only pace over barren, ugly ground when he should have been roaming the veldt, trumpeting his awesome power. The pen was dusty and barren, gray and unappealing, with moldy hay in the corner and not even the usual mynah birds for company. (I'm delighted to report that the zoo was in much better shape when I visited for my reunion—or maybe I had filtered the whole scene through the eyes of a lonely seventeen-year-old far from home.)

One day when I could step out of my own sadness and look at Francis rather than identify with him, it occurred to me that he was undoubtedly large enough and strong enough to give a good yank on either the chain or the railroad tie and be free. I did a little research and found out that elephant calves born in captivity were chained from near birth to a tree. Every few weeks, the calf would be chained to a larger tree. As the elephant got bigger, so did the tree. Obviously at some point, there wasn't going to be a tree large enough to withstand any real resistance from a several-ton elephant. But by then the chains were in the elephant's mind, and the size of the tree no longer mattered. It was the chains in his mind that were holding Francis captive. He had gotten so used to being tethered that he expected to be restrained. There was no tree big enough to withstand Francis's power, but he expected to be enslaved, so he was. Hank, I wonder what chains are keeping you from breaking out of your sad and lonely pen. Maybe they've gotten weaker, or more likely, you've gotten bigger and stronger. Expecting to be weak is a dreadful mistake.

PERSISTENT PATTERNS

✳

My father cheated on my mother. Every boyfriend I ever had cheated on me. Both my husbands were liars and philanderers, so I guess I shouldn't be surprised that the guy I'm now seeing is sneaky and underhanded too. I guess I just expect too much when I hope that there is one righteous man still alive on the planet. —CECILIA, 44, GRAND RAPIDS, MICHIGAN

Cecilia, I think your problem is expecting too little rather than too much. You expect everyone to let you down, so you're always prepared to be miserable. If people don't fail you, you just raise the bar, so they'll falter sooner or later. I'm sure you're not doing this consciously, because it obviously doesn't make any sense, but that's the real kicker about expectations. They're almost always unspoken and unexamined.

What do you think might happen if you made a list of the specific kinds of behavior you find acceptable and unacceptable in a potential mate and then discussed these with your friends, both male and female, and gauged their reactions? Could you abide by your own rules and standards? If your friends think you're on the right track, then your next step is to monitor how you act around men who turn you on.

Do you send contradictory messages about trust and acceptance because you assume that sooner or later some testosterone-soaked being will disappoint you? Could you discuss what he thinks is fair? Instead of sitting by the phone or raging when he's late coming to pick you up for dinner, could you ask him to give you a call if he's going to be late? The unpleasant alternative is expecting him to read your mind and know that you will worry until he arrives. Communication takes courage, but it is more effective than whining or nagging. Can you live in the present rather than dredging up old hurts or projecting future ones?

If you expect to be cheated, you are likely to adopt the tone, body language, and vocabulary of an adversary, which can be a self-fulfilling prophecy: "Hey, she doesn't trust me anyway, so why not . . . ?" Only someone with great strength of character is going to reward your nastiness with kindness and fairness. Why run the risk? Talk about what both of you want, take the chip off your shoulder, and decide if the two of you like each other enough to be honest and caring.

It is fair and reasonable to negotiate our desires in a relationship, but that must be done on the basis of what we *want*, not what we *demand*, from a position of assumed moral superiority. Giving up the need to control another's behavior is a sign of trust, mental health, and openness to experience. If you're involved with someone you do not trust, respect, or like, why are you wasting your time? Interaction can be far more stimulating and exciting if you let go of the need to control the outcome.

Think of how you respond when someone demands something of you. Suppose that you intend to offer someone a ride to a store and then that person says, "It's your turn to drive; I drove last week." Her demand makes you feel cheated out of the pleasure of giving. Even if you had no intention of offering to drive, it's unlikely you'd become gracious in the face of a hostile demand. Someone saying, "It's your turn to buy dinner," likewise deflates the fun of your plan to treat them. When you feel the pinch of someone's expectations, it's perfectly acceptable to offer what you want while explaining that the weight of their expectations robs you of the

expectation is the death of serenity

spontaneity and joy of generosity. If you're feeling the weight of someone's expectations, it's okay to acknowledge your feelings rather than to angrily storm out or passively allow yourself to be manipulated. You can also stop expecting things from others and allow yourself to be pleased and surprised by what they offer. Hey, worst-case scenario: if you don't like what's being handed out, you can begin negotiating for what you want, whether we're talking the way he asks you out for a first date or how you plan your wedding or your retirement party.

Imagine all the time and energy you will have for yourself if you're not waiting for the phone to ring or the promotion to come or your birthday party to be announced. You can take a class, make a friend, write a novel. The anxiety of waiting is replaced by the freedom to live in the moment and be pleased and surprised by whatever happens. If the outcome isn't what you like, begin at that moment to do what makes the most sense to you. Instead of imagining the worst and wasting all that time sorting through horrible what-if's, you've got the actual situation to cope with and use as a jumping-off place. You can take a deep breath and deal with real problems rather than imaginary ones. Focus always decreases anxiety. You can focus your energy rather than fritter it away worrying about whether or not someone else will deliver what you expect.

Cecilia, if you chill out a little and stop expecting to be betrayed, you may even gain some serenity, some of that peace which allows us to act from strength rather than panic, anger, or fear. Serenity allows us to be the rock in the stream around which water can circulate rather than a tiny ship bobbing on a storm-tossed sea.

This serenity allows us to calm our physiological responses to stress. The big fancy cortex on top of everything else is very sophisticated and good at analyzing, but all that analysis can really slow us down. If our cave ancestors had to rely on it to keep them safe, we wouldn't have the option of sitting around waiting for the phone to ring; we'd be mulch.

ANXIOUS ANTICIPATION

✳

I'm anxious all the time. I got in a car accident last year, and while I wasn't hurt, since then I can't quite catch my breath. I seem testy all the time and kinda antsy. —D.J., 59, SAN JOSE, CALIFORNIA

D.J., sounds like you've got a panic attack going on here. You're accurate about the initial trigger being your accident, but it's possible you've had a panic response even before the collision. As you and your body well know, during an anxiety attack your heart beats too fast, you can't catch your breath, you feel light-headed, and your fingers and toes tingle. The symptoms can make you feel as if you're having a heart attack and as if you might actually die.

The bad news is the way it feels; the good news is that without this response to real or imagined danger, no primitive humans would have survived. Our ancestors, who had quick responses to danger, could outrun the saber-toothed tiger or holler at an enemy who'd had too much fermented berry juice and thus live long enough to pass on this genetically encoded response to us. Without so much as a conscious thought, our body responds instantly to a real or perceived threat.

This first line of defense is also known as the fight-or-flight response, which is terrifically descriptive. In order for your loin-clothed predecessor to react quickly to the sight of a mastodon rounding the bend, his muscles had to be able to respond quickly. This response demands lots of oxygen, which has to be delivered by lots of blood to fuel these rapidly metabolizing muscles. The body has to move available blood away from less necessary areas like digestion for just such an emergency. The body is suddenly converted from a placidly grazing, ho-hum-calm veggie to a lean, mean, sweaty fighting or fleeing machine. This is a major and mind-boggling transformation.

This fight-or-flight reaction that is making your life miserable also changes you from mild-mannered Clark Kent into Superman, complete with piloerection—known to the rest of us as goose bumps—presumably so that if you have hair, it will stand on end and make you look really big and mean and fierce. All these responses are terrifically helpful in scaring tigers away, but they're not all that useful or comfortable when you get passed by a reckless eighteen-wheeler going eighty, or when you finally decide to ask your boss for a raise, or when you run into an old love while you're wearing your rattiest clothes.

If you can find a quiet place in yourself, you can be in control of your behavior not only on the highway or on the way to work but during the really hairy situations as well. This quietude can be found through any of the following activities:

expectation is the death of serenity

- Prayer
- Meditation
- Chanting
- Visualization
- Relaxation exercises (slow contraction and relaxation of muscle groups)
- Square breathing (inhaling to the count of four, holding to the count of four, exhaling to the count of four, holding to the count of four)
- Candlelit bubble baths
- Long walks on the beach, in the woods, or in the park
- Short naps
- Exercise
- Any activity that reminds you of who you are and allows you to ask what you would like to do

D.J., you can never erase the memory of your accident, but you can control your physical response to that memory. Once you're calm, you can opt for behavior that will work for you, both immediately and in the longer term. You can allow yourself to trust your neighbor but tie up your camel at night or, if you're not a Bedouin, check your tires, wear your seat belt, or chain-lock your door. You can expect nothing but be prepared for anything and thereby increase your sense of well-being and safety.

Once you stop expecting, you can start accepting, not in a fatalistic way but by understanding what you can change (almost exclusively your own behavior) and what you can't. You can then begin to find the courage to work on yourself, the calm to accept other people's choices, and the wisdom to know where you stop and another person starts.

For those of us who view ourselves as active participants in our own fate, serenity takes a little getting used to. But in the long run, it really does allow us to direct more energy to that which we can affect, and we can let the rest go.

If you need a metaphor, think of the whale, the largest living mammal, whose throat is only twelve inches in diameter, which is probably a quarter the size of a hippopotamus's throat, a muuuuch smaller beast. You might ask yourself, why would the world's largest living mammal have a throat that is only a couple of times larger than yours or mine. The answer to the question of the size of the whale's throat is . . . that's the way it is.

Some things in the world just have to be accepted without logic. The trick is to know what has to be accepted and what can be questioned. There are things you can expect till the cows or whales come home, but . . . that's the way it is. How much time do you want to spend worrying about something that is beyond your reach or understanding?

If you can stop *expecting* anything of anyone other than yourself, you can ease up and get on with your life. Know who you are and what you want and what makes you happy. All those questions and answers are in that quiet part of yourself. Go visit, quietly and often.

SHRINK-WRAPS

EXPECTATIONS THAT WILL ERODE YOUR EQUILIBRIUM

Cars will stop at red lights: Only personal injury lawyers are enriched by this expectation.

If I love you, you'll love me back: Love is a gift, not a contract.

I know how you feel: No, you don't. We are separate beings, and expecting that any two people will have the same reaction is irritating and inaccurate.

Our children will follow in our footsteps: Only if we're on the way to Baskin-Robbins or the bank. Otherwise, our kids will find their own way in the same way that we diverged from our parents' path.

If it worked once, it will work again: Think of a single-use camera, a Kleenex, or chewing gum. All of these are once and only-once products. If something worked once and it worked really well, go ahead and try it again. But be prepared for progress, which means change. Remember, *things* change considerably less than people and situations.

If it tastes bad, it must be good for you: The cod liver oil school of thought was invented so we'd swallow the cod liver oil. Now there are chewable vitamins that taste like candy.

Still waters run deep: A passive-aggressive is still passive. Another word for still waters is stagnant. In order to communicate, it's crucial to *say* something.

Gratitude: Do something because it makes sense to you and enjoy it on that level. Expecting others to respond in kind, to grovel, or even to write a thank-you note is superimposing your value system on people you love. They won't love you back for demanding their response.

3

selfish is cool;
mean is not

*If you don't take care of yourself first, you can't be
there for anyone else.*

Selfishness has gotten a bad reputation. Even the dictionary is confused about whether this is a worthwhile attribute or a character defect: "concern for one's personal interest" or "caring unduly or supremely for oneself"? And this is after listing 126 other "self" words. You can see the problem: what is appropriate and who does the defining. Allow me. We call people selfish when they don't do what *we* want them to do. The first person who leveled the term at us was Mom, who was probably right. Children think primarily and nearly exclusively of their own needs, and it is the parents' job to expand their view of responsibility to include others. When someone calls us selfish, we are instantly reduced to the role of scolded children, which is why "selfish" is such a powerful and demeaning term. I intend to offer the antidote to this toxicity by pointing out that if you can't take care of yourself, you're going to be dependent and needy, which will doom anything other than a parent-child relationship (and a very young child, at that). On the other hand, if you're interested only in yourself, what's the point?

※

*Before we were married, my husband said I was the most important thing in
his life. Now that we've been married twelve years, he's turned into this selfish*

ogre. I come last, after his parents, his friends, his job, his car, and even his rot-
ten golf. He even spends more time with the kids than with me. When I ask him
where I come in, he just complains about how hard he works and what a good
guy he is. Do men become more selfish as they get older? —CHARLOTTE, 38,
WHEELING, WEST VIRGINIA

Charlotte, before we turn this into a man-versus-woman thing, have you noticed that we never call anyone selfish unless he's got something we want and he's not willing to share? We're selfish when we take the last piece of pie, when we don't offer spare change to the panhandler on the street corner, or when we take the only available parking space. No one is ever accused of being selfish for not sharing a cold, a hard-luck story, or an IRS audit. Sharing is great if you've got enough to go around and you're willing to do it with a smile.

It sounds as if your husband feels like his time cupboard is pretty bare right now, and your making him feel guilty won't help fill it up. I'm not saying you don't have a legitimate point—sharing time means sharing yourself—but your method isn't going to work.

Remember, all of us move toward pleasure and away from pain. If dealing with you is painful, your husband will spend even less time with you. For example, have you been tempted to say, "See how much fun it is to spend time together? Why won't you do it more often?" That's a sneaky way of complaining while trying to make him feel guilty. At that moment he'll withdraw because you've made the experience painful. Then you're left feeling surprised that he doesn't want to spend more time together. Sound familiar?

Both of you are probably a lot busier than you were when you were dating. Your husband didn't necessarily move you down in his priority list, but during courtship, you're his main goal. Once the objective has been achieved (marriage, let's say, the literal golden ring), he moves on to the next objective: success at work, dealing with aging parents, being a good dad, and working harder at friendships he neglected while he was pursuing you.

I agree that you could benefit from more time, but calling him selfish won't work. You want him to spend more time with you, so figure out how to do just that. Also sort out how to have more time to do what you want to do on your own. It's a dreadful mistake to make him the gateway for all your fun and recreation. You, too, need to be able to make yourself happy.

Charlotte, make sure that you don't consider yourself unselfish because you've donned the hair shirt of a martyr or are just afraid to say no. If you can't say no when you mean it, then when you say yes it will sound grudging and sullen and your gift of time will either be poisoned or a contract in disguise. Gifts and contracts are two different categories: a gift is without conditions; a contracts says, "I'll offer you something in *exchange* for something else." It will make you both unhappy if you confuse the two, especially if you disguise a contract as a gift by not defining the attached string.

The two of you might be in the market for both a gift and a contract. If you said to your hubby, "I'd like to take you out next week at a time that's convenient," you could give him the gift of a well-planned night out doing something *he* enjoys doing that you would ordinarily resist. Most ancient cultures practice ceremonial gift-giving as a basis for doing business; a gift paves the way for a future contract. A willingness to be generous makes both parties feel more confident of a fair outcome. So once he appreciates your thoughtful gift, you might negotiate a gentle contract that says something like this: "How about next week you plan something fun for us to do?" No pouting or surliness, please.

Now that we're clear that giving isn't always what it's cracked up to be, let's look more closely at the negative press that selfishness has received. If "unselfishness" is defined as "giving without need or expectation of return" then "selfishness" has to be one of two things—either giving with the expectation of return or not giving at all. By the dictionary definition, the only way to be unselfish is by giving a gift; any contract (where we agree that one can expect something in return) is selfish. Whoa, major limitations here.

One of my favorite philosophers, the King—Elvis Presley, of course—had TCB (takin' care of biddness) as his motto. If you're taking care of business and *you're* the business at hand, it makes no sense to feel guilty: you're just doing your job.

For a moment, pretend you own a factory that employs many people. If you decide to invest in another business which drains so many of your resources that you can no longer meet your payroll, you're certainly not going to be viewed as a wonderful businessperson or a model citizen. The entire community is more likely to view you as negligent, inept, and incompetent, and you will become an object of contempt rather than pity.

When it comes to thinking about our time and energy in a businesslike way, men have the edge, since they have been taught to think about business from the cradle. Charlotte, if instead of viewing yourself as long-suffering Saint Charlotte the Martyr, what if you thought of yourself as a CEO making management decisions about your time and energy? You might make very different choices and have much more fun. A well-run emotional life works on the same principles as a well-run company, with a balance between giving and taking, investment and return, profit and loss.

Staying in business is sound both economically and emotionally. The question is how to run a profitable, stable, ethical relationship, whether it is personal or professional. How can you be selfish in a good way and still have enough resources to share? How can you lead a life that works for you?

If your life doesn't work for you, then who is it going to work for? On the other hand, if your whole life is *only* about you, what's the point? Being completely unconnected and uncaring about other people means you're going to wind up lonely and sad and just taking up space. So how much selfish is okay? The answer is easier once we agree that the word "selfish" itself has gotten an undeserved bad rep.

Instead of deciding that the word "selfish" is an insult when you applied it to yourself, what if you thought of yourself as "sovereign" and "independent"—making sure that you have a place to stand that's your very own. Think of how generous you feel when things are going well, when you get a letter from a friend or a kind word or a smile from a stranger. Those are the days when you are most likely to lend a quarter, a hand, or a favor.

Selfishness means being able to create situations that make you feel so good about yourself that you can afford to give away some effort, some patience, and some goodwill. If taking a few minutes for yourself, and spending a few dollars more for lunch makes you a nicer person, for heaven's sake, do it. Your selfishness will radiate goodwill, and goodwill has a ripple effect. Let me tell you a ripple-effect story. . . .

One day I was at a pay phone, rummaging through my pocketbook looking for a quarter when the guy next to me, who was also using a phone, wordlessly held out a quarter. I thanked him and called my machine and went rummaging again when I had a call to return. My knight in pinstripes silently proffered yet another quarter, finished his call, smiled, and went on his way. Later in the day while waiting for another phone, the person in front of me was looking for change. By now I had secured quarters of my own and gleefully offered the stunned woman a quarter. This lovely scenario could not have occurred if I hadn't had quarters to offer.

No one can offer what she doesn't have, Charlotte. Figure out things to do for yourself that make you happy. Make sure you regularly restock your emotional larder. Once that's done, you can help others. This isn't selfish, it's survival and sound economic policy.

HELP THYSELF

*

My girlfriend is seriously into cocaine. I really love her, and she says if I cared about her, I'd try it too. I grew up in a really strict household, and my parents would kill me if they even knew I was hanging out with her. I don't want to lose her, but I don't want to lose my self-respect either. —ROBBIE, 19, PORT ARTHUR, TEXAS

Robbie, I commend you for your compassion, but we have to look at this situation realistically. In helping someone else you have to make sure of two things: (1) that you have something valuable to offer, and (2) that it doesn't cost you too much. If in trying to help your friend, you wind up betraying your parents' trust or actually trying cocaine, what have either of you gained? Martyrdom, even for love, is suicidal. In order to save others, you have to be able to save yourself. You know that what your girlfriend's doing is wrong, both for her and for you. Jumping into the swamp of drug addiction to prove your love is folly, not love. The purpose of selfishness is survival. If you don't survive, you can't help anyone.

*

My parents are getting older, and I try to visit them at least twice a week. I have three kids under six and a part-time job. My husband is great about helping out, but the house is always a mess and I'm so tired most nights, I can't calm down enough to sleep. —FRANCESCA, 31, SIOUX CITY, IOWA

Francesca, you've got to give something up. I personally would forget about having an immaculate house, being the domestic goddess that I am. For you, on the other hand, maybe this isn't the best time to be working outside the house, or maybe all of you could have dinner with your folks when you visit. I'm really worried that you can't sleep, Francesca. Your health has got to come first, because as long as you're healthy, you've got time and if you've got time, everything can be sorted out eventually. If you're feeling good, you're easier to be around and you have the energy to act and learn. If you're sickly, you'll need someone to take care of you, and dependency is depleting for both the giver and the taker. How, then, to be healthy?

The basics are easy:

+ Don't do things that will make you sick.
+ Don't think thoughts that make you sad.
+ Don't hang with people who make you doubt yourself.
+ Don't indulge in out-of-control behavior.

I know you feel that you're short on time as it is, but try to find an hour a day (okay, a half hour a day) to focus on these five things:

1. Knowing yourself.
2. Discovering what makes you happy.
3. Learning how to ask for what you want.
4. Accepting what can't be changed.
5. Realize and accept that you will change and that others will change.

Then you can keep:

+ paper and pencil handy
+ a journal
+ quiet when in doubt

There really are some things that you can't change about your life right now, Francesca, but there are also aspects you can control. The more clearly you can distinguish the two, the more selfish you can be in finding ways to stay calm and focused. Good health is both physical and mental. The absence of disease doesn't make you healthy if you feel miserable. If you're so stressed that you can't sleep, you aren't healthy, even if you don't have the flu. Your emotional well-being directly relates to your physical health. By good health, I mean the way you feel after a good night's sleep, a good workout, or a gorgeous sunrise—full of vim and vigor and ready to take on the world.

I can't tell you how long you're going to live, but I can give you some hints about how to be as healthy and happy as you're willing to allow yourself to be.

The first rule is to know yourself, which is a lot easier to say than do. Think of how often we're told as children that we don't feel what we feel. A child says, "I hate you, Mommy" and is told, "No, you don't hate Mom." Sure she does—at that moment. Every society needs to socialize its young, but being told that you don't feel what you feel will cause a sense of loneliness and loss. If we aren't our feelings, what are we?

✳

I find myself dreaming of an old girlfriend. I really am happily married, but in my dream this girl is performing sexual things on me that make me blush. I feel like I'm cheating on my wife. —BYRON, 48, LITTLE ROCK, ARKANSAS

Byron, chill. It's okay to indulge yourself in your dreams. What I'd like for you to do when you're wide awake is be a bit more selfish. It sounds to me as if there is something missing in your sex life with your wife, or maybe you're unconsciously wishing for the good old days. Are you feeling burdened by work or responsibilities? Do you miss an old friend? Are your parents more dependent on you than you feel comfortable with? Don't beat yourself up, but also *do not confess your dream to your wife!* To be happy you have to know what you want. Dreams are the way for us to allow unconscious wishes to bubble closer to the surface. Be willing to be brave and selfish; ask for what you want in bed, at the office, and from your friends, so that your life will feel better than your dreams.

You're entitled to dream and to figure out what you really want, Byron. The tricky part is figuring out exactly what that is. I'm a great believer in writing things down as a way of getting down to the basics of who we are and what we want, since all of us have been talking for a lot longer than we've been writing. Writing requires more focus and concentration.

Byron, I want to teach you to be your own doctor on a day-to-day basis, so you can take care of your head and heart and everything else. You can be your own diagnostician and decide when and if you need consultants. I want to supply you with a doctor's black bag (in this case, I suppose the bag should be Browne) that doesn't contain a stethoscope or drugs, but does contain

A blank tablet for capturing thoughts
A dream catcher, for believing in your imagination
An empty cigar box, for holding on to things that matter
An energy bar, to remind you that you are what you eat
A jump rope, to link movement and joy
A tube of sunscreen, to protect you from too much of a good thing
A warm blankie, to allow you comfort and security
A feather, to tickle your fancy and anyone else's
A merit badge, to reward excellence
A mirror, to keep track of who you are
A jack-in-the-box, to temper your fear of the unexpected
A puzzle, to challenge your ability to search

Selfishness is self-indulgent only when it completely excludes the consideration of anyone else's welfare. I want you to be less selfless and more attuned to who you are. You'll be surprised how much nicer and more giving you can become once you are really aware of who you are and what you want.

This imaginary Dr. Selfish kit allows you to keep track of your thoughts and feelings, awake and asleep. It can provide a private place to hide and be quiet, a source of energy as well as a guide to both the external and the internal world. You can examine yourself for symptoms of intimacy and kindness, the ability to survive surprise and hard tasks. You can know by learning and learn by doing. "Mean" is how we act when we're not getting what we want, so if getting what you want is selfish, learn to be selfish. Here's how to use what's in your Dr. Selfish bag:

Blank tablet: This can be a spa for your psyche. Paper is a cheap alternative to a therapist. It's a private place to sort out your feelings and figure out who you are and what you want. This tablet, taken before bedtime, can relieve insomnia by getting your thoughts out on paper and allowing your unconscious mind to work on problems during sleep. The purpose isn't to write deathless poetry but to scribble the down and dirty details of your life. And please don't leave it lying around for others to read. If you've got something to say to someone in your life, say it face-to-face, not by letting him "discover" your journal—that's really mean. In this journal you can focus on what you know about yourself. What you don't know is harder to come by, but one of the best resources of that hidden self is our unconscious mind, which is sometimes revealed in our dreams, as you've discovered, Byron.

Dream catcher: I spent much of my youth in the Southwest, where I learned to make dream catchers—delicate webbed ornaments that hang by the bedroom door to catch our nighttime fantasies. (A paper and pencil by the bed works just as well, but not as whimsically.) Dreams have mystified humans since the dawn of time. Early civilizations viewed dreams as portents—gods communing with mortals. Remembering and understanding our dreams can take a little practice. There are a lot of books about dream analysis, but the actual content of the dream is known only to the dreamer and dreams are often in code: negative and positive are mixed together, as are time frames, desires, symbols, and reality. The work of dreams needs to be done during the day with your eyes wide open. Paper and pencil beside the bed will allow you to write down any remembered details of the dream before you get out of bed, since the gossamer threads of the disappearing dream seem to be disrupted by movement.

Details are especially important in recurring stress dreams, the kind where you're running down the railroad track chased by a man in black or where you can't move or you're late for class and the room numbers are blurred. The original cause of the stress may have long since disappeared but the emotions have been filed away and are now trotted out to focus attention on something that happened during the day. Once you get into the habit of it, you can actually direct your dreams to come out the way you want. You may even wake up in the middle of the dream with the interpretation intact.

Undoubtedly part of the reason nighttime is so laden with psychological possibility is that it is one of the few times when most of us are alone. In our society, when adults want time to be alone, they are often labeled—yeah, you got it—*selfish.* Women, especially, seem willing to deprive themselves of solitude, whereas men wisely reserve time for hunting, fishing, reading the paper, or watching a game, and they often spend this time quietly and alone.

Self-awareness is most effectively and efficiently accomplished alone. The quiet place inside where the self can turn off and tune in is as crucial to a sense of well-being as good nutrition. Solitude is truly digestion for the soul, which may be why so many of us have such an active dream life. If you won't pay attention to your basic psychological needs during the day, you'll holler at yourself at night. In the interest of a good night's sleep, figure out the location of that quiet place.

Cigar box: As kids, we had special things that we thought were worth hanging on to: a ticket stub, a bird's feather, a cracked marble. As adults, we need a cigar box to hold what is crucial to us, whether those things are tangible possessions or special memories. Some things are important to share; some are too private. Each of us has to be aware enough to decide what we should "selfishly" hold back. Telling a secret can be either loving or hurtful, and it's important to realize this before we blurt it out. Byron, telling your wife about the memory of your ex-girlfriend would be mean and pointless. Be selfish enough to figure out what your dream means. We are our past as well as our present, and an awareness of our "treasures" gives us insight into who we are and who we want to become. What we share and what we withhold will determine the tenor of our relationships. There is no formula that says when sharing the contents is loving or when it is damaging, so we have to decide for ourselves.

Energy bar: This is a twofold reminder—that we are what we eat and that we are what we do. I promise not to lecture you here about good nutrition, cholesterol, or health; the energy component is what's important here. Doing something feels better than doing nothing. So jump, holler, and move around, indoors or out. Sunlight helps, and exercise can do wonders. Even people who are clinically depressed feel better if they take a walk for as little as twenty minutes a day, so get off your duff and remind yourself that if you're not using your share of oxygen, you're going to upset some hardworking tree in the rain forest. If there were such thing as a passivity bar, how would it be advertised? One bite and you'll feel victimized? Be selfish about your body and its need for movement. Eat less, sing more, take deep breaths, or take a different path. (I'm not talking New Age here. Just cross over a block sooner and see what's on the other side of the street.) Ask a question, read a book, do something—anything—different. You'll like it either better or less, but you'll learn something. Your disposition will improve and you can share your energy secrets with anyone who'll listen.

Jump rope: This is an unsubtle reminder to be selfish about taking the time to exercise, not only because it's good for you but because moving is part of your physical heritage. When you were a kid, you couldn't sit still. You got cranky and out of sorts when you were confined. Every day was a chance to get sweaty, dirty, and happy. Your brain and your body are still not separate systems. Both will get dull without stimulation. Your body isn't your brain's suitcase, so try a sport or a bath or a sprint, but use your body. Heads thrive on novelty too. Talk to a stranger, learn to paint, join a discussion group, take the "wrong" side of an argument. Exercising your options, both mentally and physically, is the ultimate act of selfishness in the best possible way. Being stingy with your body is the ultimate meanness.

Sunscreen: Too much of a good thing can be toxic, whether it's time together, vacation, sex, fun, food, or sunshine. Being prepared allows us to temper indulgence with perspective and impulse with consequence. Knowing our own skin type means we can protect ourselves and not become sunburn victims. Sunscreen is also a reminder to get off your duff and go outside. Look, I love air conditioning, electric lights, and hot water as well as the next person, but before all of this, there was an outdoors with a sky that couldn't be reached and a ground that didn't have to be vacuumed. Outside is a way of putting everything in perspective. Grab your sunblock and get out of the man-made structures in order to remind yourself of what was here before you and will be here long after you're gone. Get outside of your house, your own zone of safety, but protect yourself just enough.

Warm blankie: My daughter, like my sister, had a blue blankie that she schlepped around until it was gray and threadbare. Neither my chicklette nor my sissy could go to bed at night until the blankie was tucked in with her. Babies need to feel secure to sleep. Adults seem to need sleep to feel secure. The victim virus is much less likely to take hold if you've gotten some z's.

I have a theory that the shark is the meanest and most unpredictable of all living creatures because it doesn't have a flotation bladder and therefore has to keep moving and can never sleep. If you don't get enough sleep, you're going to be *really* cranky. Be selfish enough to sleep when you need it, and learn how to make yourself feel safe and secure. Insecure insomniacs exemplify "mean."

Feather: This will remind you to giggle—an undervalued activity. Life can certainly be serious and important, but a sense of glee can make the difference between feeling you're in charge of your own life and feeling that it's all out of control. Unless you're a bird, a feather is only for fun, so remind yourself that it's good to indulge in a moment of selfish pleasure; it's mean only if it's at someone else's expense. You don't actually have to use a feather. You can simply launch a snowball fight, draw outside the lines with your favorite crayon while lying on your belly, or jump on a bed, preferably your own. Eat your dessert first, finger-paint, or play air guitar. If you've gone a couple of days without giggling, what are you waiting for? Just because we're grown-ups doesn't mean the sense of fun has to evaporate from our lives. If you're not sure what to do, find some kids. They'll explain. When someone calls my program with a particularly gnarly issue, I try to get him to laugh. I know we're almost home free when I hear a giggle, which signals a quick and unexpected change of direction and perspective.

Merit badge: Your merit badge is a reminder that you're part of a larger whole, that selfishness must have its limits, because we stop at some point and other people and their desires begin. There is value in kindness as well as excellence. In this relatively impersonal world, doing something for someone else reminds you that *you* count. You've undoubtedly seen the bumper sticker that encourages you to perform random acts of kindness. How else do we acknowledge that we're really here and mean something? Kindness is a gift of and to ourselves, which makes it the ultimate form of selfishness if you think about it. Yippee, a way of feeling good about doing good, so enjoy! Meanies need not apply.

Mirror: None of us can safely or comfortably allow another person to get close until we're okay with our own face in the mirror. If you think it's vain and selfish to look at yourself in the mirror, how are you going to know yourself? If you're always trying to keep people at a distance because you're afraid of what they'll see, I guarantee you're going to be viewed as a mean person. Intimacy is an act of trust; it says, I'm okay and you're okay and we'll trust each other to be kind and know we can withstand the friction and abrasions that occur when two people bump up against each other. "I want you" is always a selfish statement. It's mean only when it's followed by "I don't care if you want me." Negotiation takes time, but intimacy is the sunshine of relationships. Without investing the actual hands-on, thinking-about-you time, a parent, a spouse, a kid, a neighbor, even a pet will not only be less nurtured but also less available for a hug and less a part of what keeps us healthy and grounded.

When I was seeing patients in my private practice, I required couples to spend an hour a day together, alone, without interruption as a condition of the therapy: one hour of intimacy. It was amazing how disruptive most of them found that basic requirement. "No wonder they needed help," you smugly say. Yeah? When was the last time the two of you spent an hour together just talking about feelings and not griping or focusing on the kids or the mortgage or what went on at work? I'm sure you've heard that alarming statistic that dads spend less than seven minutes a day with their kids and that couples spend about the same amount of time together. Intimacy requires trust and maintenance, and both take time. The time can be a quiet walk, a phone call, any way of demonstrating an emotional commitment by sharing time, the most valuable resource on the planet. Don't allow understanding friends to make it easy for you to neglect them.

At one point in my life, I lived in a huge chocolate-brown, ten-room, red-roofed hundred-fifty-year-old Victorian monstrosity of a house on a cliff overlooking the north Atlantic in a summer community in Hull, Massachusetts. I had fallen in love with the house when I lived across the street and moved into it when my daughter was three months old. It had never been lived in year-round. (You could tell the direction of the wind by walking from room to room. I had the world's largest sweater collection for visitors, and my daughter slept in a snowsuit the first winter.) I was constantly entertaining people who would call up and invite themselves over for a weekend. I found myself explaining to my *real* friends— who, because they were friends, were much too polite to impose—that I had no time for them because I was entertaining. Struck by the irony and aware that I wasn't any better at saying no back then than I am now, I devised a nifty little scheme that offered people accommodations at the house in the winter or fall rather than summer. It instantly separated the folks who really wanted to see *me* from the folks who wanted a free summer weekend at the beach. All of a sudden I had much more time for the people who liked me and whom I called friends.

Jack-in-the-box: This is a reminder that if you're not selfish enough to know who you are, you're going to be defensive and mean when things don't go as expected. This is really a shame because as selfish little kids we all understood the unabashed glee of the unexpected. Surprises are fun! As a baby, you loved having the silly clown pop up and startle you. As adults, we come to fear surprises because they make us feel out of control. We come to associate surprise with the word "nasty," as in "a nasty surprise," like a note from the IRS, a flat tire, a run in a stocking, or a burst pipe. Surprises don't have to be negative; they can be just a bit disruptive in a *positive* way. A horror movie can help teens deal with fear of going out into the big bad world alone by offering threats in mini-doses in a controlled environment. In the same way, carefully planned surprises can give us confidence to deal with the ones we didn't anticipate or plan. They can also teach us flexibility, which increases our resilience. We need to be self-aware enough to know our characteristic response to the unexpected, whether it's delight or horror.

Puzzle: I've put the hard task at the very end, hoping to convince you that I was on the right path with some of the easier, more fun stuff. A challenge might be the ultimate act of self—"Can I do it? Am I up to the task?"—but it is also the way we define our existence. As a society we've learned to take the easy way out, unfortunately. We believe that if it doesn't come easy, we should let the whole project go because it wasn't meant to be, whether we're talking about love, cooking, or child rearing. But remember the first time you tied your shoe for yourself? It was *really* hard. It wouldn't have been hard for your mom or dad to do it and you very likely begged for them to do it. Your chunky, sweaty little fingers kept getting tangled up with the loop. But remember the elation the first time the knot stayed tied? Doing hard stuff is what makes us feel good about ourselves. Doing the easy stuff is fun occasionally, but we take less pride in it because it's easy (even if other people don't know how easy it was). Attempting something you're not at all sure you can do is how we grow and learn and feel proud. Not succeeding offers a direction and a tangible goal. Being bored will make you mean as fast as anything I know, so be selfish and keep yourself challenged. Accomplishing a difficult task is the true basis of self-esteem, because you value something that you did.

Take these steps to keep yourself in good mental and physical health:

- ✦ Stay positive.
- ✦ Be consistent.
- ✦ Ask for help when you need it.
- ✦ Take responsibility for your actions.
- ✦ Decide to be happy.
- ✦ Understand your feelings.
- ✦ Be aware of others.
- ✦ Be brave enough to matter to yourself.

In a word, be selfish. If you'd like to try majoring in mean, just do exactly the opposite.

SHRINK-WRAPS

SELFISH REALITIES THAT ARE COOL

In the bad old days the ultimate act of selfishness was to indulge in lots of sex. Talking about it was considered more than a little tacky and if you mentioned a partner, you were downright mean. These days, with long work schedules, frightening communicable diseases, and Viagra, talking about sex is considered perfectly okay, but now we've got a new unmentionable *s*-word that is the symbol for indulgence. Just as the old *s*-word elicited giggles and sly glances, so does the current *s*-word: "sleep." (Does this mean we're overstimulated or just pooped?) The similarities don't stop there either. If you don't believe me, just take a quick look at the following and ask yourself if you didn't use to use these statements to explain your bedroom needs in a far different light than you might today:

I never get enough.
It can really clear up your skin.
A quickie can really perk you up.
When's the last time you got enough?
It makes life worth living.
It changes everything.

It makes you see things in a completely different light.
It's embarrassing to want too much.
You get caught up on weekends.
You feel that everyone else is getting more than you are.
It changes your attitude.
It puts a sparkle in your eye and a bounce in your step.
It is referred to obliquely as "going to bed."

Getting enough of what you want without depriving anyone else is the ultimate act of selfishness and sanity. Not knowing what you want or how to get it is going to make you mean. Ergo, be selfish: make yourself and everyone else happy. Amen.

4

we're responsible for our behavior; feelings just happen

Everybody has bad thoughts. It's bad behavior that separates the good guys from the bad guys.

When *we equate* thought and deed, we give up responsibility for our own behavior. Thoughts just pop up! (Try *not* thinking about a cool lemonade on a hot day. Or try not to think of Christmas when you hear "Jingle Bells." Pavlov showed that you can unconsciously link unrelated thoughts in a dog's mind, so why should humans be any less susceptible?) We are judged by what we *do*, not by what we *think*. This distinction is crucial because it allows us the freedom to explore our feelings without guilt and to understand the link between thought and behavior so we can be responsible for how we act. And, yes, you're correct, I don't think there should be a verdict of "not guilty by reason of insanity." Either you did it or you didn't.

FEELINGS, WHOA, WHOA, WHOA . . . FEELINGS

✴

I am a Christian man and I love my wife, but I would be less than honest with you if I didn't admit that I sometimes break the Ten Commandments in my mind. I am ashamed to confess I have had lust in my heart. —JIMMY, FIFTYISH, PLAINS, GEORGIA

Okay, so this particular ex-president has never actually called my program, but he was brave enough to admit publicly what lots of us have only felt privately. We have somehow become convinced that we are as liable for our thoughts as we are for our actions. Maybe it's because several major religions have traditionally regarded certain thoughts as impure. As a result, we feel ashamed of angry thoughts, fantasies of revenge, and sexual images. It's important, however, not to confuse things we can't control with things we can control. Jimmy, I'm here to tell you that you are responsible only for what you do, not for what you think.

Most people over the age of five know the difference between right and wrong. Most people know what they *should* do, but between knowing and doing there is a lot of room for denial, rationalization, avoidance, sin, and redemption.

In days of yore, this question of control and responsibility was painted in terms of an ongoing battle between good and evil. The prize was nothing less than our souls. The idea of good and evil using the soul as a battleground was a dramatic metaphor that completely absolved the individual of responsibility, although being absolved of responsibility wasn't always fun. You weren't responsible for your bad behavior because you were possessed by evil spirits, but because it wasn't your fault you could get burned at the stake or dunked or otherwise painfully exorcised of your demons.

✳

I see these kids from broken families all the time. It's not their fault they have no respect for law and order or their teachers or me. Right—these are just rotten, no-good kids. I'm tired of all the excuses. —OFFICER KRUPKE, 44, WEST SIDE, NEW YORK CITY

You got me again. Officer Krupke was a character in the musical *West Side Story*, which predated the current sloganeering about the breakdown of the family structure in America by more than thirty years. The song was intended as a satirical look at society's wimpy approach to juvenile delinquency.

These days, bad behavior is still attributed to broken homes or deprived upbringings, but now we also can add chemical imbalances and genetic predisposition to the list. I'm not sure whether possessing a chemical imbalance is more harmful to society or to the individual. The problem with this chemical "understanding" of behavior is that it makes human behavior a result of biochemistry, like a huge bubbling cauldron on the stove: a little meat, a little potato, a dash of salt . . . whoops, too bland. Free will and personality are ignored, which reduces us to a Campbell's soup recipe. It's hard to hold soup responsible for anything.

There have always been psychological conflicts between the easy way and the hard way, the childish and the more mature parts of the self. Freud was the first to describe these conflicts as the ongoing war between the id and the superego, that part of ourselves that wants what it wants when it wants it and the part that understands consequences. The warden (super-ego) watches over the boiling cauldron of desire (the id), and the actor (ego) determines what happens—unless the individual is completely repressed or totally without conscience. In this scenario, behavior is most appropriate and healthy when it is balanced between the two opposites of desire and duty.

Denial is the result of ignoring internal information (our feelings) or external information (others' behavior). Because denial doesn't change reality, it leaves the individual less prepared to act in an appropriate way. Conscious denial allows us to ignore hunger pains while we finish a project or to swallow our anger when our boss is late to a meeting. Unconscious denial means we're not even aware of what we're hiding so our behavior seems erratic and unpredictable, as in a panic attack, a phobia, or a bout of crying for no discernible reason. By treating our feelings as culprits, we are less likely to be aware of our responses which are as much a part of who we are and how we act as an allergy to peanuts or a love of opera.

Until we understand and acknowledge our impulses (sexual, venal, angry, whatever), we deny our true self. I stress the difference between thought and deed because knowing the difference allows us to have control over our behavior. If we fear our *thoughts*, we're not going to see what's going on. Keeping ourselves in the dark because we're afraid to turn on the light of understanding will leave us clueless about our thoughts. Since feelings lead directly to behavior, ignoring the trigger means behavior will seem random, and if it's random, we aren't responsible for it—but *it isn't random and we are responsible*. Understanding and acknowledging our feelings gives us a blueprint of options that can be altered, acted upon, or discarded.

Officer Krupke was full of beans then and now. Regardless of how we were raised, we must be held responsible for our actions. Ignorance about our own behavior doesn't mean we're any less responsible.

The best way to combat this "it isn't my fault" or "I'm a bad person because of my thoughts" notion is to understand that both saints and sinners are tempted to ignore the pain of self-awareness. Once we understand our feelings, we've got to make choices, and choices are risky. It isn't unreasonable or wrong to want life to be easy, choices to be obvious, and conflict to be minimal, all things being equal. Unfortunately, all things are seldom equal.

✳

My twenty-two-year-old daughter is very busty, and when I comment on how tight her shirt is, she calls me a dirty old man. She is really stacked, but I was just trying to point out that she was going to attract guys' attention in that getup. Should I just keep my mouth shut? —DEAN, 54, PHILADELPHIA

Dean, I know it's confusing to be a dad these days, especially if your adult children are staying around the house a lot longer than you did when you were young. Your daughter needs to understand that you love her and are occasionally able to see her as an adult, which is confusing to both of you. On the simplest level, I would stop commenting on her wardrobe and body parts, but I think we're talking about a much more complex issue here.

A number of years ago I gave a lecture to the California State Police Convention, at which I was asked to explain the increase in sexual crimes within the family. I rather unsuccessfully tried to convince them that incestuous *feelings* were neither new nor unusual. In fact, there are no universal taboos against things that do not exist or that occur infrequently. Societies have taboos against behavior that is frequent but unacceptable. The incest taboo was originally instituted to protect bloodlines when marriages were arranged and mostly political. When people began to choose their marriage partners on the basis of sexual attraction, the problems escalated.

If you think about it logically, being attracted to a younger, more pliable version of the person one married is to be expected (think of how often partners in second marriages resemble the first spouse). The situation has gotten even more complicated as more and more adults live with stepchildren and other children who are not their biological offspring. In those situations, blood ties don't even exist to inhibit the adult's response to a child who looks like a younger, smoother version of the adult he found attractive.

Make no mistake: Incest is illegal and immoral. It betrays the natural and appropriate confidence and trust that children deserve to have in parents. The *feelings* are not the problem; the willingness to *act* on those feelings is a horrendous problem. If we equate feelings and behavior, we lose control over the behavior. Thoughts and deeds are quite different. Good people not only *can* have bad thoughts; they *do* have bad thoughts. As long as these thoughts are not acted upon, good people are still good.

Men, in particular, are more and more confused about exactly what is expected of them as father figures and husbands. The old notion—"If I go to work, make a good living, bring home my paycheck, and don't fool around or get too drunk or violent, I'll be considered a good guy"—has come and gone, leaving a lot of shattered egos in its wake. Weak egos resist temptation significantly less well than strong ones, which makes it even more crucial for us to allow our thoughts to roam but our behavior to be corralled, and we must also understand the difference.

As I explained to my rather shocked audience of California police officers, feeling sexually attracted to someone in your care isn't unusual or evil. Acting on that feeling *is*. Good people do have inappropriate feelings. The difference between heroes and villains is not feelings but behavior. If we don't distinguish between the two, then people are going to feel guilty for their feelings, and once you've felt guilty for just feeling something, why not go ahead and do it? If the thought is the same as the deed, there is no reason to stop bad behavior—and then we are lost. The first time we step over the line is the hardest. The second time is significantly easier. Anything that allows that slippage must be avoided and anything that acts as an obstacle is to be prized. The distinction between thought and action is exactly that barrier. Without it, the person who dreams of killing his boss and the one who actually goes berserk with an Uzi are the same. Clearly, we must hold killers and cheats liable for their actions, but are we

we're responsible for our behavior; feelings just happen

to punish people for just *thinking* about murder or adultery? Get real! Thoughts are not the same as deeds, and they may in fact act as pressure valves to keep us on the straight and narrow.

THERE IS A DIFFERENCE BETWEEN KNOWING AND DOING

✳

I really want to be a good person, but I yell at my little brother, diss my mom, and talk in class. I don't know what to do to become a better person. —KAITLIN, 14, DECATUR, ILLINOIS

Sweet cakes, you know perfectly well what to do; it's just that there's a difference between knowing and doing. You know what to do to make your mama happy, your teachers delighted, and your brother love you. It's just the *doing* that's hard.

The first and best way to control our impulses is to understand that there is a difference between thought and action. The second tenet of responsible action is that *knowing* the right thing to do doesn't mean that the right thing will actually get done. Knowing that Häagen-Dazs isn't good for your diet may not prevent the 4:00 A.M. trip to the freezer. If on the other hand, we can understand our hunger and the impulse to hit the fridge, we can build up our resolve rather than beating ourselves up for even *thinking* such a thought. That enhanced sense of self can help you decide to give the pint of vanilla Dutch almond to your next-door neighbor or the dog. Hey, if you're feeling really desperate, you can even paste a nude picture of yourself to the inside of the freezer. Until we give up the notion that *doing* the right thing is as easy as *knowing* the right thing, we're unable to offset our less than glorious impulses.

If you start from the premise that you already know the right thing to do 90 percent of the time, you can use your energy to figure out how to behave in a righteous way rather than just preaching the right thing to do. You can begin to solve problems rather than lecture, analyze rather than criticize, and learn rather than label.

Kaitlin, pretend you're trying to earn good behavior merit badges for a whole week and see what happens. If all the adults in your life (and your crummy little brother) don't faint from pleasure, I'll be surprised. Bet you'll be happier, too. Try it for a week: what do you have to lose?

LABELING MAKES IT SO

*

I've been married for only six weeks, but I've inherited the world's nosiest mother-in-law. She wants to know what we're doing for the weekend, what we had for dinner, when we're coming over, and are we pregnant yet. I love my wife, but I'm not sure I can take this busybody in my life for the next fifty years. Any suggestions? —MORTON, 23, PUEBLO, COLORADO

Mort, believe it or not, the solution is in your head: if you define your new mom as nosy, you'll avoid her questions, and as you withhold information, she'll feel left out and nervous, so she'll start grilling you. You've labeled her as nosy, so even if she just says "How are you?" she confirms your opinion of her. What if you viewed her as a caring woman who loves her daughter and wants to seem interested in you? You might relax and offer her a bit more information voluntarily, which would quell both her anxiety and her curiosity. If that doesn't work, you can tell her I said she's a buttinsky and she should butt out.

The way we describe a situation can often create a self-fulfilling prophecy. As my favorite college professor, Dr. Trenton Wann said, "By describing, you bring into being." For example, if we define ourselves as evil because we had an unacceptable thought, we allow ourselves no way to counteract the impulse. Evil people do evil things. On the other hand, if good people have bad thoughts, they can remind themselves of their goodness, not in a sanctimonious or denying manner, but as a reminder of the importance of looking in the mirror and being able to face ourselves.

When we call our children stupid, we leave them no opportunity to learn. Stupid people are by definition incapable of learning. Smart people who haven't quite caught on yet may make mistakes, but stupid people can only be stupid. Hey, like my mama says, "What's the point in being stupid if you can show it off?"

We sculpt our universe by how we describe it. Optimistic people live in a happy world, but a pessimist's universe is always bleak and morose.

A year or so ago I was invited to give a seminar to a large group of paralegal secretaries. The organizer agreed that each participant could submit one written question having to do with work or a personal dilemma. I would have these questions a week before the seminar so that I could base my speech on the secretaries' concerns. (Yippee, my fantasy of giving a relevant speech was being granted.) I patiently waited as the time grew nearer. Three days before the scheduled date, I still hadn't heard from the organizer. Several times I called and asked when I could expect the questions. Finally, the day before the speech, in response to my increasingly frantic phone calls, he calmly informed me that *he* had decided I should speak about "difficult people."

I took three cleansing breaths and tried to explain in my calmest, most professional voice that this was idiocy: once you describe people as difficult, you will see them as difficult, and my strategy was exactly the opposite. (Note: I did not point out to him that *he* was unreliable and untrustworthy. "Remember, self-fulfilling prophecies," I muttered.) Trying to make my point, I emphasized that once you've decided someone is a pain in the neck, even if he says "good morning," you're going to ask yourself some questions:

+ "What did he mean by that?"
+ "Is he just trying to soften me up?"
+ "When will the other shoe fall?"

Still trying to remain calm, I sweetly allowed, "I'm not suggesting we all go through life with a silly grin plastered on our faces, but to give that much power away to someone you honestly believe will abuse it seems unwise, unnecessary, and unreal." Completely unmoved by my combination of charm and panic, he responded, "The topic is already listed in the program."

I now had to decide whether to back out of an impossible situation or respond to the challenge of giving a speech on a topic I hadn't chosen, didn't like, and didn't believe in. If your life's work is being a media psychologist who teaches people to do the best they can do with what they've got, you have to rise to the occasion or view yourself as a hypocrite.

Dressed in my most grown-up designer suit with a starched blouse, restrained jewelry, a matching scarf, and shined shoes, I asked the two hundred paralegals why they would choose to victimize themselves by labeling their bosses as difficult. From that moment on, the speech was a laboratory experiment on the challenge of communicating without a shared worldview. For two rather bloody hours, they tenaciously held on to the opinion that I simply didn't understand how difficult their burden was, while I cheerfully and steadfastly suggested that they were making their situation worse rather than better.

If you want to make someone your enemy, you point out threatening differences between the two of you. If you're looking for ways to solve a problem, you look for shared goals. This approach is even more important if the other person has power and you don't. A difficult person is going to be . . . difficult. Conversely, a reasonable person who is frustrated might appear to be a stinker, but if the frustrations can be resolved, he can return to being reasonable. I desperately tried to convince the paralegals to look for the underlying causes rather than labels by suggesting ways of behaving in situations that were more familiar and less power-based. (Almost all the bosses were men, and most of the paralegals were women.)

"What would you do if your best friend acted the way this 'difficult' person is acting?" I asked. "You'd likely not tolerate it. Why not? Because it's wrong. Then why tolerate it here? Is it because he's the boss? What makes him the boss?" I asked the hostile but temporarily attentive audience. "You believe he has the power—but the power to do what?"

"To make my life miserable," shouted a red-haired woman in the back.

"No, they don't have that power," I said. "They have the power to fire you, but if you feel that your boss is a bully, you have the power to quit. Remember that bullies thrive on power and intimidation. Don't give a bully power. Keep it for yourself!

"If you can accept that you have power too, then you can redefine the situation and find different ways to act," I continued. "What do you think would happen if you said, 'I could be much more efficient if you told me what I was doing *right*'? Or 'When you holler at me, I become flustered and my work suffers.'"

I could feel the mood of the room slowly changing—if for no other reason than that I had not let the "difficult" redhead bully me. I could see heads nodding in agreement. Encouraged, I continued: "How about saying, 'I would be delighted to get your coffee, but it takes about forty minutes a day and I would much rather spend that time organizing your files; so tell me how you'd prefer I spend the time.'" Would you get fired for saying that? Unlikely, unless you were unpleasant or whiny or belligerent, because—bottom line—employer and employee need each other. Neither is irreplaceable, of course, but both want the same thing: to get the job done. Anything that facilitates getting the job done is good, anything that impedes it needs to be examined and either modified or removed.

Most people aren't born difficult. Don't enter into the land of paranoia that says only difficult people get to be bosses. Head honchos are sometimes demanding and sometimes impatient, but they're usually impressed when someone does a good job. If you're doing a good job and your boss doesn't appreciate your efforts, you can be sure that someone else will. Perceiving someone as difficult means you're going to be defensive and nervous around him rather than open and flexible, and your cringing will make you seem ineffective. Remind yourself that your boss didn't spring fully armored from the head of Zeus; he must have been an underling at some point. Asking him about his first job may reassure you that you're not doomed to be an underling forever, and the resultant conversation will establish a more human bond between you and him.

Learning how to deal with someone else's power as well as your own will make you a better employee today and a better employer tomorrow, when it's your turn to be in charge.

Mort, I know you wanted to focus on your personal life, which is always more complicated than your professional life. The good thing about work is that it's always about effectiveness. The tricky relationships happen outside of work. You can always find a different job with a different boss if you're good at your job. If you're not, figure out why and either polish your skills, learn what you don't know, or find another kind of work to which you're better suited.

If you're married to a difficult person, ask yourself why. Why did you marry her in the first place? Why do you stay with her? Has she always been this way or did she change? If she changed, when and why did it happen and what can you do about it? If you have a difficult friend, should you negotiate or dump him? How about a difficult child? You have the power here, so make sure you're not giving up too much or too little.

You didn't pick your mother-in-law, and you can't divorce her, but you can give up your anger and your preconceived notions and see what happens. And please don't complain to your wife about her mom; you'll just start a war. We may not be crazy about our kinfolk, but if anyone badmouths them, we'll go for the jugular.

In dealing with difficult *situations*, remind yourself that the only behavior you can control is your own, and that is the behavior you must not only understand and control but also monitor and modify.

CHANGE IS EASIER SAID THAN DONE

✳

You're always telling people to sit down and write out what they really want, but I'm not so sure I know. It's a lot easier to say than to do. —KAREN, 38, CANTON, OHIO

Karen, for heaven's sake, *everything* is easier to say than to do except "supercalifragilisticexpialadocious"! But it's worth the effort, especially when it comes to self-knowledge; so let me see if I can guide you through this. Changing your attitude or behavior requires courage and vision. Unfortunately, the only time we *want* to change is when things are awful and awful undermines our sense of self, which makes it difficult to do something new. *Saying* something is easier than doing it, especially if we're talking about behaving in a new way. You have to start by figuring out what the problem is, and only you know that. No one can tell you what you want or how to feel, but those are the building blocks of your existence. Living a meaningful life takes more concentration than fooling around. Don't let anyone stop your progress by saying, "It's easier said than done." Just do it if it makes sense and stop talking about it if it doesn't. No whimpering allowed.

Don't let anyone rain on your parade by pointing out that "easier said" stuff, but do be willing to evaluate someone else's idea instead of just dismissing it. Years ago I was the Monday Night Shrink on *Thicke of the Night* before Alan Thicke went on to fame and fortune on *Growing Pains*. My first night on the program, I asked the audience to raise their hands if they agreed with the statement: "Prestidigitation predicts parsimony." Some raised their hands. I then asked how many disagreed: a slightly larger number waved their hands. I then asked how many wanted to know what the hell I was talking about, and a virtual avalanche of hands went up. I was trying to make the point that ideas are for using not believing. If what I say makes sense to you, use it because it makes sense, not because I have a degree or you "believe" in psychology or the world according to Dr. Browne. Don't believe gurus—be willing to try out an idea. If it works, illuminates, eases your load—hurrah! Make it yours until it stops working. Test out your ideas! Don't just believe.

Our willingness to seek easy answers has given rise to a cult of gurus who say things that seem right but don't mean anything. I was giving an object lesson in the importance of filtering other people's ideas through our own sensibilities. The vast majority of the audience realized that what I'd said was gobbledygook—intentional, but nonsense nonetheless. Ignore people's credentials; if what they say makes sense, accept it because it makes sense and reject it if it doesn't.

The responsibility for running our own lives is ours alone. Figuring out what makes sense and what doesn't isn't easy, and it's going to change as both we and circumstances change. If you understand up front that it's your life and your responsibility, then you can complain less, make fewer excuses, and focus less on other people's mistakes and more on your own. You'll make fewer costly mistakes if you look beyond the obvious and realize that when something sounds too good to be true, it probably is. Making your life a masterpiece isn't any easier than creating any other valuable work of art. The advantage here is that you get to be the only important critic of the project.

There are very few valuable shortcuts in this life, but since life will be over well before most of us are ready, who needs shortcuts? Do the work, put in the time and effort, and enjoy your stunning creation. Be willing to evaluate rather than simply accept or reject the criticism. Consider the source. If you can learn from your critics, alter your plans. If they're just being mean, don't believe 'em. Let them design their own lives.

Ideas aren't all that difficult to come by, but the task of implementing them can be hard. Ideas are fantasies until they're workable. Making those ideas reality is hard but valuable work. All of us are assigned the same task: to make our time on earth meaningful. How we do that depends on our ability to know who we are and what we want, and to know our strengths as well as our weaknesses. This self-knowledge is the raw material on which we build our sense of ourselves and of others. Our feelings are the impulse; our behavior is the structure. As we learn more about ourselves, we can do more with the material at hand and fashion an increasingly useful and valuable structure that defines our existence. Other people's structures can be inspirational and instructional but don't be intimidated by them. This is your life. Get on with it. Enjoy.

SHRINK-WRAPS

IRRESPONSIBLE BELIEFS

Only the good die young: Does this mean that if you're old, you're a bad person?

If the good Lord meant for us to . . . (fill in the blank): The good Lord gave us brains to figure out how to fly an airplane, curl hair, and grow better beef.

If you kiss your elbow, you'll turn into a boy: Guys seldom admit to wanting to be girls and most girls decide by the time they're through with junior high school mixers that it's kinda cool being female after all.

USABLE IDEAS

The best is yet to come: This is a worthwhile belief that will increase your chances of remaining sane.

Payback's a bitch: Combined with "Vengeance is mine, saith the Lord," this idea should keep most of us out of the revenge business.

Living well is the best revenge: Living well is the best anything.

We get the face we deserve: Given the fact that we can't pick our parents, this is probably more or less true as we age. I *still* think I should look a bit more like Audrey Hepburn. Still, beauty is in the eye of the beholder.

There's no accounting for taste: That's what full-length and rearview mirrors were invented to emphasize.

No one has it all: In spite of the woman's movement, this is basically true. There is a vast difference between wanting it all and having it all. The odds of having a lot of what you want increase if you happen to have a wife who will pick up the laundry and take care of the kids. What most working women need is a wife.

If you don't ask, you don't get: Asking doesn't guarantee receiving, but it increases the probability.

Don't ask, don't tell: This makes sense not only for gays in the military but for all of us anytime we're tempted to confess, complain or commiserate.

Your prayers will be answered: Sometimes the answer is no.

God helps those who help themselves: It's a little hard to tell who's responsible for success, but doing your part certainly increases your chances.

5

romance is the poison of the twentieth century

Unrealistic expectations mean never being satisfied with what you've got, and romance is the ultimate unrealistic expectation.

Romance is the Peter Pan theory of life—an unwillingness to grow up, grow old, and deal with reality rather than always looking to some fairy-tale future where everything is wonderful. Romance deals only with the promise of what *might* be, never with the pleasure of reality. Competence, conflict, and work have no place in a Never-Never Land of children, fairy dust, and believing in the impossible. This willing suspension of disbelief dooms any reality to a pale, dirty second place in which the unreal offers the seduction of instant pleasure without any work. For flowers to grow, they need soil, sunshine, and water. Relationships need the same cultivation to blossom.

In the world of romance no one ever has to say "I'm sorry," which means everybody is either completely self-righteous, furious, or both. Flesh-and-blood relationships rely on the possible and the probable. Romance is a belief in unicorns with flowing manes and single horns when real horses with sinewy muscles and pounding hooves are perfectly lovely creatures, especially if you're interested in going for a real ride.

"LOVE" VERSUS "IN LOVE"

✳

I've been married for thirteen years to my high school sweetheart. I have the perfect life: he's a great guy, I've got two wonderful kids, we've got two houses, and I love him, but I'm not in love with him. I told him that he should move out. He says he's crazy about me and if I want to leave, I should do it, but he's not budging. What effect will my leaving have on the kids? —GENEVIEVE, 42, EAU CLAIRE, WISCONSIN

Ah, Genevieve, the old "I love him, but I'm not in love with him" dilemma is a commonly voiced, reasonable-sounding statement that is positively lethal! I have no idea whether your marriage is viable or not, but it appears that you don't know either. You sound as if you have succumbed to one of the truly dangerous lies of male-female relationships: that it will always be the way it was in the beginning: the excitement, the fun, the tingles, the fizz, and the novelty. Genevieve, novelty is a one-shot deal.

As a nation we are in love with the notion of being in love. If I had a nickel for every caller who echoed your plaintive wail, "I love him, but I'm not in love with him," I would be a wealthy woman. What does any of this mean, for heaven's sake? What is love and what is being in love? We all know the symptoms of falling in love, but that's just the sizzle; relationships that endure and nourish are based on the steak.

We subscribe to the fantasy that love is effortless, spontaneous, instant, and independent of the work of self-knowledge or getting to know someone else. This nutsy notion is why we invest so heavily in the fantasy of love at first sight: no waiting, no embarrassment, and no work.

Genevieve, I can just hear you muttering under your breath, "Boy, Dr. Browne's taken her mean pills today. She doesn't understand how much I crave that feeling. Somewhere out there there's someone who can make me feel tingly and brand new. I want to feel the way I did when I first met my husband, when we couldn't keep our hands off each other. I loved discovering that he liked lilacs and leather and that everything including me was shiny, shimmering, and new. What's the problem with a little fantasy now and then?"

At the risk of sounding like the ogre who lives under the bridge, let me assure you that you're not alone, but when it comes to love relationships, any diversion from reality can be really dangerous.

Is this the moment for you to be thinking about sunning yourself on a beach somewhere with a piña colada and a new man nearby? I think not. We've got trouble right here in River City. So let's knuckle down rather than trying to escape.

I know this isn't what you were hoping to hear. After all, I'm talking logic and you're talking passion, so let's try it your way for a moment. Let's say you are now the lovely divorcée. You wait a whole year after the divorce is final, and then you find a brand-new, wonderful man who

+ loves you and your children
+ has never been married before (why deal with his ex?)
+ is an orphan (who needs another mother-in-law?)
+ is independently wealthy (why worry about money, for heaven's sake?)
+ gets along famously with your kids, but not too famously
+ thinks the father of your children is a great guy, but not too great
+ shares your politics, religion, and stance on makeup
+ never flirts with other women
+ loves your friends, but not too much
+ has your initials (who wants to buy more towels?)
+ will love and be loved by you exactly the same way *forever*

Sounds a little improbable, yes? We have all been seduced by romance—hearts, flowers, sparks, and fireworks—because romance, by definition, is an imaginative story, an exaggeration or distortion, an appeal to the emotions and passion with a focus on grandeur rather than reality. So romance is a lie. Even the dictionary defines it as a "picturesque fiction."

Genevieve, the way to sort it out is with my old standby, the trusty, inexpensive paper and pencil. Do some reality testing by asking yourself what works and what doesn't. What can you do to make yourself and your marriage better? Are you bored or unhappy with how you look? If your life isn't exactly what you had in mind, be willing to look back at what you had in mind and evaluate it. Don't allow a perfectly good relationship to go stale because you're not working at it or looking at it realistically. Talk about what the two of you want and what you are willing to give up to make each other happy. That kind of communication is the nuts and bolts of building a viable relationship.

Ask yourself this: "What do I want?" Don't you dare allow yourself to say abstract nonsense like "I want to be happy." What kind of behavior would make you happy? Be specific for yourself and your husband. If you're not having at least one date with each other every week, you're missing an important way to keep things fresh and fun. I'm not talking about going to the local greasy spoon and complaining about the kids. I'm talking surprise and silly.

Fantasy is about doing nothing but daydreaming. Reality is about doing the best you can with what you have. If it's not good enough, fix it or leave it, but don't fantasize about what might be. Make what you want come true. Believing in fantasy weakens our ability to function, and anything that weakens our ability to function is the enemy.

Romance is the idealized version of life, an unobtainable perfection. Unfortunately, romance is the difference between being happy with what you have and always longing for what might be. In theory, having a goal that is beyond our reach could motivate us to better behavior and loftier aims. The problem is, however, that we can't reach that lofty goal, so we're left feeling dissatisfied and restless. The true romantic is never satisfied with reality but always searching for perfection, and the search is littered with false starts and broken hearts. When we're just learning about love, we indulge in crushes, or infatuations—love with training wheels—until we have the emotional maturity for the real thing. Grown-up crushes are heavier because we actually expect things to work out, at least occasionally. A kid has the attention span of a gnat, so daily crushes are relatively painless. Not so for a sane adult. Any entertainment of the "crush" is more than offset by the pain of dashed hopes. Expecting the next ride to be wilder, the next thrill to be bigger, the next person to be sexier is a way to never experience pleasure in the present.

A vivid way to understand the dangerous seduction of romance is that television commercial where a hunky man in a tux slinks toward a gorgeous woman, who breathlessly awaits him at a table set with linen and polished silver and crystal. A perfect rose in a priceless vase symbolizes their future bliss in a room with gently wafting gossamer curtains. The whole scene is slightly out of focus making the situation dreamy and slightly hallucinatory. As the man gets closer to the woman, he tries to casually and suavely lean on the table, which begins to tip. In trying to get his balance (good metaphor, huh?), he catches hold of the edge of the tablecloth and, in slow motion, pulls everything off the table, including a goblet of wine. As he loses his balance and begins falling, the focus changes to his ladylove, whose look of anticipation and adoration is replaced by one of horror and disbelief. The commercial is for a stain remover. It is also a sly commentary on our wish for romance, which blurs the edges and offers us life slightly out of focus. Romance is the longing for fantasy made real, a willingness to trade off wish for truth, sweetness for nutrition, short-term for long-term.

REAL PLEASURE

✳

We've only been married four months, but somehow it's just not the same. She used to call me four times a day just to say she loved me, but now it's only once or twice at most. I was afraid this would happen. I guess the honeymoon is over.
—CAMERON, 22, SAN BERNARDINO, CALIFORNIA

Cameron, it's a comfort to know that men share this lunatic romance notion of life. Think about it for a moment: who else calls you every day at work just to say "I love you"? Who else would you *want* to call you daily? This isn't even counting the hug and kiss you get when you leave the house in the morning and the super-duper one you get when you arrive home after work. I am not trying to totally banish romance from your life as long as you accept it for what it is: a fairy tale that takes our fondest wishes and frees them from any reality at all. Romance is about loving someone because of who you'd *like* her to be rather than seeing and adoring her for who she really is.

How many of us have hollered, "Love me for who I am, not for who you want me to be." Romance denies that possibility. I want the two of you to grow more and more in love with who both of you are, not who you pretended to be. That's going to mean working out a lifestyle, not a courtship. I want the two of you to have the resilience that comes from reality, not fantasy. We are all in love with the idea of someone instantly knowing and loving and accepting us—the myth of unconditional love. Most of us are, of course, completely unwilling to *offer* it. Instead, we say, "Hey, I don't have to do business with you if you hurt my feelings"—or if you lose your job, lose your mind, or lose the car keys again.

If we're not willing to offer unconditional love, it's a bit unfair of us to expect it. "But if you *loved* me . . ." has got to be one of the most plaintive, overused, and futile phrases in any language. Most disagreements have little to do with love and mostly to do with different perceptions of how to express that love.

This isn't meant to make you feel dumb or alone. All of us have been brought up to believe in the concept of romance. Women believe a cool dude will ride up on a white charger and carry them off into the sunset. Men believe that they will round a corner and a gorgeous, curvaceous vision will appear and not only knock their socks off but cook, clean, bear beautiful children, and never argue. Of course, in both fantasies, everybody will live happily ever after.

The point isn't the trappings, it's the trap. These sticky, silly fantasies aren't limited to the very young, the slightly worn out, or anybody else who should know better. *Everybody* is in love with the ideal of an emotionally satisfying shortcut. These romantic notions, including the soul-mate notion, are truly the poison of the twentieth century. Romance poisons by discoloring, tainting, and contaminating otherwise viable interactions. Never have so many people been seduced by a fantasy that has the very real potential to ruin perfectly good, reality-based relationships. Longing for what might be allows reality to wither and die, unnurtured and unmourned, until it is too late.

KNIGHTS IN SHINING ARMOR

✳

My wife, Guinevere, is much younger than I am. When we first got married, I gave her everything and idolized her. She embodied all that was good and pure in womanhood. She was my reason for living; she tamed the beast inside me. Then she had an affair with my best friend. I'm trying to decide whether or not to burn her at the stake. —ARTHUR, A REAALLLLY LONG TIME AGO, CAMELOT, ENGLAND

Arthur, you sound like a prince, er, king of a guy. Who would have guessed you even had access to a phone. Then again, maybe you just magically transmitted your thoughts to me. I'm sorry you're so upset, but in a way, you've got only yourself to blame here. It was you who started this whole romantic perfect-love notion. It's a real burden to live up to, and it sounds as if Guinevere got exhausted. I'm not excusing her bad conduct—there is *never* an excuse for adultery—but rather than burn her at the stake, have you thought about asking Merlin if he does marriage counseling? Maybe you two can have a reality-based relationship in which you don't lord it over her all the time and you stay home a bit more and see her as the woman she really is rather than as some impossible ideal that makes her feel inadequate. Maybe you could admit that both of you have sexual feelings and that lust isn't so profane and horrible that it has to be sublimated into something chaste and sacred. I know you've convinced your knights that unconsummated love for a woman can give them hot blood in battle. I just don't think a woman's favor in the form of a rose or a hankie is going to suffice where knights are concerned.

By setting up an impossibly unrealistic ideal of the sanctity and purity of women, you might have hoped not only to dictate a chaste standard of conduct for your knights but also to keep your young wife out of harm's way.

This ideal was supposed to keep men challenged and women unobtainable. Voilà! Safe and chaste wives, including yours, would allow you and your men to go off and fight holy wars without worrying about the little queen back at the castle. The problem is that you may be a great king, but you're not a terrific psychologist. Romance is *fantasy* and lust is reality.

This romance stuff allows you to fantasize like crazy while keeping everything calm. However, Arthur, these days Merlin has been replaced by call-in psychology talk shows, and even the peasants have access to reliable birth control, lots of leisure time, indoor plumbing, and antibiotics, so you don't pass dangerous diseases on—and if you do, you can cure most of them.

Romance gets really dangerous because the usual constraints that you took into account disappeared. A woman these days doesn't have to behave herself to avoid being stoned to death for contracting an infection or conceiving a bastard child. Just as you were ahead of your time, perhaps your wife also saw into the future. Or then again, maybe she just had the hots for Lancelot.

VARIETY PACK

*

I met the girl of my dreams after dating a lot of different women. She's every-thing I've been looking for—smart, sweet, petite, and single. We met in a chat room on the Net and talked for three weeks on the phone, and I've visited her twice. This last weekend we spent two days together, and by the end of the weekend, we didn't have anything to talk about. Should I be worried? — LUCAS, 36, NEWPORT, RHODE ISLAND

Lucas, you should be very worried. It seems like you've fallen in love with the idea of falling in love. I think there are two parts to your dilemma: (1) you're hooked on variety, and (2) now that you're ready to settle down, you're in a rush to find the perfect woman.

If you value variety over intensity and quantity over quality, I'm sure you sometimes feel quite alone, even when you're on a date. Your previous romantic style sounds like the guy who spins plates on top of poles: he gets more and more plates spinning and everyone knows it's only a matter of time till the whole thing comes crashing down, but in the meantime he sure has a lot of variety going, doesn't he? The real question is—is the excitement worth the crash? If you don't mind being alone with a lot of broken plates (or hearts), maybe. But if you want something to show for all your work and effort, maybe variety isn't all it's cracked up to be. Sounds like you've noticed that playing the field no longer acts as a deter-rent to men and women coupling, but only as a deterrent to them coupling happily. All of a sudden there is ease of introduction but tons of unrealis-tic expectations, free love but no free rides, access but no acceptance, and with it all, a completely nonsensical notion of love.

All of which, I'm delighted to hear, you've discovered. My concern is that now that you may feel you've wasted so much time sowing your wild oats, you're in a terrible hurry to get with your ideal woman. The problem with meeting someone on-line is that you have no idea who she really is. False intimacy only fuels the romantic fires, and the two of you haven't taken the time to learn about each other. Now that you don't have much to talk about, I'm concerned you may be doing your old variety routine once again. Why not slow the whole process down and give some serious, specific thought to who you are, who she is, and what you are looking for in a mate? And let the romantic claptrap go.

GREENER GRASS

✳

I'm going to get married next week, but all of a sudden my fiancé's best man is looking really dreamy. He's tall, dark, and handsome and drives a great car. —
NADINE, 27, CHERRY CREEK, COLORADO

Nadine, it's perfectly normal to have pre-wedding cold feet, but don't warm them on the best man's back. His dreamy looks are a distraction from the very important questions you have to answer: do you love your fiancé, and do you want to marry him? If so, keep your hands off the next best man. If you're not sure, postpone the wedding.

This isn't about love or even lust. This is about conjuring up an all-new romantic notion so you don't have to deal with your very real feelings. Longing is much more acceptable than lust: the ache rather than the release, the pain rather than the pleasure. You are subscribing to the "grass is always greener" philosophy. The unknown man or woman will always have more romantic appeal than the known.

Groucho Marx stuck his tongue firmly in his antiromantic cheek when he said, "I'd never join any club that would have me as a member." Rejection hurts, but to the romantic, it can be better than acceptance. The daydream of "might have been" takes up more time and poetic space than the actual business of negotiating a successful relationship. Rejection is painful but easy because it can keep the fantasy alive on the basis of *someday*. . . .

Romance is the sophisticated version of *The Rules:* silly, impossible, and dangerous to any long-term stability, the institutionalization of a lie. Romance is what makes last Christmas better than this one or any other one, your first love your best love, your deceased grandmother more wonderful than any woman who ever lived. Romance ignores the reality of today. It emphasizes the past over the present and the promise of the future over anything you currently have. Whew, talk about making yourself miserable.

Nadine, you need to resolve two things immediately: to keep your distance from your *fiancé's* best man, and to decide whether your fiancé is the best man . . . for you.

REALITY CHECK

✳

I went to my first boy-girl party last weekend, and it was awful. I thought it would be fun to dance with this ninth grade boy who looked like Tom Cruise, but he glommed on to me and slobbered all over me. When I told him to cut it out, he never asked me to dance again and didn't even smile at me all night. —
LAURIE, 14, BATON ROUGE, LOUISIANA

Laurie, just because someone looks like Tom Cruise, doesn't mean he'll act like Tom Cruise. Maybe even Tom doesn't act like that in real life.

Your idea of how guys should act came from the same place as everyone else's—from the movies and television. We are most likely to believe in these screen fantasies when our reality isn't much fun, which it may not be at your age. Don't worry, you won't be fourteen forever, and for now you can get to know guys who may not be as gorgeous as Mr. Slobber but will be much nicer. If you're really smart, you'll get to know them as friends, so when you're ready to settle down, you will know who you are and who he is beneath the surface. That way you can be happy with who he is and how he makes you feel, rather than believing in someone who looks like your fantasy but makes you unhappy. You may even be willing to look at some guy who looks real and not fantastic.

I'm not saying you can never go to another Tom Cruise movie or send another Valentine or watch Leonardo DiCaprio in *Titanic* for the millionth time. I just don't want you to confuse Cinderella's wicked stepmother with your dad's new wife or Saint George's dragon with your new history teacher. I'm saying that if you believe your fantasies, you're going to mislead yourself. If you *use* your fantasies, you can strengthen your sense of who you are.

Fantasies can tell us a lot about the distance between what we have and what we want, which can be a blueprint for how to make yourself happy. Pretend you're designing your dream house. You can map out the kind of building you'd like and where to put your doll collection and your private stuff. If you change your mind, you can erase your diagram and start over again without spending a cent on bricks and mortar until you've decided what you really want. Then one of these days, you can go about turning your dream into a reality rather than just scribbling. You can even find a real person to live there with you if you want.

THE SEVEN DEADLY WHIMS

Some dangerous myths are so ingrained, we take them for granted. For those dedicated to reality-based relationships, let me help you weed out some pesky, sly wolves in lacy clothing:

+ I'll know when my love comes along.
+ The worse you treat 'em, the happier they are.
+ Men are interested in only one thing.
+ Women are interested in only one thing.
+ Love is better the second time around.
+ Bodies don't lie.
+ Variety is the spice of life.

I want to dissect each of these seven deadly whims without reference to a caller's problem because we *all* fall prey to each of them. I don't want you distracted by how they relate to any life but yours!

I'LL KNOW WHEN MY LOVE COMES ALONG
(Some enchanted evening)

This is a treacherous belief for several reasons:
+ It assumes instant recognition, which is always a bit dicey.
+ It leaves you wide open to the folderol of love at first sight and all the accompanying headaches and heartaches.
+ You will base a relationship on information you don't have, the equivalent of building the Empire State Building without a foundation and hoping it won't fall over as it gets taller and taller.
+ This approach also assumes that if your initial reaction to someone isn't gangbusters, you should write 'em off.

Passivity is the hallmark of this notion, which assumes that a really wondrous person will just wander by and you won't have to do or say anything—or even get your buns up off the couch. Love will simply happen and it'll be destiny. Well, far be it from me to argue with destiny, but this is your life and you will feel better, more in control, and less a victim if you do some of the choosing. Women who have been bred to be passive and girlish (heaven knows I was) need to be very careful here. We complain about men who always need to be in control, but what if this is the result of *our* passivity and cowardice, not *their* aggressiveness and arrogance? Make no mistake, passivity is cowardice. The good news is that we can do something about it.

In this disabling fantasy, everything is based on how a person looks, which is really silly if you think about it. Remember all the people who didn't appeal to you when you first saw them but who later became your friends? I'll bet there were also people you really responded to at first, based on some mysterious chemistry, but who turned out to be major disappointments. Great physical beauty is usually about choosing the right parents, and chemistry is, well, chemistry.

So come on, let's be a bit more reasonable, a little slower to judge, and a good deal more active in our social lives.

The Worse You Treat 'Em the Happier They Are
(. . . and my problem is that—I'm just too nice . . .)

This is a theory for masochists who actively choose misery. All of us get bummed occasionally but *choosing* martyrdom is a glorious waste of time. "Too nice" is a manipulative phrase invented by someone too scared to be himself or herself.

Trust me: there is no such thing as "too nice." However there is such a thing as being a doormat, which is not sexy, acceptable, or lovable. Why would you let anyone walk all over you? Not because you're nice but because you're sad or afraid. This is bogus "nice," and once you've defined yourself as wonderful and everyone else as hateful, you're distancing yourself from intimacy by being afraid the other person might hurt you (because you're so sweet and lovely and he's so powerful and mean). Irritating, yes?

Inherent in the "I'm terrific, you're a cad" worldview is the assumption that you can read someone else's mind well enough to figure out what he wants and just give it to him without being honest or sincere or even thinking about what you want. Manipulative *isn't* nice, passive *isn't* nice, and phony *isn't* nice. If you believe that someone will love you if you're dishonest and deceitful, you're being clueless.

The freedom to be exactly (or almost exactly) who we are means you don't have to remember what you told somebody or who you were pretending to be. It also cuts down on whining—"but I tried so hard" or "I loved you so much" or "I was only trying to please you." Asking someone to be grateful because you love her is unworkable. Again—love is a gift, not a contract. Give or don't give, but understand that wimps bring out the bully in most of us. You don't have to tolerate being treated badly, so be neither a wimp nor a bully; just be yourself. When in doubt, honesty and kindness are an unbeatable combination. Sexy, too.

This assumption is the most dangerous of the fantasies, since it encourages bullies to find martyrs to beat up on. If we aren't treated well in a love relationship, what's the point? Don't believe this myth for even a millisecond.

MEN ARE INTERESTED IN ONLY ONE THING
(Sex? Hmm, sex? Let's see . . . sex . . . oh, yeah, sex . . .)

Our moms warned us about it, *Playboy* confirmed it, our minister lectured about it, and our health teacher confirmed it: men are sexual predators who cannot control their impulses. Therefore it is up to women (because nice girls have no sexual impulses) to control the situation and get the best deal they can before they are overpowered by these animals who will seduce and abandon them. The message is loud and clear. Men are interested only in sex.

Right, let's just condemn half the world's population in one untrue, depressing statement. Sentences that imply *all* or *none* of *anything* should be instantly suspect. The world is very big and complicated, and generalizations ought to be treated with a certain amount of skepticism. If the one thing men are interested in *is* sex, understand that in a survey I read in *Psychology Today* nearly ten years ago, 25 percent of male college seniors were still virgins. Men are interested in cars, computers, lawn mowers, holidays, money, baseball, dating, and other people. Beware of paranoid fantasies, and be willing to find out what men are interested in.

WOMEN ARE INTERESTED IN ONLY ONE THING
(Shopping? Money? Size?)

Here we go with the generalizations again. If men are interested only in sex, then perhaps all women are looking for security—a nice rich guy who wants to settle down, right? Because women have historically been the ones with less power, finding a powerful and wealthy male was traditionally the only way a female could be certain she and her progeny could be protected. Before she granted any sexual favors, it was important to seal the deal. We're nearly to the millennium, and things have obviously changed, although women may still be warier about sex, because no matter how sensitive he becomes, no man is ever going to get pregnant. Most men and women today, however, can make sure that they don't have babies if they don't want to.

Pregnancy may still be no-man's-land, but women are learning to support themselves. Marrying for money has gotten too expensive in terms of self-respect. Men and women are approaching the notion of mating on the basis of personality and sense of humor and cool Caesar salad recipes rather than bust size or bank balance.

LOVE IS BETTER THE SECOND TIME AROUND
(Relationships are like waffles; throw out the first one)

"Better" is a relative term. My concern here is that if things aren't perfect the first time, rather than trying to figure out what went wrong (not whom to blame but what happened), there is a very great likelihood that the same problem will arise again. Not only are we creatures of habit, but we behave in ways that create a pattern. Unless we are willing to look at that pattern and learn from it and do something different next time—choose a different kind of mate, perhaps, or behave differently or have different expectations—love will not be better the second time around. It may even feel worse, because the unhappiness of doing the same ineffective thing the second time will be compounded by the sadness left over from the first time. The situation will continue to snowball. Don't assume anything will change unless you change it.

BODIES DON'T LIE
(My love meter always points north)

Well, yes and no. They may not lie, but they can mislead. I'm a great fan of chemistry, but I don't want you to assume that your body can take over where your brain used to be. Your body can tell you a lot about sex and warmth and cold and sweat, but your brain has to tell you about caring and kindness and commitment and caution. Body and brain working together are gangbusters, but try to run your life if one or the other is turned off. You'll be lonely if you live only in your head and bruised if you think only with your body.

VARIETY IS THE SPICE OF LIFE
(I'm married, not blind)

Have you ever noticed that when people say this they're never talking about cooking or decorating but always about cheating? Once you and your mate decide to be sexually exclusive, you need to decide what fidelity means to each of you. Don't assume you're both on the same wavelength. Believing that the only way to be stimulated is with lots and lots of partners is a way of limiting the depth of any one relationship, of using other people to keep any one person at arm's length.

Variety can be scary, dangerous, and costly, and there are many other really good ways of not becoming bored with someone. Honesty and trust allow you to dig deeper and deeper, and depth may be your reward for working hard at understanding who you are and what you want and listening carefully to who that other person is and what he or she wants. There is a terrific movie called *Lovers and Other Strangers*, with Anne Jackson, Gig Young, Bea Arthur, and a very young Diane Keaton, and written by Renee Taylor and Joseph Bologna, two married actors who are still together. By looking at a large extended family of couples who come together at a wedding, the movie delightfully makes the point that we can never really understand another person, but working at it is a really cool goal for men and women to share. The patriarch and matriarch, who have a seemingly solid marriage, admit to infidelity; an engaged couple have questions; the bride and groom nearly call it off; and a bickering husband and wife make up in the bedroom. The movie makes the point that marriage isn't perfect, but the intimacy it offers is unique and special, and not easy to come by.

If you're afraid that your relationship is doomed or that everyone else has an easier time of it, or if you're afraid to let smoke get in your eyes from a forbidden passion, go rent *Lovers and Other Strangers* and cuddle up with your sweet babboo. Hunker down to spend some serious time getting to know each other for real.

SHRINK-WRAPS

ROMANTIC REALITIES THAT WILL KEEP YOU SIZZLING

ROMANCE	REALITY
You take my breath away.	I'm suffocating.
She loves how I take control.	She says I'm a control freak.
He makes me feel like a million dollars.	If I had a nickel for every screw-up.
Don't stop.	Don't start.
We always agree.	She never has an opinion.
How did we find each other?	I can't believe we ended up together.
He's lost without me.	He'll never ask directions.
We love being together.	We never go out.

REALITY-BASED LOVE SONGS

"I'd Really Love to See You Tonight": I'm lonesome and a bit horny, so hey, what do you say? No promises. You're on your own.

"Smoke Gets in Your Eyes": When you're in love, you will not see all that clearly, and you're likely to shed a tear or two. If only there were Visine for the heart.

"Slow Hand": Hey, good sex is about taking your time, considering your partner, and asking for what you want. Maybe good relationships are about the same thing. What a concept.

"Lyin' Eyes": This window-to-the-soul stuff is nice to think about, but how good are most of us at reading our own facial expression, let alone anyone else's?

"Sometimes When We Touch": Passion is real and misleading and can make both men and women want to cry, hide, or cling. This is a good song to sing at the top of your lungs when you're alone, to remind yourself of the confusion inherent in loving and intimacy.

"Do That to Me One More Time": Asking for what you want doesn't guarantee you'll get it, but it sure increases the probability and is healthier than that "if you loved me, you'd know" nonsense.

"Torn between Two Lovers": If you can't choose, then don't marry either lover. Take a step back.

"Dust in the Wind": Life is fleeting, so don't sit around waiting for someone to make you happy, but understand that you've got to live with yourself.

"All I Have to Do Is Dream": Fantasy is easy, but—duh!—there's no payoff; that only comes with reality.

"Will You Still Love Me Tomorrow?": No promises of everlasting love should be taken seriously. Go slowly, date a friend, and pay attention to what's going on. Tomorrow and next week are reasonable time frames, but the past is the best indicator of the future so build carefully, slow down, relax, and enjoy.

"I Don't Know How to Love Him": Two people who really love each other are not necessarily good together. It's important to be able to mesh style and energy and expectations.

"Stay a While": Short-term chemistry can be deceptive, so be willing to go slowly and get to know each other.

"Bridge over Troubled Water": Being able to count on someone, especially when things get dicey, is a lovely basis for a long-term relationship. If you can't count on your partner, then what's the point of staying together, even if the relationship seems hot, hot, hot.

"Those Were the Days": Don't confuse memory with reality or who you once were with who you've become.

"Your Cheating Heart": Not only will your heart tell on you, but so will Call Waiting and Caller I.D., so there.

"I'd Love You to Want Me": Wouldn't we all. It's much more fun to be loved than to love, 'cause whoever cares least controls the relationship.

"Help Me Make It through the Night": It's not romantic, but it's honest. Need is a great short-term basis for a relationship, but, man, does it get tiresome in the long run.

"Too Much, Too Little, Too Late": Sometimes we get a second chance and sometimes we don't.

"Killing Me Softly with His Song": Be careful with whom you spend your time because we're all affected one way or another.

"Breaking Up Is Hard to Do": So be careful—not fearful, just careful—going in.

6

go for short-term pain and long-term gain

Get the icky stuff out of the way first, so you can enjoy everything else for a long time.

voiding pain and moving toward pleasure is a basic animal instinct. We humans have become sophisticated about this pleasure-pain thing because we can contemplate the consequences of our behavior. It is this ability, for instance, that encourages us to lie. We did it, we knew it was wrong, but we did it anyway, and we are now trying valiantly to avoid the fallout. As children we were taught—and as adults we chose to forget—that lying usually makes things worse. If we didn't have these big ole fancy brains atop our necks, we wouldn't be tempted to lie because we wouldn't be able to understand the uh-oh's of our behavior.

Let's face it: the short-term answer to any dilemma is to bail out. That approach assumes that there won't be a morning after to deal with and that a problem avoided is a problem solved. Fat chance. If we assume that there are hassles in every life (and there are), the question is, do you want your hassles fresh or stale? The advantage of a fresh problem is that it hasn't had time to deteriorate. Solving a problem *now* instead of allowing it to grow into a serious obstacle cuts down on the anxiety of knowing it's still lurking. Putting off till tomorrow what you're worrying about today, just means you get to worry about it for an extra day before you start working on a solution.

I know this sounds eminently reasonable, but every time you even *think* of telling a lie or taking the easy way out, whether you realize it or not, you're trading off short-term gain for long-term pain. As grown-ups we try to opt for as much gain as possible with as little pain as possible.

✳

I've always been a hard worker, at home and at the office. Even when I was a kid, I burned the midnight oil, always kept my room clean, and did my chores. It seems like no matter how hard I work, other people get more credit. Nobody really appreciates me no matter how hard I work. I just wish everyone could see how hard I work without me constantly reminding them. —JON, 51, LOS ANGELES, CALIFORNIA

Wow, Jon, it sounds as if they'd better put up a statue for you soon. I know it's not much fun when other people don't respond to our obvious wonderfulness. If you're having a blue meanie day, knowing that isn't much comfort: folks are focused on their own lives. These insensitive louts (okay, so they're really not that awful, are they?) probably figure that you do what you do because you *want* to, which actually isn't a bad formula. This self-sacrifice stuff isn't what it's cracked up to be, is it? It's the fault of those exercise gurus who have convinced us that we won't be beautiful on the outside until we've suffered.

This nonsense isn't new. It's just that historically, sacrifice focused on the *soul,* not the body. Somehow, instead of hair shirts and flagellation, we now use spandex and sit-ups. Not only do exercise videos and personal trainers encourage us to push ourselves and go for the burn, but more than half of the U.S. population is on a diet most of the time. We've come to believe that deprivation will make us more gorgeous. The idea that pain is a wondrous and ongoing part of life has made self-denial popular to a degree unseen since the Middle Ages. Martyrdom may look great in paintings (arrows piercing flesh, whips delivering punishing welts to the backs of ecstatic saints), but it's a pain in the neck to live with.

Jonny, I'm afraid you've become an attention junkie. After all, a saint without an audience would just be a masochist with no place to go. The implicit contract between the saint and the spectator is "I did something difficult and painful for you, and now you owe me big time!" Your gratitude is the price of admission, for the true self-sacrificer can never receive enough gratitude.

Which gets us back to the issue of short-term and long-term goals. If the pain is short-term and there is an obtainable goal, we're not talking martyrdom, since the pain is merely the down payment on the long-term benefit. Masochism, however, is an investment in misery; a tiny amount of pleasure preceded by huge amounts of pain—bad idea!

So where's the trade-off here? How can you invest enough effort to be successful, but not so much that your lifestyle is based on your deprivation and other people's gratitude?

The key to differentiating between investment and needless sacrifice is understanding that nothing in life comes without a price tag. Payment is sometimes expected to be made in the form of money, but much more often it's time, sweat, reputation, or tears. Once you understand that basic reality, you have to decide how much pain seems reasonable.

Jon, do what makes sense to you because it makes sense to you. If your boss applauds, terrific: it's icing on the cake. If he's ungrateful, the cake is unadorned. You're responsible for the cake. If gratitude is the price of your cake, let them eat something else. If you wipe that smug grin off your face you may find yourself much more appreciated. If not, at least you're not schlepping around a humongous attitude that's making you bitter and churlish. Lighten up: do what you *want* to do. Enjoy your job, your choices, and your life, you little dickens.

DESSERT FIRST?

✳

I'll graduate from high school in June, and I'm trying to decide what to do. I've got a chance to go to college, but I'm not that great a student. I have a chance to start as a manager at the local Burger King when my girlfriend's brother goes into the Marines. My parents really want me to go to school, but the money is looking real good to me right now. —SAM, 18, DULUTH, MINNESOTA

Sam, the world is divided into two kinds of people: those who eat dessert first and those who don't. (I don't think we even want to contemplate people who never eat dessert.) Do you do what's expected of you so you can get the payoff, or do you want the payoff first to cushion the bitterness of the inevitable? I know more schooling sounds like a bummer and the idea of some jingle in your pockets sounds terrific, but the amount of money you can earn now is likely to be severely limited in the future by your lack of education. This is a classic case of short-term gain versus long-term pain or short-term pain versus long-term gain. Sounds a little like algebra, right? Whenever you have a choice, take your licks up front, especially if it's going to be relatively quick.

When I use the word "pain," I'm talking about effort that is out of the ordinary, trouble taken, and unpleasantness endured. The Protestant work ethic has convinced us all that the longer we defer gratification and endure suffering, the greater will be the payoff. It's easy to understand how this works as a political philosophy: if you can convince the peasants (that's us) that the more suffering they endure on this earth, then the greater will be their payoff in heaven, which will come later—much later.

An entire lifetime without pain is a fantasy. Sooner or later payment is always due. Avoiding all discomfort is impossible. Indulging in unnecessary pain, however, is just plain silly and a terrible waste of time and resources.

Sammy, it's not just about job versus school or money versus poverty. The question is whether what you're doing now makes any long-term sense. Don't take offense at the question; we all indulge in shortsightedness from time to time. Think of all the instances where we just avoid taking consequences into account. Each of these acts provides brief gratification while we ignore the long-term consequences. These actions are initially easy but costly, since they ignore the long-term consequences.

I'm now going to give you a complete course in the "Thou Shalt Avoid—for the Rest of Thy Life" All-Time Hit Parade, whether you decide to pursue "higher" education or not.

Love at first sight
Throwing caution to the wind
Exit speeches
Company Christmas party frivolity
Switching lines at toll booths and grocery stores
Swearing
Gossip
Letting your hair down
Spoiling kids
Tennis weekends
Crash diets

Love at first sight: By rushing into a relationship we trade off short-term pain (embarrassing questions, awkwardness, and uncertainty) for long-term pain ("But I thought you wanted to have kids . . . liked visiting my parents every weekend . . . wanted to travel"). It's dangerous to commit ourselves to a stranger based on precious little and often ambiguous data.

Throwing caution to the wind: This is just the generalized version of love at first sight. It's a willingness to believe in good luck, angels, divine providence, and a benign universe. You throw caution to the wind when you cross the street without looking both ways, buy a stock on a whim, believe in your horoscope, or put your faith in the Tooth Fairy or the Great Pumpkin. Flying off to Never-Never Land without leaving a note for your parents is self-centered, unreliable, and childish. Subscribing to the Peter Pan school of life is like slamming out of a room to make a dramatic exit and finding yourself walking the plank. If you've got nothing left to lose, ignoring consequences might not be all that risky. But if you've still got parents, your self-respect, school tomorrow or a curfew, beware of dramatic gestures and pirates and crocodiles lurking on the beach.

Exit speeches: This is the notion that all is lost and you can't make anything worse. Of course you can. Once you've been fired, why shouldn't you unload your complaints about the lousy work conditions, your philandering colleague, the sticky-fingered cashier? Three words: letter of recommendation. Even more succinctly, two words: small world. Burning your bridges behind you is the ultimate short-term gain, long-term pain scenario.

Company Christmas party frivolity: A big party can be an exit speech waiting to happen. To understand the idea of *company* and *party* in the same sentence is a contradiction in terms. Work is about competence, parties are about fun. It's seldom a good idea to try to combine the two. I know, I know, these parties are fun in the short run, but you want to be able to determine when you leave your employment, so beware of company Christmas parties, picnics, affairs (yeah, both kinds), and even work-based friendships. It's fine to go to the company party, but dress conservatively, drink seltzer, and behave as if you were at a church social. On December 26 it's better to be an employed fuddy-duddy than an out-of-work party animal.

Switching lines: This is the behavioral manifestation of the grass is always greener. The switch from a slow-moving line is inevitably based on the belief that doing anything is better than doing nothing and that movement is the same as progress. We all know, however, that as soon as you change lines the cash register will malfunction, the clerk will go on her break, or the person in front of you will launch into an argument about the accuracy of his bill. When we get frustrated, the idea that we are exerting *some* control over a stubborn world is tempting, but are we buying anything but more frustration in the longer (not even very long) run? Whether you're thinking about switching jobs, mates, phone companies, or heating systems, be sure you do the research rather than just changing for the sake of change.

Swearing: Losing your temper is always costly whether it is expressed verbally by swearing, flinging an insult, or by slamming out of a room. Ah, the pleasure derived and the cost exacted. This is the verbal equivalent of picking your nose in the car: you assume that no one else will notice, but swearing is costly and almost always comes back to haunt you. If nothing else, it gives someone permission to return the favor by swearing back at you. This is the way wars are begun, a terrifying example of *reeaaalllly* long-term pain. Sometimes you don't actually have to swear, but just find yourself thinking, "I really shouldn't say this but . . ." *Stop.* You're just about to trade off your credibility by saying something you ought not to have even thought.

Gossip: All that needs to be said here is that what goes around comes around. If you said it about someone else, all they need to do to ruin your reputation is say that you said it. Yikes! Gossip is tempting, but it's incredibly dangerous.

Letting your hair down: This is a polite way of describing a temper tantrum, having too much to drink, flirting with the boss, figuring no one will ever know. You'll know, and so will all the wrong people. Think of it this way: once you've let your hair down, Rapunzel, who's going to put it back up? And what about all the tangles and loose pins? If you like it down, why bother to put it up in the first place? I know, you know that hair is a metaphor here, so don't lose it.

Spoiling kids: Never is the difference between short- and long-term goals more evident than in the raising of children. There is a huge difference between a successful child and a successful adult. A successful child is easy to raise—obedient, quiet, cute, and docile. These words would not be used to describe a successful adult: adults need to be self-reliant, creative, and independent. Giving a noisy child what he wants in order to keep him quiet will create a narcissistic bully who views the world as functioning solely to meet his needs.

Tennis weekends: You'll end up with a sore elbow and a trip to the emergency room to check out your heart, which isn't used to such strenuous exercise, unless you've spent some time before the weekend getting in shape. If this is the only time you play, you'll hurt yourself to no purpose. This is the blitz approach to life, which holds that preparation is a waste of time and you should just go for it. It's the same philosophy that results in torn ligaments because stretching seemed like a waste of time and because skiing lessons are for wimps.

Crash diets: The emphasis here is on the crash. A crash breaks things into tiny, irreparable pieces. The exhilaration is indeed heady, but the sudden stop is dangerous and deadly. Long-term benefits are seldom accidental; long-term disasters often are. If the goal is to do anything more than fit into that special outfit by Saturday night, the lasting benefit requires patience and discipline, which offer short-term pain leading to long-term gain. It's easy enough to lose weight quickly: just stop eating. The problem is that to continue the loss, you have to continue to starve . . . and, hey, death isn't the goal here. If you start eating again, your starved little body is going to go into storage mode so that it won't be so vulnerable next time there's no food around. Shazam! Weight-gain city.

If this whole section seems to be about exerting some sort of order over your life, you're definitely paying attention. Discipline means considering consequences and deciding they're worth paying up front. I don't mean to sound like your aunt Gertrude, but when in doubt, always pay at the beginning and keep an eye on the true value of what you're paying for, so you're not on the road to martyrdom.

As a general rule, when in doubt, do the unpleasant stuff first while keeping an eye on the long-term goal so you don't get convinced that wretched is as good as it gets. In theory, the younger you are, the more emotionally flexible you are. When you're young, acquiring experience in lieu of money is a sound investment in your future, so volunteering makes sense. Sam, when you're old, volunteering can keep you active and involved. Emotionally, most of us are slightly more flexible when we are young than when we get older, so taking the knocks early rather than late makes some sense in terms of elasticity. It is also much easier to be poor early in life rather than late. Given the choice, also be gorgeous as late in your life as possible. You won't feel that you're losing anything you had when you were young or that the best is behind you and you'll develop a lot of other nifty skills like compassion and conversation, and maybe you'll even learn a trade. I myself plan to be gorgeous when I reach ninety and not a minute before.

GO FOR IT

✳

There is this really attractive woman in my building. I keep running into her in the elevator. We smile at each other. I'd love to ask her out, but I'm afraid she'll just think I'm an old coot. Is there any way to find out if she's interested or not?
—ELMER, 68, WALTHAM, MASSACHUSETTS

Elmer, of course there's a straightforward and simple way to find out if she's interested: ask her out. If you've survived nearly seventy years, you've undoubtedly taken some chances in your life. This one sounds as if it's worth taking. I know it doesn't seem snazzy that we are a country that practices the cult of cool. If anybody sees you sweat, you lose points. The underlying idea is that everything comes easily to the chosen. Elmer, don't you believe it. Some people are better at looking cool, but everybody has sweat glands. Believe in "no guts, no glory."

First of all, easy doesn't give you any sense of satisfaction. If you find tasks easy and other people applaud, you may assume that either you must have done something wrong for it to be so effortless or that you're about to be unmasked or both. To a certain extent, we all buy in to this "impostor phenomenon"—the idea that we're all in over our heads and it's only a matter of time before the thought police come and carry us away. Maybe the idea of asking her out makes your heart beat fast and your palms sweat, but she can't read your mind.

If you think about it, accomplishing a challenging task is what makes people feel good and productive about themselves. If you don't immediately succeed, you can feel stimulated when you try again, and feel accomplished and proud when you summon your courage and ask for a date with your dreamboat. Elmer, you may also be able to exorcise some of those junior high school demons lurking in your psyche as a result of being short or scared when you were thirteen and that cute little redheaded seventh grader liked the captain of the Little League team and ignored you. There really is life after high school and you're living it.

You may be fooled by folks who seem to have it made, but making it look easy and having it be easy aren't at all the same thing. Fred Astaire practiced his dancing six to eight hours a day so he could appear to glide weightlessly and effortlessly across the floor—and occasionally over the walls and ceiling as well—in *Royal Wedding* and *Funny Face*. Don't take my word for it: go rent *That's Entertainment!* Like Astaire, most gifted people started out with some talent and then practiced and practiced and practiced until they appeared to have been doing it all their life—which they very likely had, but just not as well. Hard work is the hidden polish to most people's shine.

✳

Everything comes easy to my sister. She's smart and pretty, and everybody likes her. I'm big and clunky, even though I'm two years younger. Why can't I be like her? —*MARIAN, 12, BEAUMONT, TEXAS*

Marian, you'd hardly recognize a diamond when it comes out of the ground. It needs to be cut and polished and worked on to become a "natural wonder." Like diamonds in the rough, we are all projects under construction, works in progress. The question then becomes when and how and for how long we need to do the work. As your authoritarian parent might say, "Spend time on the basics: a firm foundation is a much better investment than spending a lot of time diddling with the doorknobs and trim." (I know your parents don't talk exactly like that, but you get the point, yes?) Things that seem to come easily to some people aren't necessarily that easy and even if they are, so what? This is your life and there are things that you're better at than your sister. If you focus on yourself and work hard on what's important to you, I'll bet you'll be a lot happier. And when it comes to friends, all of us have to work hard, sometimes to make them, but always to keep them.

Pain is inevitable in life, and it makes sense to get it over with as soon as possible. The real trick is to not be embittered or hardened by the pain. Don't learn to love it, but do learn to use it. I'm not talking about pain with a capital *P.* I'm talking about the do-able—for example, waitressing to pay your way through school so you can make more money and have more freedom later, or going slowly in a relationship so you know who both of you are. Remember: if something seems too good to be true, it is.

In a nutshell, this chapter is the lesson of the frog: no frog will jump into boiling water, but if the frog happens to be resting in a cool puddle that gets heated by the sun, the frog will get scalded since he got hot gradually and didn't jump out of the water until it was too late.

✳

Make sure the price you are paying is within your budget and be certain that you value the prize. Be willing to evaluate from time to time and holler "ouch" if necessary, but understand how really tempting and dangerous it is to take pleasure first, with payment on demand. If you want all this distilled to its essence: Go for short-term pain and long-term gain.

SHRINK-WRAPS

The concept of short-term pain for long-term gain is never more evident than in friendship. A true and lasting friendship takes time, patience, communality of interest, and enough time to trust each other. Most of us love the idea of having a friend, but the real work of remaining friends seems too overwhelming and tedious. We confuse friends and acquaintances and call them both friends, but there's a difference between a Friend with a capital *F* and a friend with a small *f.* The kind we long for is much harder to be than the one we often are, and it quickly comes down to that short-term—long-term equation again:

A friend identifies himself when he calls; a Friend doesn't have to.
A friend looks uncomfortable when you start whining: a Friend says you've been whining about this same problem for a long time.

A friend tells you what is going on with her; a Friend asks what's goin' on with you.

A friend thinks you're cool; a Friend has seen you cry.

A friend brings wine to your birthday party; a Friend either throws the party or comes early to help you cook.

A friend complains that all families are the same; a Friend knows your parents and their pets' names.

A friend goes to movies with you; a Friend chats for hours.

A friend tells you the name of a good hairdresser; a Friend tells you when you've gotten a bad haircut and gives you a massage.

A friend introduces you to her friends; a Friend tolerates your friends.

A friend asks for understanding; a Friend understands you.

A friend offers companionship; a Friend offers acceptance.

Okay, so you're convinced you want a Friend. Yeah, but can you *be* a Friend rather than a friend? The task becomes significantly easier when you think about long- and short-term investments. Short-term pain in friendships comes in the form of mistakes, resentment, and stubbornness, but as uncomfortable as each is, without mistakes, we don't learn. Without remorse, we don't develop a moral code. Without fear, we don't understand consequence. Without resentment, we don't understand our relationship with others, without stubbornness, we don't develop a sense of self.

7
people do things for reasons

Even though it may not be obvious, there is always a reason for action.

T*he world is* divided into two kinds of people: those who think logically and those who are nincompoops, right? Wrong. Logic just means a system that is internally consistent. Believe it or not, there is no such thing as human action without reason. When we look at someone else's behavior and deem it nutty, we are simply unaware of the link between that person's thoughts and actions, but a link does exist. Once you accept that you and everyone else act on the basis of interior logic, then you simply look for the clues, assemble the pieces, and ask for explanations. Think of it this way: it's much more fun to play detective and figure out what's going on than to play lion tamer and feel you're only a chair and a whip away from chaos.

✳

My boyfriend is crazy. All of a sudden, he just up and quit his job, bought a motorcycle, and said he was leaving in ten days to find himself. Is there a way to get him committed for psychiatric evaluation before he completely blows his cork? —RITA, 38, LINCOLN, NEBRASKA

Rita, luckily it's really difficult to get people committed against their will. If it weren't, we'd find ourselves institutionalized every time we violated someone's notion of appropriate behavior.

I know you're upset, but instead of viewing your boyfriend's behavior as loony or taking it personally, what if you widened your perspective to include his behavior from *his* perspective? I don't ordinarily recommend that people attempt to read each other's minds, but in this case, let's make a partial exception. If we assume his behavior disturbs you but makes sense to him, we can begin to ask what reasons he might have to buy a motorcycle or take off on short notice. In some ways, I'm asking you to walk a mile in his Doc Maartens. Your questions then become both more abstract and more to the point: How can we ever really know another person? How can we predict our own behavior? How do we learn to trust one another? Or a great deal simpler, like, "Why are you leaving?"

All of these questions can be answered only if we understand that

+ People do things for reasons.
+ The reasons are knowable.
+ There is a consistency of response—in other words, given the same circumstances, a similar response would be likely.

Unless you are willing to believe that the world is completely chaotic and that all behavior is random, Rita, you, like the rest of us, act on the theory that people behave in predictable ways. For example, we feel safe in predicting that someone who is never late will be on time, that a person with a good sense of humor will likely enjoy a funny movie, and that someone who is on a diet won't order German chocolate cake for dessert. Obviously we are human and not robots, so behavior is never completely predictable, but in order to interact with one another, we act as if there is a connection between thought and action, even if it's not obvious.

We make this assumption not only when we interact with others but also when we examine our own responses. We assume that we, like everyone else, will not act "crazy." And even when we do get a little wild, it's in a predictable, relatively controlled way. For lack of a better term, we label this assumption "sanity." When these behavioral assumptions are upended, we say things like "I don't know what came over me" or "I wasn't myself" or "I was drunk." All these statements are further examples of what we label our ordinary, predictable, and unremarkable actions.

Many behavioral patterns are learned. The newborn will suckle when a cheek is touched, and cry when hungry, but it is the parent who learns to distinguish a newborn's cry of anger from one of frustration or fear. Most of what we expect from each other and ourselves is learned either by trial and error ("What happens when I say poop in front of Grandma?") or by rote (two times two is four). This isn't a news flash, but it is extraordinary how often we forget these methods of learning when we seek to understand behavior—our own or anybody else's. Rita, you and your boyfriend learned how to be adults in the same way.

The path to knowledge begins at birth. At first, an infant is constantly amazed and amused by a pop-up toy, not understanding the predictability of the top popping open and the puppet emerging in conjunction with the handle being turned. Every time the funny face pops up is like the first time. After repeated examples, the child begins to associate a part of a song that is played with the pop-up and waits delightedly and expectantly for the thrill of seeing the clown. When the child gets older and smarter, he either abandons the contraption for a less predictable toy or he takes the whole mechanism apart to figure out how the puppet really escapes the box. Throughout this experience, the child is learning that the behavior of the clown is predictable, which is true for all the learning that follows: "Mom gets mad when I throw my food. Dad hollers when I hide the remote control. The dog snaps at me when I pull his tail."

I know your boyfriend is well past his childhood chronologically, but if you think about this outline of how a child learns, you'll understand how to deal with the guy today. We're going to look for the patterns that were laid down long ago and are still in place.

Rita, my guess is that, while you don't like your boyfriend's behavior, it is not completely surprising to you. If your best girlfriend asked you how her boyfriend could cheat on her, you'd likely remind her how she said he was flirtatious with the waitress on their first date, how charming he was to her sisters, and how absolutely flat-out leering he was to his secretary at the company Christmas party. My guess is that your boyfriend mentioned his daydream about traveling or his restlessness or how he really envied guys who could just pick up and go. Most people will reveal everything we need to know about them in the first fifteen or twenty minutes after we meet them, if we only bother to notice.

Don't beat yourself up here. Even being a professional student of human behavior isn't always all that helpful. At one point in my life I had been seeing a man for six or seven months and was trying to decide how to deal with his seemingly erratic behavior. He seemed either needy or angry all the time, ranging between furious temper tantrums and stony withdrawals. Finally, in a moment of insight, I remembered how angrily he talked about his mother on our first date. If I was nurturing, he was mad because his mother smothered him and tried to make him feel guilty, and if I was aloof, he was mad at me for not taking care of him. This guy needed to be in therapy, not dating a therapist. If I hadn't been behaving the way we all behave on first dates (sort of dreamy, eager, and nervous), I would likely have paid much more attention to the fact that somebody who's furious enough at Mom to mention it to a stranger has some serious issues going on.

Very little behavior is random, so if we are confused by how we or someone else acts, believing there is a discernible reason gives us a head start on understanding that behavior.

If you view the world as unpredictable and random, understanding behavior—yours or anyone else's—is problematic. Who knows what will happen next? There is no way to forecast or control it and therefore no way to feel safe. Any change is to be avoided and feared since nothing is certain to begin with. This is the stuff of which horror movies are made. It might make for an entertaining film, but it's a pretty limited and unhappy way to lead your life.

If, on the other hand, you believe that there is some order to how things work and how people behave, then the job is to discover the underlying rules of human behavior. Allow me to reiterate that

+ People do things for reasons.
+ The reasons are somewhat predictable—which means consistent.
+ The reasons are usually discernible—which means knowable.
+ Trying to read any mind other than your own is a futile waste of time.

It's important to remember the last rule, because while there is always a logical connection between thought and behavior, the logic may not be obvious to you. It doesn't have to be. It only has to be logical to the actor, and it always is.

Once you can accept that human action is not random and is unpredictable only to the audience, not to the actor, you can start with your own behavior and ask yourself why you did what you did. Surprisingly, this is not always obvious. Remember that

- ✦ We do not always do the right thing.
- ✦ We sometimes regret our behavior.
- ✦ We often ignore the anger, envy, or greed that prompted us to behave badly.
- ✦ We sometimes miscalculate the impact of our actions.
- ✦ We try to distance ourselves from bad behavior.
- ✦ We occasionally act impulsively without considering options.
- ✦ We may act in a habitual way that is no longer appropriate—for example, "You used to think it was sexy when I undressed you in the car . . . sprayed you with the hose . . . shaved off half your mustache."
- ✦ We don't always assess our own behavior, which is kind of like never checking our gas gauge to see if our tank is full.

WHAT WAS I THINKING?

✳

I'm always screwing up. I choose the wrong men, the wrong jobs, the wrong friends, the wrong roommates. I get to the point where I just figure, what the heck, and do whatever because I'll just louse it up anyhow. —VERONICA, 27, DES MOINES, IOWA

Veronica, this Bud's for you. You're not looking at the reasons for your behavior. There is a direct connection between your feelings and your behavior and when you ignore both, your behavior seems random and whimsical. In reality, it's neither. If you begin to sort through your feelings, you can understand your behavioral options rather than just doing whatever. All of us make mistakes, but if we're willing to go back and reconstruct the path that led from the feeling to the action, we can understand what better choices were available and make them the next time. Your unwillingness to look at your behavior is your biggest problem at this moment.

We can be unwilling to look at our own behavior clearly because we are

- Ashamed to face up to the reasons for our action.
- Thoughtless; unwilling to take the time to examine our options and too ready to act on the basis of ease or fear.
- Clueless or unwilling to study consequences, both immediate and eventual.

Confusing other people is risky but often acceptable. Being confused by others is nearly inevitable. Confusing yourself is really pointless. Feelings just happen, but how you behave is always an option and therefore controllable and crucial.

The reasons for our own behavior can be less than obvious. Even once we are willing to look, we can be

- Ignorant and unaware of our own motives
- Uncomfortable with our feelings
- Conflicted and ambivalent about our choices

Naïveté is expensive innocence. Ignorance is seldom cute and never helpful. Cuteness is endearing only in babies, who need someone to take care of them. It is unacceptable in adults, who are expected to know what they're doing.

If you don't know yourself, you're in quicksand. You're a builder without material, tools, or a plan. The "Duh, like I didn't know" approach is pointless and reckless whether it's "I don't know what came over me" or "I don't know what to do next." It's bad enough when you're your own loose cannon. When this uncharming ignorance is part of a relationship, we're talking serious jeopardy. "I don't know why I love you like I do" is a statement of *danger* not love, both to you and to your lover. If you don't know what you value, how can either of you build on it or enhance it or make sure it's a part of your life? Eyes wide open is the only way to go through life unless you really love bruises and disasters.

Veronica, instead of deciding that your only options are misery or a nunnery, what if you decide to figure out why you keep making the wrong choices. Don't be tempted to return to those dumb acts.

You now understand that ignorance isn't a reasonable lifestyle choice, so let's move on to why people are so reluctant to do a little *self*-analysis. The reason is the big *D:* discomfort. It's embarrassing to be back in the same old stupid place again. All of us get embarrassed; the danger comes when we internalize this embarrassment and it becomes *shame*, which is doubly damning because it can leave you feeling important about feeling bad. It's such a strong word—shame. Carrying around your own private punishment chamber is terribly burdensome.

Veronica, don't let yourself get stuck in a hell of your own making. If you find yourself in a rotten place in your life, move on as quickly as possible. Don't create such a place. Don't get stuck there, and don't revisit it once you've left. If you see the pattern, you can change the pattern. That's good news. It just takes some work.

✳

I'm a churchgoing man and I try to lead a righteous life. Still, not only am I tempted but sometimes I succumb to several of the deadly sins: I feel angry when someone passes me in the car, I'm envious of my brother's new car, and I realize that, at heart, I'm fairly slothful. Do you think I'm damned? —CLAIN, 32, PEORIA, ILLINOIS

Clain, I'm a psychologist, not a theologian. As a psychologist, I'm delighted that you are so aware of your feelings. Once you can accept that feelings don't ask to happen, then you can sort out your options. If you allow your lazy feelings, your anger, or your envy to make you feel ashamed, you're going to undermine your own ability to control your behavior. You're going to begin thinking of yourself as a bad person. What do bad people do? Bad things! You're stuck in a nasty prison of your own making.

If, on the other hand, you understand and accept that you are human and can be tempted by your brother's car, a nap in the hammock when the lawn needs to be mowed, or the impulse to swear at a rude driver, then you can exercise your options. You can visit car dealerships and start saving, hire a kid to cut the grass or do half and then take a nap, or sing along with the car radio at the top of your lungs. You can politely, if wistfully, turn down invitations to do what you know is unwise, or you can consciously choose to indulge, but not because you're at the whim of your emotions. If you are unwilling to accept your urges, you are going to be powerless to behave in a way that allows you to look at yourself in the mirror. Accept those imperfect thoughts and understand them. You can then build barriers against them (don't ride in your brother's car), find a therapist and explore sibling rivalry, or sublimate your resentment and competitiveness by making your garden more flamboyant than his.

PREDICTABLE PATTERNS

✳

I seem to be attracted only to "bad girls," but I'm getting to the age where I'd really like to settle down, get married, and raise a family. I'd like to marry a "nice girl," but I don't seem to be able to break this pattern. I'm not having any fun anymore. —VICTOR, 32, ANN ARBOR, MICHIGAN

Victor, ambivalence is a natural and predictable part of life. Internal conflict is inevitable because feelings are with us from the beginning. Conscience is a later development. Your madonna-whore complex (the idea that women are either saints like your mom or sinners like your girl-friend) isn't unique to you (or it wouldn't already have a name), but it won't be resolved until you sort out the feelings behind the behavior. Are you afraid you'll marry someone like your mother? Are you afraid you'll become like your father? Have you adopted a lifestyle based on being a bad boy? Is it hard for you to grow up? Does responsibility make you break out in hives? Got to face your fears, Vic, or I'm afraid you'll continue to be haunted by them.

It is not only possible but probable for all of us to entertain contradictory urges—for example, the wish to be loved and the desire to control; the need to feel powerful as well as a longing to be taken care of. Until we are willing to examine these conflicting sensations, our actions will reflect whatever feeling is most dominant at the time. Our behavior will seem random, out of control and downright bizarre. In the most extreme case, someone who is unable to sort out thought from behavior, imagined from real, internal from external, is viewed as schizophrenic. Still, unexamined, urgent emotions *can* be cataloged and controlled if we have the courage and the energy to exert control over our impulses.

If it's difficult to assess your *own* motives, it's truly futile to worry about anyone else's. Yeah, other people are doing things for reasons, but they may be unable or unwilling to explain those reasons to you. Invest your time and effort in profitable pursuits: stick with what is knowable—yourself.

KNOW THYSELF

✳

I hear you talk all the time about knowing who you are. Even my philosophy professor said, "Know thyself." But where do I start? I've been trying to please others ever since I was born. I was Daddy's good little girl, then the perfect girl-friend, then the perfect wife and mother and friend and daughter. I'm not sure I've ever pleased anyone, and I have no idea how to please myself. Help! —
JANINE, 42, GREEN BAY, WISCONSIN

Janine, you're asking the *perfect* questions: "Who am I, and what do I want?" These are the keys to the psychological kingdom of happiness. How then do you begin to sort through your own motives? While you once tried to please your dad, are you still trying to do so? When you bake a cake, are you looking for gratitude from the kids, patterning yourself after your mom, or trying to sabotage your diet? When you're figuring out who you are, there are two fundamental places to start:

1. **Problems:** Things just aren't working. However, beginning with a mess means there's very little risk of screwing things up, since things are already lousy and you have a lot to gain if you can make your life better. Make sure you look at *why* something isn't working, rather than just what isn't working.
2. **Changes:** Behavior that has recently changed is fresher and more obvious. If you can start with *when* the change occurred, you'll have a general idea of why.

Since we've already established that people don't do things out of the blue very often, start looking for the *why*. Pay attention to *what* you're doing. It's easier to see than the why. Once you can establish a link between the *what* and the *why*, you can explain yourself to you. I'm not talking about the kind of explaining that's necessary when you get caught misbehaving. I'm talking about being honest with yourself so you feel good and grounded about why you're doing what you're doing. Once you begin doing things because they make sense to you, you'll have a much nicer time in your own skin.

When things go well, note them and ask yourself if there is any way to improve the situation or push the envelope a bit. This way, you can focus not only on how to avoid pain but also on how to seek and achieve pleasure: the clue to being a happy, serene person.

If something has changed, look first for the obvious. If you hear hoofbeats, think horses, not zebras. Zebras are nifty but relatively uncommon, so always start with the usual, not the unusual. Ruling out the obvious is less tantalizing, but a much better use of time and effort. Once we've figured out the likely cause, let's move from the zoo to the roof.

When I lived in that big old house on the ocean in Massachusetts I learned a lot about life from my roof. When it leaked, the first place to look would be directly above the leak. Often the hole in the roof was a long distance from the wet ceiling. I learned to find the leak by tracing the water backward to its source. I remembered from grade school science that water seeks its own level, which is the line of least resistance. Water doesn't go uphill and it's not going to turn corners, but it can get blown by the wind. So I learned to find the source of my leak by thinking like water. (I just made up the rule of roof leaks, so don't be too disturbed if it sounds unfamiliar.)

Janine, tracing your own line of reasoning this way is a little drier but a bit more challenging than figuring out what sprung a leak. Water doesn't feel guilty, ashamed, or embarrassed. Start with the problem and trace it backward, asking yourself what's most likely and you'll end up at your source. If you think of yourself as tracing the leak, you can remove some of the potential embarrassment that occurs when we dissect our own motives and *really* dig deep. If you think about plumbing your own depths, you won't be tempted to avoid painful subjects that make you blush.

Understanding your own reasoning process is heady stuff. Don't be seduced into thinking you know how everyone else thinks, just because you've sorted yourself out. You're not them, so please remember that people do things for *their* reasons, not yours, but they may not be aware of this rule. Also keep in mind that they may be unwilling to be quizzed about their motives by you. "Why," after all, is an incredibly important thing to ask yourself, but don't ask it of anybody else. Other people may not know their own motives or may be unwilling to admit their motives if they do know them.

Why ask why? Asking why will antagonize other people, but should stimulate your own self-analysis. Most of us react badly to being asked to explain ourselves, so ask the question only of yourself. Ask *yourself* why, so you'll *know*. When you know, you can decide what to do. Once you begin looking at your own behavior, you can more easily see patterns:

+ Were you a stubborn kid who had to stand up to a bossy big sister? Are you now a bit pigheaded and intractable as an adult?

+ Were you a musical teenager who dreamed of being a rock star while plotting revenge on all those really popular kids who ignored you? Now, as an adult, are you conflicted about whether rock music is a career or a hobby?

+ Were you a runt with a hot temper? Now that you're tall and strong, do you still occasionally lose your temper when you feel that people are ignoring you and treating you as though you don't matter?

+ Has the problem with your difficult dad translated into trouble with authority figures or finding people to date who will take care of you without smothering you?

Janine, the search for self is a search for patterns. In the patterns you will see the blueprint of who you are and how you can change.

Several months ago a twenty-three-year-old woman asked me to help her figure out why her husband wanted to drop out of graduate school when he was nearly ready to propose a thesis topic. She said, "It doesn't make any sense; his grades have always been good." She was perfectly willing to continue to support them both. She deemed his behavior "crazy." I said, "If we assume that he has a reason that makes sense to him, what might it be?" Silence. I said, "If you had finished your course work and it was time to come up with a thesis topic, what might make you want to quit?" In a quiet little voice she responded, "I'd be scared." Bingo. A marriage saved, a technique learned, an insight gained.

While it would have been unwise for her to assume that being scared was her husband's only motive, she at least moved away from the assumption that he was crazy and that she could change his mind. Once it occurred to her that he might actually have a reason for his behavior, she was more willing to listen so that he would be more willing to look at his behavior and actually talk about his feelings with her.

Whether you're thrilled or appalled by someone else's behavior, you may not be able to figure out exactly why he is doing what he's doing, but perhaps you believe there's a link between thought and action. You don't have to understand the link, but it is wisest to assume that it exists.

Again, Janine, whether you're looking into your own head or trying to scope out what somebody else is doing, remind yourself that people do things for reasons—all people, not just those whose behavior you like. In negotiating compatible patterns of behavior, believing that both of you are doing things for reasons allows you to begin with *why* you're doing what you're doing and giving the other person the same respect. You don't have to risk launching World War III by looking shell-shocked and bellowing "You're crazy!" or "What could you possibly have been thinking?" or "Why in hell did you do that?"

Instead, you can calmly say, "This is *why* I said this (or did this or want that). Tell me what you want, and let's see if we can sort this out." When in doubt, you can calm down by quietly asking yourself, "If I had just done what he did, what might I have been thinking?" or "If I didn't feel threatened by his behavior, what might I see?" It's amazing how many sane options open up when you use this technique. Your reasons aren't necessarily going to be anyone else's, but by getting in touch with your reasons, you are at least opening yourself to the possibility of learning the other person's reasons.

At very least, you will learn to avoid the button *A* approach to life: every time I push button *A*, *B* pops up, and I hate *B*.

Listen up: stop pushing button *A!*

SHRINK-WRAPS

MOTIVATIONAL REALITIES

Blood is thicker than water: This is undoubtedly true from a chemical standpoint. What it means is that while we may not be crazy about our family, we are the only ones who are allowed to criticize them. During your children's teen years, it is also wise for you to remember that given a choice between hormones and heritage, sex will win. Blood may be thicker than water, but it's thinner than Love Potion Number 9.

Power corrupts: You don't have to think politically to see that this is true. Just remember the first time your parents left you in charge of your little brother or sister.

We'd all rather be praised than punished, but we'd rather be punished than ignored: This is true from the moment of birth on.

Bribery works better than guilt: Study after study has proved that positive reinforcement is effective and negative isn't. Everyone knows this except parents and office managers.

If you've adopted any of the following as your theme song, you're looking for pity, not a party, and you've got to figure out why you're opting for misery.

PROZAC MUSICAL MOMENTS

"If You Leave Me Now": I just love emotional blackmail, don't you?

"Release Me": Oh, please, asking someone to make it easy for you to do what he doesn't want you to do is more than a tad unrealistic, don'tcha think?

"Are You Lonesome To-night?": Right, we're both miserable, so why not console each other and be so incredibly clingy and claustrophobic that we'll make ivy and octopi look relaxed.

"I Can't Stop Loving You": Let's talk obsession here. This isn't love; it's a therapeutic issue. Get help.

"Only the Lonely": Talk about the theme song for a pity party parade. Everybody gets the blues sooner or later, and the only way to be sure you'll never get your heart broken is to put yourself on house arrest.

"Why Do Fools Fall in Love?": All of us have to be a little bit foolish to give up our personal sovereignty and let someone else begin to know who we really are. But what's so bad about being foolish from time to time?

"Tears on My Pillow": Yeah, yeah, yeah, we've all been there, but why make it a world-class, going-for-the-gold misery sweepstakes? Take a couple of days off and indulge in a pity party, or get a rubber pillow.

"Raining in My Heart": A meteorologic metaphor. Crying is okay, as long as it doesn't become a lifestyle choice, which is more than a little manipulative.

8

attitude: hey, dude, it's everything

We can't control what happens to us, but we're in charge of how we respond.

L*et's face it;* everybody has bad days, but when they become a lifestyle or an excuse, it's time to look in the mirror and firmly resolve to do the best with what you've got and stop the complaining. Being a Pollyanna or tiptoeing through the tulips isn't the result of a medication overdose; it's simply a willingness to be an active participant in your own happiness. The good news is that you truly are the architect of your own well-being. The bad news is that this signals an abrupt end to the tendency to whine, complain and blame. I think, in the long run, you'll view it as a reasonable trade-off.

PITY PARTIES

✳

I was born under a cloud. No matter what I do, it doesn't work. My mother hated me, my father ignored me, and my brothers and sisters used to gang up against me and beat me up. Kids in school made fun of me. I had no friends then, and I've got no friends now. Even my husband and kids ignore me. I'm lonely and tired. Why do you think some people are cursed? —NANCY, 48, BOISE, IDAHO

241

Wow, Nancy, talk about your big league bummer bash. Could it be that even *you* don't like being around you? This attitude of yours will make you unpleasant, wrinkled, and lonely 'cause nobody is going to want to play with you.

Nancy, I want to tell you the old story about the dad who had twin sons. One son was horrifyingly cheerful, and the other complained about everything. Being of an experimental mind, Daddy decided to see if he could disrupt these tendencies. He filled one room with every toy and gadget and video game imaginable. I mean, we're talking a shiny red bike, a toy train set, computer games that make those irritating noises, and all sorts of sports equipment, including the latest big league uniform. This room made FAO Schwarz look inadequate. The other room was crammed full of . . . well, manure. The frustrated dad sent his first son, Wayne Whiner, into the playroom and the other twin, Charlie Cheerful, into the doo-doo room. An hour later he visited Wayne who complained that dad had neglected to buy Tickle Me Elmo. Charlie hardly noticed his dad's appearance in the room, so busy was he with a shovel, figuring with all the manure, there must be a pony in there someplace.

You and I both know people who have very little and are cheerful, happy, and generous. Conversely, there are folks who seem to have lots of money, good looks, a great job, and a fine education and yet they are grumpy and miserable. The question is, "How come?" The answer is ATTITUDE!

Meanwhile, back in the twin tale, we also know that Charlie Cheerful has gobs of friends, is loved by his teachers, and always gets an A for effort. His brother, Wayne Whiner, may have more brain power, but he never gets invited for sleep-overs and is the last kid picked for the team, even though he's a pretty good athlete when he's not pouting. No matter what Dad or the world offers Wayne, he'll never be happy until he decides to be.

Nancy, with that monstrous chip you're carrying around on your shoulder, it's surprising you can walk at all. I know you're not very happy, but, kiddo, we've got to teach you to get out of your own way. If someone delivered four dozen roses to you at this moment, you'd distrust the giver's motives and point out those pesky thorns. Obviously your life is not completely without contact: you're married and you have kids. If I hear you correctly, you have a relationship with your siblings, even if it's not a very happy one. What happened to make you so bitter? Whatever it was, it seems to me it's high time to sort it out, give it up, and get on with your life. I don't want you to spend another moment being quite so miserable.

To a very large extent, we are not responsible for what happens to us in this life, but we are completely responsible for how we respond to what happens. Let's not worry about our dysfunctional family upbringing, our culture, or our religion. Certainly, all of those factors can influence us, but that's why adulthood was invented, so each of us could choose what works and what doesn't work. Blame is a waste of time and energy. It will keep you locked in your unhappy past and at the whim of the person to whom you have given your power. If you can think of yourself as doing the best you can with what you've got, you'll find yourself in a much healthier, happier place. You'll be able to minimize the pathos, which will make you a lot more socially acceptable. You can free yourself to live your life and stop victimizing yourself.

Once you decide to stop being a sacrificial lamb, you can sort through your options. This doesn't mean that only terrific things will happen to you from now on. You might still get headaches and not resemble Cindy Crawford, but you'll spend a whole lot less time anticipating the headaches and cursing your parents for their gene pool. Nancy, when you decide that you've spent enough time being miserable your life will take a turn for the better. Have you ever gone to the movies when you had a stomachache and completely forgotten about your malady during the movie? You made a conscious choice to pay attention to something else.

Not convinced? Remember back to when you stayed up all night with a brand-new love? You probably felt a lot different in the morning than you did when you stayed up all night studying. The sleep deprivation is exactly the same; the difference is in your attitude. Nancy, don't take my word for anything. Just spend a day looking for positive stuff, smile, compliment people, and see if the world doesn't become a better place for you. If it doesn't, you can return to being grumpy.

THE OLD DYSFUNCTIONAL-FAMILY BLUES

✳

My boyfriend says I shouldn't get mad at him when he hollers because that's how he was raised. He says his family is more dysfunctional than mine. —LAVINIA, 28, HOLLYWOOD, CALIFORNIA

Jeez Louise, dueling dysfunctions? I truly don't think you want to go there, and even if you do, I definitely don't. Everybody's family—and I do mean everybody's—is dysfunctional. I'm not sure where this national obsession with blame began, but it's past time to put the whole family-as-doomed-destiny thing to rest. How you respond determines who you are. We are our choices and not the choices of our parents, our religion, our sex, or ethnicity. We choose how to behave. If you're not happy with your boyfriend's behavior, talk with him about it. Don't let him duck the issue by invoking the Ghost of Family Past. You're here, this is now, get used to it. The dysfunctional family blues are a variation on "Woe is me." Let's all repeat together: "I'm in charge of my own life. I'm responsible. I can function."

Neither you or your boyfriend had a whole lot of choice about how you were raised, but nowadays you can choose your own behavior. You can opt to be happy and content or restless or searching. And, honey, you're twenty-eight, and I'm assuming your boyfriend is at least out of high school, so both of you are definitely adults chronologically. If you're feeling a little less than adult, take comfort in the fact that sometime between twenty-five and thirty-five, we all begin to figure out who we are and who we want to become.

✳

My twenty-one-year-old daughter and I have always gotten along well. Even when she was a teenager, she was respectful. Now she won't even talk to me without sneering. It's like she hates me, and I swear I don't criticize her or try to run her life. —MAY, 43, LITTLE ROCK, ARKANSAS

May, your daughter is right on schedule. I know it's hard on you, but sometime during our twenties, most of us begin adopting a more adult perspective on life, and often the first casualty of these years is any affection for our parents that survived our teen years. In some ways, this decade is Adolescence, Part Two. The first part, the teen years, serves to weaken the cord that binds child and parent so the young person can begin to establish some personal independence by the time she is old enough to vote. The second civil (or not so civil) war, which often occurs during our twenties, is an assault on the parents themselves, rather than just on the parents' values. Anything that isn't exactly as we hoped in our own lives gets blamed on their lousy parenting.

When we begin to understand our limitations in an adult world, we often want to blame someone. What better target than our parents? We've already launched ourselves toward independence, emotionally and financially. Our friendships are still relationships between equals. Our love life can take up a lot of time, so it's tempting to toss overboard the least crucial and heaviest baggage—Mom and Dad. This is the payback that mothers mention when they say, "You should only have children like you."

Just as most people are aware of the terrible twos, when an infant takes her first lurch toward independence, and can therefore be prepared, the turbulence of the teen years is expected. Nobody ever tells you about the fearsome fours or the sullen sixes or the enigmatic eights. There are ongoing stages in a child's life: times of progress and consolidation. The consolidations are the quiet years, the forward movement, a bit harder on both parent and child. The second adolescence of the mid-twenties is as unanticipated as the fearsome fours, but equally important to maturation. Relax, if you can, and stay focused on yourself—who you are now, who you would like to be—and try to understand that your daughter is going through a rather painful but necessary phase.

If your parents are still alive, ask them how you behaved at that age, and try to remember how much you blamed them. Your daughter would be better served to leave you out of her struggle, but you can't really tell her that. Remind yourself that all her other phases passed and so, most likely, will this one. If you can keep your perspective and your sense of humor, and refrain from overreacting, all concerned will fare quite well.

GOBS OF GUILT

✳

I feel guilty all the time. I don't spend enough time with my kids. My wife complains that I'm cold and indifferent to her. My mother is recently widowed and she needs me. I'm in sales, which is a really competitive field. I try to get in a workout a couple of times a week, since my dad had a bad ticker. It seems I can't please anyone, and when I try to find some time for myself, I feel even worse. — RON, 48, WHEELING, WEST VIRGINIA

Ron, you've got to take a deep breath here and relax. Guilt is feeling good about feeling bad, and it's a colossal waste of time. Let me tell you a story. In the first few weeks after I first separated from her father, I took my daughter on a skiing trip.

Sure enough, on the first evening, my husband showed up. He "just happened to be in the neighborhood"—some four and a half hours from home! I felt trapped and finally opted for guilt by being pleasant but not inviting him to stay. When I later related the story to a girlfriend, I wailed, "He makes me feel awful. I guess I should have asked him to dinner." My friend, being older and wiser, calmly replied, "He can only *try* to make you feel guilty. You own your very own private guilt supply. Only you can choose how to respond."

A lightbulb went on in my head, even though she was only partially right. We are not responsible for our feelings, only our behavior. I may have been *feeling* sad or remorseful or, yeah, even guilty (that most useless of all emotions), but how I *behaved* was completely up to me.

Action is a feedback loop. Just as Anna in the musical *The King and I* explained to her son before meeting the king of Siam, you can choose. She pointed out that by whistling a happy tune when you're afraid, you can fool not only the people you fear but yourself as well.

Ron, you've got a lot on your plate. Feeling tired and under the gun all of the time doesn't help anyone. Adding a huge dollop of guilt is only going to sap more time and energy out of you than you can afford to lose. You need to sort through your priorities and get much better at scheduling. If you block out certain specific time periods to spend with your kids doing special things, and if you schedule private time for yourself and your wife to keep the spark alive, you'll feel more in charge of your time and your loved ones won't feel that they're always begging for your attention. Make sure you budget some time for yourself, even if it's going grocery shopping alone on Thursdays after work without the kids. You might also want to figure out where you learned to be so good at guilt. Cut yourself a little slack, schedule your time, and chill out a bit.

THE BLUE MEANIES

✳

Politicians stink! They lie and cheat and steal. There's no reason to vote, no reason to care. The church is outdated; marriage is a joke. My college "education" is a crock. My girlfriend abandoned me for no reason. I don't trust anyone, and anybody who does is a fool. The world is a really horrible place. —FRANKLIN, *20,* PHOENIX, ARIZONA

Whoa, Franklin, you've got a bad case of the college senior blues. Leaving school can often feel traumatic, but it sounds as if you're unconsciously giving yourself a reason to dig a hole, jump in, and retire from the human race. Could I possibly negotiate a cease-fire between you and the rest of the world to see if there isn't something that makes you happy or at least doesn't irritate the daylights out of you? In my experience, when people are so completely unhappy, it's usually because they've just had a major disappointment on the emotional front.

Is it possible that your girlfriend took a piece of your heart as well as her stereo when she left? That can give anyone a major funk attack. It's amazing how that one special person can change our world from gray to blue and back again, depending on whether the relationship is cooking or not. She isn't the first and probably won't be the last to do a little damage, but don't allow one nasty experience to taint your perspective on love, life, or women. Since there is so much other emotional turmoil in your life right now, being upset about a relationship must feel like the final insult. Keep your upsets separate and deal with them one at a time. When you have only the heartbreak left, you may not feel much happier, but you'll feel much saner.

I know it's hard to see the world as a good place when your heart is aching, but "the world is a lousy place" is a pseudo-sophisticated riff on the older and less hip "woe is me" theme. Being negative may seem hip and trendy, but you'll be totally miserable, and folks will avoid you like the plague, which will just make you lonelier. Bummer.

Frank, attitude is the template we place over our unruly and unreliable emotions that allows us to behave appropriately and trust ourselves to be consistent and reliable. What if we designed a field experiment together: For the next week, try to appear confident in class and at get-togethers. Try being polite to an adversary. Laugh at an insult. Let a tear drop from your eye during a sentimental movie. Choose how to respond and watch the difference it creates in your environment.

A word of caution: I'm not encouraging you to become superficial or to play a part without regard for your feelings. I'm suggesting that feelings are the raw material of our lives and behavior but that you can shape and pattern them without fundamentally distorting or denying them. I don't want you to become a hypocrite, but you do need to realize that you can choose how to behave and how to respond. To use a simple and straightforward metaphor, just because you're hungry doesn't mean you have to eat immediately. You can be really tired but still stay awake at a dinner party. You can be intensely angry without lashing out or striking someone. You can acknowledge your hunger but still eat slowly or settle for a cup of coffee because you're going out for dinner in an hour. You can even chow down on a Big Mac. It's not so much what you do as understanding that you have a choice about doing it. If you have a choice, there is no victimization, no one option, no destiny, and no whimpering.

MIXED SIGNALS

✳

Men are always hitting on me. I go into a bar to have a drink and they're all over me. When they find out I'm not dying to have sex with them but would like to be friends before I hop into bed, they disappear. I must be doing something wrong. —DONNA, 48, SACRAMENTO, CALIFORNIA

Donna, you've either got to assume that all men are pigs or that there's something *you* can do to send different vibes. Let's start with option number 2 or you're going to have to find a convent! It sounds to me as if you're sending either mixed or easily misinterpretable signals. Are you careful about how you dress? If you were going to be on the cover of a magazine, would it be *Cosmopolitan* (sexy, low-cut, clingy, and available), *Field and Stream* (sporty, casual, rugged, and functional), or *Working Woman* (businesslike, no-nonsense, authoritative)? Ask an honest friend to stand you in front of a mirror and be brutally frank. By standing in front of the mirror together, you can see how your friend sees you inch-by-inch.

Wardrobe is the easy part. We choose how to cut our hair, stand, talk, and make eye contact. Not only do our choices affect how others see us, but equally they are also the basis of how we view ourselves. Most of us are self-involved enough to be unaware of subtleties of body language, eye contact, or posture in other people. Therefore, most of us respond on the basis of a quick appraisal of the obvious. Studies have shown that you have about four seconds to make a first impression on someone. How you look, act, dress, smell, smile, and interact will allow others to decide how to act toward you. All these cues are a part of your attitude.

Last year I accidentally discovered how easy and basic the whole process is when I got sick the day before the company Christmas party, which was particularly upsetting since I had bought a new sequined slip dress for the occasion. It was on sale and fit as if it had been made for me alone. The tank top was outlined in navy blue bugle beads, and the dress itself shimmered with shades of blue, purple, and turquoise. (I know it sounds kind of gaudy, but, honest, it isn't.) With visions of being the belle of the ball permanently stalled in my stuffed-up head, I stayed home that night, feeling sorry for myself. Three days later, having mostly recovered from my bout with the flu, I decided, why not? I got up at my customary 5:30 A.M., donned the sequined wonder, and went to work. Hey, I bought it for the company Christmas party and I was going to work for the company, after all. Well, you'd think I was visiting royalty from the response I got. Even though I kept explaining that I just wore it for the fun of it, everyone was convinced I had some incredibly important secret high-class event to attend, all disclaimers to the contrary. I'm not sure that wearing a fancy cocktail dress to an office in which most people wear jeans is in the *Dress for Success* rule book, but it sure did wonders for my stuffy nose and sense of fun.

You can choose how to act and, by deciding, exert control over your own destiny. I couldn't do anything about the flu, but I could choose my response. People will pick up their primary cues about you from you. In this way, it's your show. You're the star, the director and the writer. The costumes, blocking, and inflection are all up to you and you alone. You can choose drama or comedy, a one-act monologue or a three-act mystery. The setting can be in Elizabethan times, in the present, or in the future. The pacing can be lickety-split or stately. The rest of the cast will adjust and the play will take on a meaning as a result of your choices.

Donna, before I let you get carried away with my stage-managing scenario, make sure the person you're directing is you. I don't want you shoving other people around the stage as it will strain your back, your credibility, and *their* patience. Manipulation is the less than fine art of trying to make someone do your bidding by making them feel guilty.

It sounds like the Donna you're presenting to the world is "sexy Donna." Think about it for a moment.

If it's true that others judge us by our presentation, or if one of your friends says she's insecure or needy, you might avoid her for three reasons:

1. We tend to believe what others say about themselves, especially when it is negative. Who better than you to know your shortcomings?
2. It's hard to be around someone who is constantly negative. Depression can be contagious. It's much more fun to be around someone who is pleasant and happy.
3. The constant need for reassurance becomes taxing. All of a sudden you feel there's not enough air in the room for both of you, because your good insecure friend old Wendy Whiner (Wayne's intended) is taking both of your shares: "Look at me, feel sorry for me, do something for me, talk about me, cheer me up. . . ." Yikes, let's get out of here.

The ultimate manipulator is the person who says, "No one loves me," and "No matter what I do, it's not right."

This unhappy and unpopular soul is creating a self-fulfilling prophecy while simultaneously trying to make the audience respond. "My happiness is *your* responsibility. You're that important to me" isn't seductive—it's scary. Beware the seduction of dependence. It's a subtle control mechanism that is hard both to recognize and to defend against. This kind of attitude is often passivity cloaked in fear: "If I make you feel important, you won't leave me." Donna, you really don't want to send the wrong message, so decode your own soul and then proudly convey who you are and see who responds.

I'm not sure it's necessary to adopt the "don't worry, be happy" motif, but it's a lot closer to the secret to happiness than "the woe is me and you'd better do something about it" theme. You may not be able to change the world, but you can change your attitude, and in that change you can affect your corner of the world. That change can have a ripple effect. You can lose the fear that underlies the temptation to manipulate by asking, "What's the worst thing that could happen?" and figuring out how to avoid or compensate for that outcome.

You can lose your anger by figuring out what you can do for yourself and absorbing the energy in activity. You can lose your disappointment by evaluating your expectations and letting them go. You can lose your self-involvement by focusing on others. You can stop being a victim by doing something. This is your life, the only one I can promise you'll get, so why waste a moment of it by putting yourself in a negative place? Figure out what you can do to change the situation or your perception of it and do it.

SHRINK-WRAP

As a final note, for my last shrink-wrap, I want to share a call I got from a woman a few weeks ago who was dying of brain cancer. She had two children under the age of eight. The doctors had told her she had no more than six months to live. Without an ounce of self-pity, bitterness, or anger, she asked me what legacy she could leave her children. She also wanted some help in arranging a lasting legacy while still leading a normal life for as long as possible. I suggested that she make a video, record lullabies, hug her kids, and when the end seemed near, let the kids stay home from school with her, since she had no wish to spend any more time in the hospital. She had set up her house so she could live there until the end.

This was a rotten break for a courageous woman who would leave her children a legacy of courage and dignity and doing the best she could with the truly lousy hand she was dealt. She will live on in my memory for displaying grace under pressure. Her attitude was more important than her cancer. She had found a spiritual antidote to physical malignancy. The thought of her still makes me cry. Would that we could all inherit her legacy, her strength, her attitude. Amen.

a f t e r w o r d

Just as evil is always more interesting than good, fantasies are more seductive than reality. Bad guys steal more attention than Dudley Doright even though we want to believe that justice will eventually triumph over wrongdoing, but we are tempted, fascinated, and distracted by the bad stuff.

Fantasies aren't inherently evil, but they are distracting and therefore a dangerous preoccupation. Unfortunately, or maybe not, we have to live our lives on a reality basis, which requires discipline, order, and courage. Rats, how come it can't be a bit more exciting? Well, if you're willing to focus on outcome rather than immediacy, some tingling might begin in anticipation of real pleasure.

Blueprints are always a bit less fun than castles in the air unless you're looking for a place to live. That's what I'm trying to provide here—not pie-in-the-sky notions but a real plan for living a happy, successful life. The bad news is that reality is harder work; the good news is that the payoffs are tangible.

If you are willing to give up the notion that perfect love is the result of being reunited with your long lost soul mate, you can begin putting in the time and effort to find a real person who loves you and whom you can love because of, not in spite of, each other's differences and peculiarities.

Once you understand that money is only a tool, you can figure out what you'd like to build with your tools and discover other tools that are just as necessary to the successful completion of your task.

You can also figure out the difference between tenacity and obsession and opt for problem-solving rather than blame. You can live by the rules that make sense to you and let everyone else do the same, even if your rules and their rules bear no similarity to each other. The relaxation of running your life and letting everyone else do the same will give you scads of free time to make money or whoopee or trouble or hay while the sun is still shining.

You may even find time and energy to read, which can give you perspective on all that you don't know or understand. You can adopt the eagle rather than the ostrich as your mascot and decide that you will never again be Cleopatra, the Queen of Denial.

As a side benefit of this newfound wisdom, you can accept (without cringing) the idea that life is complicated and that simple and easy aren't the same thing. This sophistication can smooth out the wrinkles that result from realizing that life is seldom fair by anyone's standards. "Do the best you can with what you've got" becomes a mantra worth repeating and sharing.

Your personal truth will become all the more vibrant if you realize that it is personal and that questions are significantly more important than answers. Once you can come up with the right question, you're focused and poised to sort through data.

You can also stop blaming your parents for being less than perfect and let go of the fantasy that everyone's family worked better than yours. You won't have to boycott Mother's Day or Father's Day, but you can construct a family structure that suits you and your needs rather than being encumbered by the nose-pressed-against-the-glass feeling that there really are functional families lurking just beyond the next hedge.

You can also stop cringing behind that same hedge waiting for an alien invasion of the opposite sex from another corner of the galaxy. *The X-Files* refers to a television series, not a search for chromosomal abnormalities between men and women. We already know women are XX and men are XY, but both were conceived right here on earth. We are all carbon-based, oxygen-breathing life-forms that need to learn to get along.

And what a relief to finally admit that nobody's perfect. If you're not perfect, then I don't have to pretend that I am. None of us have to hide mistakes or fake it anymore. Think about the freedom of being rather than pretending. It's like slipping off a pair of shoes that look good but are a size too small. I promise it will brighten your day all around.

Once you stop investing in ideas with no payoff but misery, you'll have energy to invest in real solutions to real problems. Just make sure that the investments are primarily personal. Telling yourself what you already know is a useful exercise in inventory awareness; telling other people what they already know is *booooring* and will make you as popular as a root canal. You will be freed from expecting people to be grateful for your criticism, and you can stop waiting for others to disappoint you. The serenity of living in the moment and allowing people to be who they are will add a note of excitement and banish bitterness.

All this free time and emotional energy salvaged from not mucking around in other people's concerns can be lavished on little old you. Yeah, you. Go for it, be selfish, it does the body good. You can take that intellectual bubble bath, massage that emotional muscle, wrap yourself a little tighter or a bit looser. Once your focus shifts to the person you can affect (you, darlin', you) you'll be easier to live with, happier, and invited to all the best parties.

Even if you're not on the A-list, you can focus on what you can *do* and never spend another moment worrying about how you feel. Your feelings are as much a part of you as your eye color and about as much under your control. Ah, what bliss to expend energy on something that is actually changeable: your actions.

I'm referring to action in the broadest sense, but if the word has some other connotation for you, well, I can tell you're not the last of the romantics and thank goodness for that. Romance is the prescription for disappointment, the basis of unrealistic expectations that can ruin a perfectly good relationship faster than a high school reunion. In a way, romance is a sexually transmitted disease and should be avoided like the problem it is.

Inherent in the danger of romance is the willingness to trade off fantasy for reality, short-term gratification for long-term disappointment. When in doubt, it makes much more sense to have a quick ouchie rather than prolonged agony. If we assume there's always going to be a bit of pain, it's wise to get it over with. Who needs the anticipation?

If you've sorted out your priorities, you're acting for a reason, and while this reason may or may not make sense to anyone else, it's the basis of your behavior. Other folks have different priorities and different rationales, but we share the link between thought and behavior. If the initial thought is different, the action may differ, but there's always a link between the two, thank goodness. How else could we figure out what's going on in our own head, let alone understand anybody else's behavior?

In the final analysis, it all comes down to *you:* who are *you,* what do *you* want, how are *you* going to get it? Your thoughts are the basics, your skills are the tools, and your actions are the work. Baby, it's you, so figure out the plan, keep your chin up and your whining to a minimum, and remember, this isn't a dress rehearsal. You are your attitude, and if you don't like it, work on it, change it, and polish it. Don't waste your time fantasizing about other people's lives or parents or bank accounts or cheekbones. The reality of your existence is waiting to be shaped by you.